The Best Day the Worst Day

The Best Day the Worst Day

LIFE WITH JANE KENYON

Donald Hall

Houghton Mifflin Company

BOSTON   NEW YORK   2005

For information about permission to reproduce selections from
this book, write to Permissions, Houghton Mifflin Company,
215 Park Avenue South, New York, New York 10003.

Visit our Web site: www.houghtonmifflinbooks.com.

Library of Congress Cataloging-in-Publication Data

Hall, Donald, 1928–
The best day the worst day : life with Jane Kenyon / Donald Hall.
p. cm.
ISBN 0-618-47801-9
1. Kenyon, Jane.   2. Kenyon, Jane—Health.   3. Kenyon, Jane—Marriage.
4. Leukemia—Patients—United States—Biography.   5. Poets, American—
20th century—Biography.   6. Married people—United States—Biography.
7. Hall, Donald, 1928—Marriage.   I. Title.

PS3561.E554Z74 2005
811'.54—dc22
[B]   2004059421

Book design by Anne Chalmers
Typefaces: Miller, Filosophia (ornament)

Frontispiece photographs, clockwise from upper left:
© William Abranowicz; Ken Williams, *Concord Monitor; Boston Globe*

Printed in the United States of America

MP 10 9 8 7 6 5 4 3 2 1

FOR L. K.

Contents

The Best Day the Worst Day

The Funeral Party

JANE KENYON died of leukemia at 7:57 in the morning, April 22, 1995. My wife was forty-seven and had been ill for fifteen months, but we had not known that she would certainly die until the last eleven days. For a week I had sat beside her while her faculties diminished, disappearing like lights going out on a hillside across the valley. I had tended to her as I could, scratching her nose, bringing water to her dry mouth. She lost the ability to speak. I studied her breathing. I touched her and kissed her, but not so often as I wanted, because with whatever consciousness she maintained, she was concentrated on letting go. It was a Saturday morning. Chadwick's Funeral Home could not pick up her body until the visiting nurse confirmed her death, and the duty nurse was out of beeper range. It took two hours to connect with the nurse, and another hour before she arrived and telephoned Chadwick's. I sat beside Jane's whitening body until almost noon. I kissed her cooling and cold lips. I spoke to her. Over the next days and weeks—when I woke in panic that I had forgotten to give her a pill, or when I returned from visiting her grave to fancy that she had been shopping and had arrived home before me—it helped that I had sat so long beside her. Still, it was long before every cell in my body believed in her death. It was a year before I could give away her clothes, and two years before I could gather together her letters and manuscripts, her unfinished poems.

As I watched her breathe her last breath, the telephone rang, my daughter Philippa calling from her house thirty miles south. I told her what she expected to hear. My children, who were not Jane's children, had cherished her. Almost every day, as I sat beside Jane over the fifteen months of leukemia—in our house, or in the New Hampshire hospital, or in Seattle where we spent five months while Jane had a bone marrow transplant—I had talked with them. The telephone, which is not my favorite device, centered the day of sickness. Often Jane did not feel well enough to speak. I talked with Jane's closest friends and my own, and with Jane's mother while she still lived. While I was talking with Philippa now, Jane's brother and sister-in-law and niece, who had flown from Michigan when I told them Jane was dying, entered the house. They were staying in Jane's mother's old flat, five miles away—untouched since Polly died three months earlier—and emptying it out. After a few minutes with Jane's body, they went back to the flat and left me to the telephone. My son Andrew was in Texas for the weekend visiting in-laws. When I called him, he offered to fly back immediately, two days before he had planned to. I told him that I would be all right. Jane's friend Caroline, who had driven on Thursday to say goodbye, called at eight-thirty. I called Alice and Joyce, Liam and Tree, all of whom had visited to make their farewells. I did not call everyone on my list until I could tell them the time of the funeral. I decided to bury Jane on Wednesday afternoon, April 26, but our minister was in Washington that Saturday and I needed to know for sure that Wednesday would do. All day I fretted over the timing of the funeral—displaced anxiety: to worry over something trivial in order to look away from the desolation at hand.

Chadwick's drove its van to the house at noon, rolled a gurney to the front door, and entered carrying a canvas sling. I shut our dog Gus into my study; I thought he would go wild, seeing them take her away. Marion and Charlie from Chadwick's wrapped Jane's body and carried her from bedroom to living room through kitchen out the front door and wheeled her to the van. I gave them the hymnbook and the order of service for the funeral that Jane and I had planned a week before. I gave them the obituary that we had composed. Gus was anxious, fretting when I let him out of my study. A reporter called from the *Concord Monitor* and interviewed me for the news story. I was able to speak easily about Jane's poetry and about our life together.

My daughter telephoned again, to propose that she and her husband and daughters come calling late in the afternoon. A basket appeared on the porch, no name attached, with a huge cooked ham, a casserole of scalloped potatoes, vegetables, bread, and a cake. I guessed who had cooked and delivered the feast. In the afternoon our minister called from Washington—and the funeral was set for three P.M. on Wednesday. I telephoned Chadwick's so that they could fax the obituary with the funeral notice to the newspapers. Then I called a dozen friends, who helped by calling other friends. Jane's old acquaintances, in New York and Boston and Virginia, canceled dates or made airline arrangements for travel to New Hampshire. I told Kris Doney in Seattle, Jane's hematologist at the Fred Hutchinson Cancer Research Center. More casseroles and loaves of bread appeared on the porch.

It was good that my daughter and her family came to visit. Allison and Abigail were six and almost three. I hugged everyone large and small. At one point Allison and I went exploring, as we always do when she visits. We stepped past the kitchen into the toolshed and stopped suddenly as if turned to stone: Facing us, propped on my grandmother's practice organ, was the placard the grandchildren had lettered and illustrated for Jane's return from Seattle to Manchester Airport, when we had come home en-

couraged, eight weeks earlier, with Jane's new marrow: WEL-
COME HOME JANE FROM SEATTLE! Quickly, neither of us
speaking, I dropped the placard out of sight. That night the families from Michigan and Concord sat at the big dining room table,
eating from the porch baskets. After dinner, I wanted to be alone.
My visitors left early and I slept in an empty bed. I kept reaching to
touch her.

The next morning at five I drove to the store where I pick up
the paper, tugging it from the bundle. Top of the front page of the
Concord Sunday Monitor was the headline POET JANE KENYON
DIES AT HER HOME IN WILMOT. Under the headline the
Monitor printed a color photograph it had used two years before
when it did a feature story on Jane, Jane smiling a foxy, flirtatious
smile as she looks into the camera with her reading glasses
halfway down her nose. I loved this photograph; Jane preferred
the more austere picture that appears on the jacket of *Otherwise,*
her posthumous selected poems. Both are true portraits—Jane
bodily, Jane spiritual—and both show the beauty that overtook
her in her forties. To each side of the *Monitor* photograph began
two long articles. The news story quoted from my telephone conversation with the reporter and from interviews she did later with
Philippa and Jane's friends. Mike Pride, who was editor of the
Monitor, our friend and a lover of poetry, wrote an eloquent account of Jane's work. I bought ten copies.

That Sunday morning I could not attend our church; going
by myself would have ripped me apart. And there were many
things to do, so many things. Talking with friends about Jane's
death helped me to avoid watching her die again in my mind. Understanding who was coming to the funeral, I arrived at a list of
pallbearers: two church friends, two old male poet friends, her
best friends Alice and Joyce, my son and son-in-law. At noontime

I let Gus out for a piddle, without attending on him, much less leashing him. Jane and I had let Gus into the yard for years, and he would not wander into the road or disappear—but this Sunday midday he vanished. Everyone who lives with dogs wonders how much they understand. Gus's existence was immensely important to me now. In the twenty-four hours since her death, I had talked to him, explaining to him carefully, in language that dogs can understand, that Jane was dead, that she died of leukemia, that she would never be back, that she had loved him dearly. This noontime, when he did not return after twenty minutes, my heart began to pound. I called his name up-mountain. I whistled. I drove the car along the dirt of New Canada Road where Jane had walked him every morning for eight years. I knew that he was looking for her. I whistled and called and clapped my hands. Was I losing Gus the day after I lost Jane? I thought of telephoning Jerry and Philippa to come from Concord and help me look. I searched for his body in the ditches of Route 4. I drove back to the house, then up New Canada again—and when I returned Gus was waiting patiently on the porch.

(For six months Gus remained in depression. He lay in the parlor day and night, a room Jane and I seldom entered, with his face on his paws, hardly looking up when spoken to. Finally he decided that I was *it*—and spent day and night as close to me as he could get. But whenever someone came to the house who had been Jane's particular friend, he went wild with joy, singing, as if Jane might walk through the door. Constantly he brought me Jane's white slippers from the bedroom, where I let them stay by her side of the bed. Always I returned them, so he could carry them again. He fetched them for a year until the pheromones dwindled away.)

The phone rang. The fax beeped as Galway Kinnell sent me a draft of "How Could She Not," his poem about Jane's death. Kris called from Seattle. Dr. K. C. Doney was the closest of our doctors during Jane's bone marrow transplant. She had found someone to switch with, taking her place on the floor of the hospital, and she would fly to Manchester on Tuesday, attend the funeral Wednesday, and fly back to Seattle Thursday. I was pleased—as I was by the *Monitor*'s attentions, as I was by the crowd at the funeral, as I was later by the public homages. All attentions to Jane were gratifying, even distracting. The mail in the first weeks was prodigious, more than a thousand letters in the first month. Every night I dictated answers. I didn't answer for the sake of politeness; answering gave me comfort. I wrote everyone, even strangers, about her last days and hours, about her brain-stem breathing, about pulling her eyelids down. It helped, to spread my sorrow and outrage onto the world. I know—I think I even *knew*—that I wrote as if this misery had never happened before, an old husband closing the eyes of his much younger wife. Many letters came from people who knew Jane by her poems only. Some had not known her work until they saw Bill Moyers's documentary, in 1993; others had heard her read five years ago, or had exchanged words with her at a book signing. There were also people closer to her, friends she had gone to school with, old teachers and boyfriends. Most letters were addressed to me at our town of Wilmot, because Wilmot was named in the obituaries, but our postal address was Danbury, and the Wilmot post office forwarded bundles of letters. One day a Wilmot postal clerk drove to the house to leave a box of letters on the porch. The women who typed my dictated letters worked long hours. One man addressed a letter to Jane, praising my work and hers, commiserating with her on the death of Donald Hall. I wrote him that he had two surprises coming.

On Monday the *Boston Globe* ran its obituary. So did the *New York Times*, the *Washington Post*, the *Philadelphia Inquirer*, and papers in Texas and California. When I had sat beside the living Jane ten days before, composing her obituary with her, I had the notion that one piece of information would catch the attention of the journalists who wrote death notices. In January while we were still in Seattle, New Hampshire's governor had proclaimed Jane the state poet laureate. I planted this information at the beginning of the obituary, and newspapers headlined: POET LAUREATE OF NEW HAMPSHIRE DIES. The long notices from the *Concord Monitor* had gone out on the New England wire. When an editor at the *Philadelphia Inquirer* read a brief item about her death, he did a search, and some of the *Monitor*'s words about Jane and her poetry turned up in a Philadelphia paper. This Philadelphia editor had been Jane's friend at the University of Michigan, and my student in the writing class where I met Jane.

Monday I took her burial clothes to Chadwick's and picked out the coffin. Jane had approved of my mother's coffin; my mother had died a year earlier when Jane was first ill. It saved me a decision, to order the identical box. Our church would seat eighty. Chadwick's arranged to erect a tent for the overflow, and to use loudspeakers. Chadwick's had suggested a photograph for the cover of the funeral program, and I brought with me Jane's preferred image of herself, the *Otherwise* photograph taken by William Abranowicz at the 1992 Dodge Poetry Festival. Leaving it at the Country Press for copying, I suffered more displaced anxiety; I was convinced it would be lost. I had three hundred programs printed for the funeral. Later I ordered more, with envelopes, so that I could send the funeral program to friends who could not attend, to Seattle and New Hampshire nurses, and to strangers who wrote commiserating. I ended printing a thousand.

When Andrew came back from Texas on Monday, he decided to drive up on Tuesday with his daughter Emily, six years old, for

calling hours Tuesday night and the funeral Wednesday. My children have always contrasted: My daughter would not come to calling hours because she could not bear seeing Jane dead; she
wanted to restore to her mind the lively woman of fifteen months
earlier. She would come to the funeral, and for her sake I would
keep the coffin closed, but she and Jerry would not bring the children. When Allison heard that her first cousin Emily would come
to the funeral, she wanted to come too. Philippa said she could,
but did she know what a funeral was? When Allison heard that
Jane would attend, in a box, she changed her mind. Tuesday
morning I drove to Chadwick's to see how Jane looked, made up
and arranged in the coffin. I had driven half a mile when I realized
that I had forgotten something. I drove back to the house to get
my glasses.

When Jane and I had chosen the outfit to bury her in, she decided that she would not wear her wig. The brush cut she was
buried with was her own hair. Chadwick's placed the coffin in the
viewing room where my mother's body lay a year before, and
where Jane and I last saw my grandmother Kate in 1975. Dead
Jane looked all right. The white salwar kameez from India, which
we had chosen for the coffin, looked pretty. I draped an Indian
scarf over her left shoulder. She looked lean, her face bony and her
crossed hands skinny, wearing her wedding ring and the ring I
gave her on our twenty-second anniversary, at the start of her
leukemia a year before, which she had nicknamed Please Don't
Die. She looked like Jane, sick Jane after fifteen months of wast-
ing. John Singer Sargent once described portraiture as that form
of painting in which there is always something a little wrong about
the mouth. There was something a little wrong about Jane's
mouth. Marion Chadwick told me that mouths were the hardest
part.

Andrew arrived with Emily on Tuesday afternoon. After an early supper we drove to the viewing in separate cars—because I needed to stay until the end, to be there for all the callers. I recognized a social worker from the Dartmouth hospital, whose shoulder I had cried on a year before. Our old doctor came with his wife, and the cousins and neighbors came. Dick Smart drove from Tilton and walked inside while Aunt Nan stayed in the car. Nan was my mother's younger sister, eighty-four now and incapacitated by a series of small strokes. Before Jane took sick we had visited them once a week and Jane did Nan's nails; Nan could not speak but splayed her fingers out, gazing at her nails to express her gratitude. Now Dick and I walked outside to the car so that I could speak to Nan and observe her grief without words. Emily appeared to enjoy herself. She approached her first dead body cautiously, retreated to another room with her father, then returned to gaze at Jane again. The next day at the funeral she told Alice Mattison: "We saw Jane's actual body." I stayed late alone, after the friends had left, and Charlie took off Please Don't Die, a pink tourmaline with nine little diamonds around it. As Jane had suggested, I would give it to Philippa. I kissed Jane's cold hard lips for the last time.

The day of the funeral was fair. Jane's daffodils bloomed in the hill garden behind the house, over the brick patio that she had laid out in sand ten years before. Maybe half her daffodils waved their bright pennants. Our housekeeper Carole Colburn came early to tidy and vacuum the house. Andrew and Jane's brother and I fussed and set out chairs. After the funeral, during the burial, churchwomen and neighbors would take over the house and put food out. Jane's brother drove to New London and bought box wine while I picked up paper cups and plates. Neighbors would bring big coffeemakers. I kept busy, too distraught for sorrow. Friends who came from a distance began to collect at the house. Kris Doney from Seattle arrived late in the morning, driving up in a rental car from a motel in Manchester. We set porch food out for lunch and visitors made themselves sandwiches. Liam Rector and Tree Swenson arrived, who had married in our back garden two years before. Alice Mattison and Joyce Peseroff, the writer friends with whom Jane workshopped, came with their husbands. Gregory Orr, our old poet friend, arrived from Virginia with Bill Moyers's television producer David Grubin from New York. Then came poets from Cambridge and Boston, from New York and New Haven, Maine, Vermont, Virginia, Minnesota, and New Hampshire: Louis Simpson, Geoffrey Hill, Robert Bly, Caroline Finkelstein, Wesley McNair, Cynthia Huntington, Charles Simic, Cleopatra Mathis, Peter Davison, Lucie Brock-Broido, Ellen Bryant Voigt, Stephen Sandy, Sharon Olds, Galway Kinnell, Frank Bidart, Lloyd Schwartz, Robert Pinsky. I kept chattering, showing people the house, pointing out our painted bed where Jane died. Most stopped briefly, then drove on to the church. The church opened at one and people began to sit down shortly thereafter. It was filled by two o'clock for the service at three.

When my family and I arrived at the South Danbury Christian Church, we found a crowd scattered outside under the tent. We squeezed through friends and neighbors standing in the aisles to sit in the front pew a few feet from the coffin with its flowers and the ribbon saying *Jane*. Kris Doney sat in another front pew beside Letha Mills, Jane's New Hampshire hematologist, who had told us two weeks before that the leukemia had returned. Kris and Letha had known each other in Seattle when Letha did a rotation at the Hutchinson while she was a hematology fellow at the University of Washington. The organist was Will Ogmundson, a wunderkind whom Jane and I had admired since he began playing at

Old Home Day when he was five, now a senior in high school. If the church seated eighty it must have stood two hundred. People packed together on all sides of the organ and the pulpit, in front of the piano, in the aisles and the entranceway. Carole was there who had cleaned and tidied that morning; Kendel and Sharon who typed for me; a carpenter friend, Peter, who had survived lymphoma with a bone marrow transplant; cousins from Sutton, Andover, and Vermont; friends we knew from the post office and the general store; Piero Caputo, the owner of our favorite restaurant; Mike Pride of the *Concord Monitor*—and every friend and helper from the South Danbury and Wilmot churches.

Some listened outside through the loudspeakers. Our minister Alice Ling led us singing "Come, Thou Fount of Every Blessing." She prayed with her gift of improvised prayer, as she had done visiting our house and by telephone to Seattle. We spoke Psalm 139:1–18, which Jane had chosen. Liam read Jane's "Let Evening Come" and "Otherwise." Our minister sang "Amazing Grace" a cappella, spoke of Christian promise, then directly about Jane. We sang "Abide with Me." Alice prayed again. We sang "Love Divine, All Loves Excelling," and the service ended. Outside the church we hugged and wept, wept and hugged while pallbearers carried Jane to the hearse. As neighbors and churchwomen prepared the house—everyone was invited—the procession headed by the hearse carrying Jane wound six miles down Route 4 past our house toward Mount Kearsarge, which Jane had climbed so often. We parked beside the plot Jane and I had bought fifteen years before.

We bought it so long ago because we were prudent and morbid and because we loved where we lived. It was a gesture that proclaimed: We will never leave our house except to be buried in this graveyard that holds people who occupied the house before us.

Buying our grave plot was a marriage to place. Behind the plot a gorge drops down at the corner of the graveyard, the end of a row of graves, a place of handsome quiet, with huge white pines rising from the top of the ravine, a few old oaks, and clumps of birch. Looking south from the stone, across the middle of the graveyard, you see a row of eight enormous sugar maples that burn late in September, early in October. Sometimes, in good health, Jane and I had walked in the cemetery with Gus and visited our plot, set out by four "H" cement markers.

It was warm, April 26, 1995. A breeze moved in the oaks and birches, and sun broke through small swift clouds. We stood in silence as the pallbearers moved the coffin onto straps over the hole. More and more cars arrived and parked on the lanes between the rows of graves. A crowd of two hundred moved slowly to gather in a big semicircle around the coffin. When everyone had gathered, Alice prayed again over the coffin. It was hard to hear her because of the breeze, but her presence maintained the memory of the church service. When she finished, the multitude of mourners stood together in silence, and no one knew what to do. The breeze stopped, leaves still. We required one more collective sigh. Robert Bly started singing "Amazing Grace," picked up by Alice Ling and everyone who knew the words, and the old hymn rose in the warm breeze over Jane's body and flew to the tops of the birches. When we stopped, anxious silence returned and thickened. It was inconceivable to leave her and go back to her house. I have no memory of speaking, but I am told that I said, "We have to go, dear," and walked to the car.

Back at the house the helpers had covered every surface with cake and cookies and cheese and coffee and wine and sandwiches. For two or three hours I wandered from group to group, table-hopping at the funeral party. Gussie went crazy and I had to put him into a little run that Jane and her brother had constructed in back of the woodshed. He barked incessantly, loudest of the mourners. I visited him from time to time, praised him, reminded him of what had happened, and commiserated. People wandered uphill toward the barn, and in the hayfield between the barn and the road. Jane's peonies and tulips were starting up, not yet blooming like the daffodils. Friends stood in the narrow patch of grass in front of the house, the Cape that my great-grandfather moved into in 1865 and extended backward for his big family. People meandered in the secluded back garden on Jane's brick patio. Over a stone retaining wall, bordered with perennials, she had planted bulbs where the hill rose to become Ragged Mountain. Uphill a few yards was a great boulder and next to it a small old wooden shack, child-size, which people mistake for an outhouse. It is a playhouse, first built for my grandmother Kate more than a century ago by her cousin Freeman Morrison, a little older than Kate and handy even as a boy, who lived in this house with Kate and her parents after his own family was burned out. The same cousin rebuilt it two decades later for Kate's girls, my mother and her sisters. I had played there when I was little, and took care to keep the roof shingled after Jane and I moved in. Now Emily and her sister Ariana, who was four, invented ways to play there together. All afternoon they ran around the little hill among the yellow and white daffodils, scooting in and out of the playhouse, flashing among the somber guests.

Gatherings of three and four people took me in with mournful affection. I enjoyed the afternoon of Jane's funeral. I embraced two hundred people beset by a remediless disappearance. As one by one and two by two they left, back to airports or babysitters or supper, I said goodbye and regretted their going. Kris drove to her Manchester motel and tomorrow's flight back across the country.

Cars left for the drive to Connecticut, to Maine and Vermont, to Boston and Cambridge, to New York City and Long Island. Our numbers dwindled to eighty, to fifty, to twenty, to ten. My children and their families and Jane's family stayed to the end. I let Gussie back in the house when we were few, and he wandered among us, looking for the one who wasn't there. My son volunteered to spend the night, but I said no. Although I hadn't wanted the party to end, now I wanted to be alone. I embraced my solitude without Jane, or my solitude in the exclusive company of her absence, as eagerly as I had embraced all day so many men and women.

Then I was alone. The volunteer caterers had cleaned up and put things away. I ate leftovers. Jane reminded me to take my insulin. Suddenly fatigue came over me and I knew I had to go to bed; I would sleep tonight. But first I drove back to the graveyard in the moonlight and said goodnight to the fresh dirt over Jane in her Vermont hardwood box, wearing her white salwar kameez.

To Eagle Pond

THREE YEARS AFTER we married—we lived in Ann Arbor, where I taught at the University of Michigan—Jane and I decided to camp out for a year at my old family farm in New Hampshire. I had spent my childhood summers there, and it was my place of all places. It was the poetry house, domain of old farmers who told stories and spoke pieces memorized when they were young, and it had been antithetical to the Connecticut suburbs where I endured the school year. Summers at the farm, with my mother's parents, I had fed the chickens and hayed with my grandfather. Jane knew how I felt about the house, where I had thrived under the love of the old people in a countryside largely abandoned to cellar holes, squared out by stone walls that lacked animals to fence in. Years before Jane and I met, I wrote a book about those summers.

My grandfather died in 1953. When Jane and I drove to the farm in August of 1975, my grandmother Kate was ninety-seven, captive to senile dementia in the Peabody Home. After she died, we would buy the place from her heirs, but for now we would take a year's leave of absence from the university—TuThu 1–2:30, cocktail parties, office hours, dinner parties, term papers—to camp out in the white farmhouse, to enjoy the solitary quiet and work on poems. When we returned to Michigan, maybe we would have sampled our future. I was almost forty-seven—Jane was twenty-eight—and I was thinking of early retirement, perhaps in five or ten years. But when we arrived with a U-Haul in August, my grandmother's health took a plunge downward. The governing past died when she died, and our lives opened to improvisation. In a week's flurry we buried the house's daughter—Kate Keneston Wells was born in 1878 in the bedroom that became ours—and Jane and I began our double solitude in the clapboard 1803 Cape across from Eagle Pond as the leaves were turning: first the swamp maples, in boggy patches by the side of the road, then the sugar maples branch by branch. These colors were the most outrageous, crimson and bright orange and Chinese red. The birches turned russet, and the oaks a deeper brown-red. We floated on the bliss of the natural world.

In September Jane first spoke of wanting to stay here forever, not going back to Michigan where I had my job and where she had grown up. While the colors were still brilliant Jane's mother and father drove from Ann Arbor and visited, admiring the house and the landscape. They saw their daughter revel in place and people, floorboards and vistas. At the same time, although she didn't complain, Jane struggled with feelings of being alien. For the first time she was living apart from the familiar, from Ann Arbor, parents, brother, which was a liberation—but she inhabited a house freighted with more than a century of another family, a house that kept the broken furniture and mothballed woolens of four generations. Over that first year, in her poems she recorded a gradual, tentative sense of connection. Day by day, I observed the burgeoning new Jane, separated from her past, and from the busy academy, in a rapture of quiet.

Danbury center is four miles north of our house in Wilmot. In Danbury after Labor Day we attended the Danbury Grange Harvest Festival Parade: a fife-and-drum corps from Plymouth, floats from our Sunday school and from local enterprises, the American Legion marching, antique cars in procession, children riding bicycles with tissue paper woven through the spokes, Willard Huntoon leading a brace of Holstein oxen, the volunteer fire department with men tossing candy to children from fire engines. Buildings and sheds of the Grange and the American Legion contained a jumble sale, paintings by Danbury painters, prize Ball jars of beans, enormous pumpkins and squashes, pyramids of huge bright tomatoes. Originally, the parade and fair had celebrated harvest. Now it celebrated an autonomy of country pleasures: The summer people were gone.

We had the house and land to ourselves as the countryside emptied out and cool autumn started. I found old notepaper with Kate's father's name on it, B. C. Keneston. Under a photograph of Mount Kearsarge, his letterhead printed "Eagle Pond Farm." I had not known that he had given the house a name. (My grandmother had told me that he bought this valley farm in 1865 because of its view of Kearsarge.) Understanding that many of my correspondents wouldn't believe "Danbury, New Hampshire" sufficient address, I appropriated B.C.K.'s invention and ordered letterhead for Eagle Pond Farm. Bob Thornly, who owned the store four hundred yards away around a curve, dispensed not only gas and food and hardware and stovepipe and New Hampshire ashtrays, but also facilitations. I told him I needed a typist and he thought of Lois Fierro, half a mile farther down the road, who handled my letters and manuscript for two decades. At the store I picked up the *Globe* every morning. We shopped there for milk and sundries. Jane bought crockery there that sits in the pantry still. In November I found felt-lined boots for winter. We dropped in at Thornly's a couple of times a day, chatted with Bob, gossiped with neighbors, and heard new jokes. My cousin Ansel told us it got so cold he saw a fox putting jumper cables on a jackrabbit. Jane called Thornly's store a continual party.

The first Sunday we were alone together, I said that maybe we ought to go to church; probably my cousins would expect us to. (In Ann Arbor, Sunday morning was devoted to recovering from Saturday night.) We went, and heard a sermon from a preacher who had helped to bury Kate, and who taught at Colby-Sawyer College twelve miles away in New London. Jack Jensen quoted "Rilke the German poet," which didn't diminish our attention. The next Sunday we went again. What most ensnared us was not references to Rilke or theology, but the community of the church. Jane called our side of the building the gene pool, because it included my mother's first cousins Martha and Edna, and their husbands and their offspring. My mother's first cousin Audrey sat just across the aisle. Edna's daughter Bertha occupied a pew with her husband Launie Brown and their two young daughters. With her taciturn husband Ansel, Edna was the church's mammalian soul, a broad vessel of generosity and fierceness, her tenderness as bright as the fire of her Democratic politics. By community we slowly approached communion. Before the end of the year, we were reading scripture and commentary. Jack loaned us *The Cloud of Unknowing*. A year later we were both deacons—who had never entered a church in Ann Arbor.

It was late October when Jane made the definitive announcement: She would chain herself to the walls of the rootcellar rather than leave New Hampshire. I was terrified; I was joyous. When I was a child, I had wanted to live here, but I abandoned the notion by the time I was twenty because there was no way I could make a living. This land that I loved could no longer sustain a farm. Anyway, I had farmed with my grandfather as a boy, and I didn't want to farm. Now, at Jane's urging, I began to think of quitting my job, giving up tenure, and undertaking the freelance life. It was a thrilling idea, and frightening because I had two children from my first marriage; the elder was in college, the younger in high school with college two years ahead. At the University of Michigan I had medical insurance, a retirement plan, and an annual income.

We explored back roads in our Plymouth and later in a beat-up Saab that we bought for four hundred dollars, so that Jane could drive to the supermarket when I went off on poetry readings. We explored the house's inside—rootcellar, milkroom, tool-shed, woodshed, barn, closets upstairs and down, a frail attic holding two spinning wheels, and the back chamber or storeroom where everything broken or superfluous had accumulated over a century: chests full of clothing, a dozen double beds, a butter churn, a last for repairing shoes, thirty or forty chairs (straight-backed, Morris, rocking), tool chests, oil lamps, carpetbags, letters, old diaries, and documents with figures measured in pounds not in dollars. We lived among the things of the dead. Jane adored her mountain, her day, and her house—and fretted less about moving into someone else's world. My habitual love of mountain and house grew greater, stimulated by Jane's.

We worked on our poems, often in the same room. A year later we would have separate studies, but that first year we worked at close quarters because we had no heat except for the single woodstove—an elegant black cast-iron Glenwood with chrome fittings, from 1910 or so. On the dining room table in the autumn, I had worked at a book about the Pittsburgh Pirates pitcher Dock Ellis. In November when it turned cold I moved my work into the living room beside the stove, Jane and I occupying chairs on either side. When Jane needed to type a poem, she set up a bridge table beside the Glenwood. We had no storm windows and no insulation. We made love on the floor beside the stove with the drafts open, arranging blankets and pillows. When it was time for sleep, I dashed into the freezing bedroom to turn on the electric blankets, as in my mother's time the family stuffed hot-water bottles under quilts. We undressed beside the woodstove. Jane was too cold to read in bed. For myself, I devised a strategy. Reading at bedtime, I used only paperbacks, which I could read one-handed, switching the book from hand to hand so that I could keep one hand under the covers warming up.

Driving in the afternoon we found villages we had never entered, hills we had never climbed, great stands of birches, intact stone walls built a hundred and fifty years ago. Jane decided she preferred November's pallor to the earlier brightness, late autumn's shades of gray and tan, the palette of analytic cubism. As the days grew short we lived mostly in the stove's proximity. Before bed I would make four trips to the woodshed with a canvas-and-leather carrier that Jane ordered from L. L. Bean. I filled the Glenwood and shut it tight so the fire would keep all night. I stacked maple and ash alongside the stove, to replenish it at midnight. (It was painful taking a frozen journey to the shed wearing a nightshirt.) On a normal morning, well below zero, I rose at five and removed ashes to expose gold-red coals, then filled the dark cavity with big split logs, opened the drafts, and returned to bed for a nap while wood blasted to warm the living room and take the chill off the adjacent kitchen, dining room, and bathroom. By six it was comfortable. We rose, made coffee, and dressed beside the stove where we had piled our clothes the night before.

In December I wrote the University of Michigan resigning my professorship and tenure. The university spoiled my bravery by refusing my resignation, giving me another year's leave, allowing me liberty to change my mind. I never considered changing my mind.

From time to time I panicked, and took on literary chores that were disagreeable. A freelancer doesn't know the source of income that will provide support in six months' time. Where will the grocery money come from? Gradually, because something always turned up, I came to accept that something would always turn up. Anxiety became less frequent. It was easier for Jane to accept the uncertainty; she had grown up in a house of self-employment.

Before Christmas I bought a chainsaw and cut a small balsam for a frail Christmas tree, inadequate and beautiful, a Charlie Brown tree. One morning when I tried to start the Plymouth, it barely turned over and wouldn't catch. I was puzzled until I checked the thermometer on the porch. It was minus twenty-one degrees—and I had not noticed: New Hampshire's cold is drier than Michigan's, and less painful. Later that day, my cousin Clyde Currier, who owned the Mobil station in Andover, installed a block heater. A plug dangled from the grill of our green Valiant, and at night before bed I plugged it into an extension cord. A timer started heating the block at four-thirty A.M. No more trouble starting, even at negative thirty-eight.

In this portion of my life I was fat and bearded. Naturally, I was recruited to play Santa Claus at the church's Christmas party for children. (My gigs multiplied. A year later I was recruited for the Danbury elementary school Christmas party, which took place at night in the Grange Hall, and for Danbury's private kindergarten, and for the Andover Lions' bingo night.) My beard was black. I whitened it imperfectly with a spray can purchased at a theatrical supply store in Concord. I needed no padding, only a Santa costume that my cousin Peter supplied me, happy to relinquish the role he had earlier played. The Christmas pageant at the South Danbury church was an annual excitement of my mother's childhood, and my grandmother's before her. It has changed and it has stayed the same. For my grandmother in the 1880s and my mother in the 1910s, it was the family's entire Christmas celebration and present-giving, except for peppermints or an orange in a stocking at home on Christmas morning. My mother and her two sisters received their presents at church: each year, for each girl, a big storybook and a new doll. (My grandmother obtained these extravagances with coupons issued by the Great Atlantic and Pacific Tea Company, which visited the farm each week by horse and wagon.) These days, we give one another few presents at the church pageant, family to family not within the family, as the big present-giving is reserved for Christmas morning at home, the way it is in the rest of the United States. At church the children receive candy canes and bags of popcorn from Santa. Before the moment of gifts and Santa Claus, Sunday school children recite, perform, or sing the pieces they have rehearsed, Christmas poems or dialogues or songs. In between, adults sing carols. Then the children dress up to perform the birth in the manger. There are shepherds dressed in cutoff old bathrobes, boys and girls both, and wise men, and someone elevates an aluminum foil star pasted to cardboard. There is Joseph, there is Mary, and a doll lies in a cradle set on straw—while narrators tell or read the story of the birth, and Instamatics flash, and video cameras record.

In 1975 Jane witnessed the pageant for the first time. I had not attended for twenty-five years. With my beard whitened and wearing red clothing, I could not watch the pageant from a pew. From the church's foyer, I peered through a crack in the door. When I heard my cue—something about reindeer—I shook the harness bells I carried and swung open the doors heaving out so-so ho-hos. After Jane and I drove home, still in costume I poured myself a Scotch to calm myself down. Jane had watched the pageant in whole joy, more and more belonging to this tiny community of people who had been born here and never left. The rural Ann Arbor she had grown up in had become a suburb of activity, a settlement of unsettlement. In Ann Arbor, as in all university environments, there was a saying: "At every party, one third of the people were not in town the year before; one third will not be in town next year." We had immigrated to the university's anti-world. Next year we would attend the Danbury Grange Harvest Festival Parade, and next year we would sit in our pew to watch the Christmas pageant. And the next year, and the next . . .

After Christmas came the coldest January in a hundred years of recorded New Hampshire Januarys. My grandmother had just died at ninety-seven, and our first January in her house was colder than any she had known. Every morning for weeks it was at least twenty below. We burned cord after cord of Channing Sawyer's hardwood. We set electric heaters in the bathroom to avoid frozen pipes. There were days when Jane sat on the frigid floor of the kitchen aiming her hair dryer at the icy plumbing that rose from the rootcellar. It was a painful month, but exhilarating, and we passed the test. In this coldest January four friends visited from Ann Arbor, one our lawyer, and we passed papers to buy the house. Other friends came for weekends, checking us out, and slept in unheated bedrooms for the first and only time in their lives. When I finished my book about Dock Ellis in February, Dock flew to stay with us as he went through the manuscript. He had grown up in Los Angeles, and in the Pittsburgh winters kept his apartment thermostat at ninety degrees. As we drove down I-89 from the Lebanon Airport, he marveled at the formations of ice like frozen blue waterfalls hanging down granite cuts at the sides of the highway. All the time he stayed in our house, he never took off his fur hat and gloves. When he emerged in the morning from a bed in the frozen parlor, he declared, with emphatic hilarity, "I'm *never—*

going to *spend*—another *night*—in that *room!*" Dock and I went through the manuscript quickly.

Everything was exhilarating that year, and the next, and the next. We kept wondering: Will we ever take things for granted? Will it ever seem *normal* to live here? Mount Kearsarge changed color over the seasons, pink or green, white or blue or lavender. Eagle Pond lay flat and white in winter, then in mud season turned livid with punky ice that disappeared one day, sinking to melt on the bottom, just before moss turned green and birches started uncurling frail leaves.

All the while I wallowed in the muddy freedom of freelancing. I began every day by working on poems, and then turned to prose. Finishing the Dock book, I started reminiscences of old poets I had known when I was young. I wrote periodical essays and short stories. An old Ann Arbor friend was editor at *Ford Times* and I sold him several things at five hundred dollars apiece. I wrote an essay on the Glenwood for *Yankee* and they turned it down; heaven knows how many pieces they had printed about woodstoves. I did book reviews and magazine pieces about baseball. I flew away to do poetry readings. I reported on manuscripts for publishers and cashed one-hundred-dollar checks. I judged contests. Sales of a textbook brought in regular royalties. An old student, now a children's book editor, commissioned me to do a riddle book for kids. Moving from one sort of writing to another, I stayed at the desk all day. In the next few years I took on a variety of commissions—more textbooks, magazine writing, editing poetry for two periodicals. Late in 1976 I finished a poem called "Ox-Cart Man," which *The New Yorker* published. Then I used the same story for a children's book called *Ox-Cart Man*, which won the Caldecott Medal for Barbara Cooney's illustrations. When Jane began to sell poems, and to give poetry readings, her income added itself to the pot.

"Love at the lips was touch / As sweet as I could bear." We lived alone in the old house heated by wood on Route 4 with the railroad running between us and Eagle Pond. March of 1976 was blizzard and melt, blizzard and melt, but in April we found snow-drops and residual daffodils and Jane began her work of twenty years, the garden in patches and strips around the house and in front of the barn. All winter in her mind she had planted her flowers. But this summer, instead of doing much gardening, we returned to Ann Arbor to pack up our books and furniture and move everything to New Hampshire. Before driving west, we ar-ranged for changes in the house. My cousin Forrest was contractor and carpenter in chief—his grandfather Forrest was brother to my grandfather Wesley—with Joe Bouley and Bob Peters helping. In the kitchen we would remove the set-tubs and the old low sink, putting in a sink high enough to work at, space for a dishwasher, drawers and cabinets under a butcher-block counter. We would replace both chimneys, one from 1803 and the other from 1865, too old to be safe. Forrest saved two bricks for us from the oldest chimney, built for the original Cape: One brick had *1803* on it, the other the initials of the brickyard in Lebanon from which oxen had dragged the bricks. When Joe Bouley took apart this old chimney he found places where the brick had fallen away to plaster and lath, which was scorched black. Joe felt sick to his stomach. All the previous frigid winter we had sent flame up that chimney.

Forrest installed storm windows. We began insulating. We bought a Jøtul woodstove, which Forrest installed in my study. In the back chamber we had found a small beautiful iron stove—very old; my mother, who was now eldest of the family, had no notion

of its provenance—which needed work, and while we were back in
Ann Arbor Les Ford, a farrier who lived down the road in Potter
Place, tidied and soldered it, so that Forrest could drill a chimney
hole in Jane's study and install the repaired antiquity. Les Ford
also restored the cast-iron Glenwood kitchen range, removing the
indignity of tubes supplying kerosene, and set it up ready for wood
in the kitchen where it had taken its place when my mother was a
girl. Mostly, Forrest and Bob and Joe put bookcases in: upstairs in
Jane's study, downstairs in the parlor, on three sides of the living
room, and all over the room in which I slept as a child next to my
grandparents' bedroom, where I would now do my work. In my
study, the bookshelves went from floor to ceiling, under and
around windows. In one place, a stack jutted out from a wall, providing another forty feet of shelving for poetry.

While we were gone my mother house-sat and culled some of
the accumulation of more than a century. Late in August I drove a
rented truck full of books and manuscript to a house with new
bookshelves and chimneys. In September, again, we settled down.
Not until next year would we spend July and August afternoons at
Eagle Pond, swimming and sunning, reading and even working
under tall white pines and oaks beside birch trees over dense moss
with red berries among wild strawberry plants. By next year, we
would live as we would live until we died, or one of us did.

The Plaid Notebook

IN 1994, January started dense with activity, like the whole year of 1993. On the tenth of the month, Jane and I drove two hours into Vermont to Bennington College, where our friend Liam Rector had initiated a low-residency M.F.A. program. On the twelfth, we read our poems there. A week later, we expected to perform together at a retirement community up the road in Hanover, but that morning I had a telephone call from Clough Extended Care, twelve miles away in New London: My mother was suffering an attack of congestive heart failure. I drove to her bedside and sat with her as she survived, quieted, slept—while Jane did duty for us both in Hanover. A week later I read my poems in Cambridge with Geoffrey Hill. Jane had expected to come with me but stayed home, feeling out of sorts. She thought she was coming down with flu, and the rest of that week continued to feel general malaise and what she called bone pain. On the twenty-ninth I flew to a conference of English teachers in Charleston, South Carolina, lectured on Saturday, and read poems on Sunday. I called Jane twice a day, which was our habit when apart. Sunday she was feeling better. Much of Monday I spent flying back. My flight from Charlotte to Boston was delayed and I missed my commuter to Manchester, New Hampshire. From Logan Airport I telephoned Jane to tell her that I would be late. I had planned to drive straight home, unpack, then visit my mother at her bed in New London. Now I would drive out of my way to stop at my mother's first, so when I got home I could stay home. Jane told me about her day. She was vexed because her Saab wouldn't start that morning when she left the New London Hospital, after they stopped a formidable nose-bleed. (She was waiting now to hear about bloodwork.) She told me how she arranged for a tow truck and telephoned her mother—Polly had moved from Michigan to a flat in our town—and how her mother picked her up at the hospital. As she spoke with annoyance about her car troubles, I wasn't listening. Some-thing in my mind put together "flu symptoms" with "nosebleed" and "bloodwork." Intuition assembles information that the mind has learned and forgotten, arriving at a conclusion that appears to come out of nowhere. I had never known anyone with leukemia, but, standing in a phone booth in Logan Airport, I heard my mind deliver the unspoken sentence: "Jane has leukemia."

Maybe my voice carried anxiety with it, because Jane told me later that when she hung up she felt suddenly frightened. She wanted someone with her, and telephoned our friend and neigh-bor Mary Lyn Ray to drive over for a cup of tea. Mary Lyn had just arrived when Dr. Foote called Jane with the results of bloodwork: "You have leukemia." Her blood count was abysmal and Dr. Foote told her not to wait for my return; she must go to Dartmouth-Hitchcock immediately—the big medical center in Lebanon, New Hampshire, teaching hospital for Dartmouth Medical School. Dr. Foote had already booked a room. Mary Lyn drove Jane to the hospital.

Several times as I flew in the little plane from Boston to Manchester, or as I drove to my mother's bedside, I shrugged away the notion that Jane had leukemia. Often in my life I had imag-ined bad news, and the fancy had been groundless. Jane had told Dr. Foote that I was going to visit my mother at the center, next to the emergency room. My mother and I had talked for five minutes before a nurse entered the room and told me that Dr. Foote wanted to see me. When I met him in a bare storeroom, he said, "I'm afraid I have bad news." I interrupted him, saying, "Jane has leukemia." Dr. Foote looked startled and repeated, "Jane has leukemia." Walking back to my mother's room I told her the news. Lucy was calm. She had lived long enough—ninety years old, forty years a widow—to remain unrattled, whatever happened. Although her mind was clear, she sometimes mixed up words, and from that day on she often referred to Jane's illness as anemia not leukemia. The mistake must have comforted her: When she was a girl, she had been anemic; look how *she* had survived. I told her now that I was leaving her directly to drive to Jane, to Dartmouth-Hitchcock only half an hour north. Dr. Foote had given me a three-by-five card on which he had written Jane's room number, her admitting physician, and the telephone number of the nurses' station. But I did not need to telephone; I needed to be beside her, and from one bed I drove to another. In the car I schooled myself to stay calm as I thought about her disease. When I was growing up leukemia was inevitably fatal to children; now something like ninety percent survive. For adults, I knew, the prognosis was less sanguine. My daughter had two friends in college who had leukemia; one lived and one died. Driving to Jane, I felt not so much terror or dread as an urgent or assertive response to danger. I don't remember weeping. "Leukemia" is a terrifying word, but at that time I did not believe that Jane would die. I felt something like the enthusiasm of engagement: *Look what we've got ourselves into now!*

Parking, I found my way to Jane's room. Mary Lyn stood beside Jane, who sat up in bed, wearing her daily costume of blue jeans and blouse, tubes attached to the crook of her left elbow. Admission had been swift, and she was already receiving a blood transfusion. We kissed and murmured. Mary Lyn rose as if to go, but I asked her to stay. As my first act I would go to the hospital florist and buy flowers. On my way out, a nurse told me that flowers were forbidden in the Bubble—the glass-enclosed pod for patients with blood cancer, who had depressed immune systems—because they can carry bacteria. For the same reason, visitors should not wear wool. I hung my poetry-reading jacket on a hook outside the Bubble and at the florist's bought silk flowers.

Mary Lyn left us. Jane told me what she knew, which was not much: *I have leukemia.* The doctors would attempt to put her into remission by means of chemotherapy over the next four to six weeks. She would lose her hair. They had told her that most people achieve remission, and we knew what happened if you did not. We knew nothing yet of further treatment, nothing of prognosis. We touched as we could, not to disable tubes and transfusion. Meantime I fussed with immediate plans. I knew that I must stay near the hospital, to be with Jane most of each day; our house was an hour away and I would not waste two hours a day driving. Jane's mother, who lived only five miles from us, would house-sit and tend our animals while Jane and I stayed in room 127 and at the Days Inn. (Polly had taken over during happier absences: a book tour, a month in India.) When I called Polly to tell her, she sounded matter-of-fact—at eighty, another survivor who could summon calm in an emergency. I passed the telephone to Jane, and mother and daughter spoke for a moment.

I had asked Polly to pack up for house-sitting, and told her that I would drive home, sleep overnight, and help her move in before I returned the next morning to Jane's side. I asked her to call my daughter Philippa, who would call my son Andrew. Polly gave my children Jane's hospital telephone number, and soon the phone rang in Jane's room. *What could they do?* They lived not far away, in New Hampshire and Massachusetts; they could help by attending to the old mothers, to Lucy and Polly. Jane told them that she wanted grandchild pictures for her wall. Philippa supplied from her resources, and delivered the next day. Andrew posed a new picture of his family of five, had it developed and enlarged and framed, and brought it with him when they visited four days later.

Crushed together into one room and one fact, we began the new routines that became our lives. I found my way to the cafeteria for the first time to eat supper, a track I would learn like the journey to my own pantry. We watched the *MacNeil/Lehrer NewsHour,* which we would do at the end of Jane's day in so many hospital rooms. We made a list of things for me to bring from home the next morning: Jane's address book with telephone numbers, her boom box and a clutch of CDs, brassieres and underpants and sweats, toothbrush and toothpaste and floss, books, and photographs from our walls. When I left Jane's room that night, I stopped at the Days Inn, just a mile away, and made an indefinite reservation.

Polly already occupied our house. She had let out Gus. She had fed him and Ada, our cat. We talked of Jane and of daily practical things. Then I needed to tell the friends, beginning with Jane's closest. I telephoned Alice Mattison in New Haven, giving her the news and Jane's number. Alice called Jane and telephoned Joyce Peseroff, third of the friends who worked on their writing together. I packed what we had listed, adding a wood engraving by Thomas Nason. I read through the letters I had dictated before my trip to Charleston, and added postscripts. I dictated new letters. I slept. In the morning I helped Polly with the rest of her moving, telephoned Jane at her room, getting no answer, and canceled our performance of *Love Letters.* (Jane and I had been scheduled to perform the play on Valentine's Day at a local college; we had done it the August before at a theater in the White Mountains.) Leaving the house to join Jane, I took an early lunch at Blackwater Bill's, where I found a poster for the canceled play. It was a good picture of the two of us, and I removed it—to thumbtack it on the wall of Jane's room. The photograph had run with a story in the *Boston Globe Magazine,* published just two months before, a piece that referred darkly to my own recent cancer. The headline read HAPPY FOR NOW.

Jane wore a hospital gown as plastic tubes delivered chemotherapy into her chest. I had been anxious all morning, out of contact, and now I felt a reassurance that became familiar whenever I entered her room after an absence: *She is still here.* When Jane had not answered the telephone that morning she had been in an operating room where a surgeon inserted a Hickman into her chest. This catheter, attached to a vein just above her heart, dangled three outlets from which blood could be drawn and through which liquids could enter her bloodstream: chemo, nutrition, water, red blood cells, platelets, antinausea medicine, antivirals, antibiotics. Her night had been busy with procedures and pain, including her first bone marrow biopsy. A nurse or doctor jabbed a stout needle into her pelvis and extracted a sample of marrow for testing in the hospital laboratory. How many times over the next fifteen months did Jane undergo this bone-hacking? Two residents collaborated to tap fluid from her spinal cord for more testing. Her marrow biopsy confirmed the diagnosis of acute lymphoblastic (or lymphocytic) leukemia, known as ALL. Further analysis would make diagnosis more particular. ALL is the form of leukemia children typically get, and recover from, but Jane was a forty-six-year-old woman.

Leukemia was discovered or named a hundred and fifty years

ago by two physicians at almost the same time, an Austrian and a Scot. Presumably leukemia—"white blood," in Greek—had been with us always, and its progress often attributed to galloping consumption or anemia. Doctors and researchers over the next decades discovered leukemia's division into myelogenous and lymphoblastic, and subdivisions into chronic and acute. For a long time it was untreatable, and it remained incurable until recent years. After 1895 radiation (the spleen for myelogenous, lymph nodes for lymphoblastic) helped chronic cases survive longer. Nothing helped people with acute leukemia. Later still, arsenic was the first chemotherapy, with similarly limited results. It was not until 1938 that we approached modern chemotherapy, and in the 1950s Dr. E. Donnall Thomas began experimenting with bone marrow transplants. At first he transplanted only the marrows of identical twins. Not until 1979 did he perform a transplant in which donor and recipient were unrelated. As with so much medicine, every decade doubles the knowledge accumulated earlier.

The day began as a continuation of shock and dread. We spoke of love as we did every day for fifteen months. I unloaded the things I had brought her, and Jane changed from a hospital gown into sweats. A nurse unhooked her from her pumps so that she could take a shower. I set up her boom box and played Messiaen. I read aloud to her. Jane wanted something to write on, and in the hospital's bookstore I bought her a plaid notebook. I did not read it until after she died. She started by writing about the day before:

> Last day of January 1994. Monday. flu? nosebleed, trip to
> Dr. Foote. His call about three hours later. Perk ["Perkins"
> was Jane's pet name for me] on the way back from

Charleston, S.C., calls from Boston to say plane was one and a half hours late. I'd called Mary Lyn to be with me—something told me to call her. I think I am dying in the car.

I brought to Jane's room my grand leather tote, an L. L. Bean device Jane gave me a dozen years earlier, stuffed with books and paper for work. While Jane dozed after her wakeful and painful night, I read and wrote. Three or four days earlier I had signed a contract to write a children's story with Babe Ruth in it—because my friend Barry Moser wanted to paint Babe Ruth—and I took out a pad of paper to begin *When Willard Met Babe Ruth*. For months I worked on this story at Jane's bedside. There's no leukemia in it—but people have wept when they read it.

The day wore on—tests and infusions, telephone calls, the cafeteria—until I went off to the Days Inn. It was the Leukemia Day, to be repeated for fifteen months. In our twenty years at Eagle Pond, Jane and I lived by routine, repeating the same motions in our big old house, schedules of work and love, reading and gardening. Now the schedule was nausea and dread, elevators and cafeteria, boredom and panic and occasionally relief. Jane vomited because of the chemicals that promoted remission and extended life. Further drugs helped to limit side effects—Ativan, Benadryl, Zofran—but engendered other side effects. Frequently I fetched her the emesis basin—hideous pink plastic barf bowl—or sought a nurse. I helped, if it helped, by murmuring sorrow and love, and in my helping of course I was helpless; such palliation as one can supply is pitiful, but one supplies it. I supplied my inevitable presence beside her, interrupted only for sleep.

That first night at the Days Inn, I walked up and down in my room trying to make myself understand what was happening, so extraordinary that it felt like illusion. Over and over again I re-

peated, or tried to repeat, one sentence: "My wife has leukemia."
Again and again I misspoke internally, and it came out, "My life
has leukemia." It can be difficult to distinguish pity from self-pity.

Mornings at the Days Inn I clobbered together a quick free
breakfast in the lobby. Coffee, skim milk, juice. I toasted two
waffles and took them back to my room to slather chunky peanut
butter on them. A peanut butter sandwich was breakfast routine
at Eagle Pond, and I had packed Teddy's Super Chunky. One
morning—as Jane recorded in her plaid notebook, and told visitors, laughing—she asked me what I had for breakfast and I said,
"Oh, the usual. Meatloaf on waffles." Maybe meatloaf, a longtime
staple of my cuisine, felt even more comfortable than peanut butter. Meatloaf Wellington was a regular feature of the cafeteria at
Dartmouth-Hitchcock, and over the next fifteen months I looked
forward to its weekly reappearance, as I did to the featured ziti au
gratin, a.k.a. macaroni and cheese. At noontime I took the elevator
to the second floor and entered the cafeteria line, filled my plate,
added a V-8, and paid the cashier. Medical personnel were
charged less than civilians, and I was so steady a customer that the
cashiers provided me the discount. Usually I ate a cookie in the afternoon. Suppertime, sometimes I repeated my lunch, especially if
soggy meatloaf Wellington perpetuated itself in the warming
trays. Often I grabbed a hamburger, cooked and wrapped at the
grill, added onion and ketchup, bought another V-8, and carried
my supper back to Jane's room, for the comfort of sitting beside
her while we watched the *NewsHour*. Usually by seven Jane was
exhausted and I left her for the Days Inn, first putting on a CD—
Mendelssohn, say—so she could drowse toward sleep through
music as she did when she was a child in Ann Arbor.

At the Days Inn I drank a beer, often with a tubal basketball
game dimly observed, while I dictated letters. For all of my adult

life, I have been a prolific writer of letters, thousands every year. Particularly after the move to New Hampshire, where Jane and I became virtually reclusive, letters were my social life; by letter I am positively gregarious. I write them in order to connect with people, whether I have anything to say or not. Now indeed I had something to say. It comforted me to keep my friends alert to what happened. Writing poems and stories by day, dictating letters by night, I required assistance. I hired Bert Hillsgrove, our retired Rural Delivery man, to bring me the mail every day from the Danbury post office together with my typed letters in one case and word-processed manuscript in another. When he arrived with the mail and the typing, he picked up tapes to deliver to my assistants for typing the next day.

Every day, my children and some of our friends telephoned Jane's room. Always I picked up the phone and reported the news before passing the phone to Jane, to diminish her telephone time. Sometimes I told friends "five minutes" or "two." Sometimes, when her suffering was acute, she could not talk with anyone. Most of my news was of headaches and stomach cramps and continual nausea; sometimes I could say that the blood count looked better. Jane could read little, and often found it impossible to concentrate enough to listen when I read aloud. In better times I read her Henry James, but now on good days it was Dave Barry—and one column was plenty. Mostly she wanted silence. Much of the time she lay dozing or trying to doze; some antinausea medicine is soporific. When I arrived each morning at six I bought the *Globe* and a large coffee and read the newspaper in the winter dawn's faint light. As she woke we talked about her night and how she felt right now. All day when she shut her eyes I worked on poems and prose: old poems from the old world and new poems about Jane in her illness, children's books, essays, notes for the new edition of a text-book, short stories. When I finished with writing I dictated what I had written anew. "Do you mind if I mumble?" "Mumble away, Perkins." Sometimes she felt alert enough to listen as I spoke the draft of a poem into the recorder. "Sounds good," she might say.

Every other day I left Jane for two hours to visit my mother, usually in the afternoon. Once a week I drove all the way home for clean clothes or further objects that Jane had thought of. Friends drove Polly to the hospital every two days. Jane's psychiatrist Dr. Solow frequently dropped by her room from his office on the fourth floor. Whenever he arrived, I took a walk. Our minister Alice Ling, who was teaching at a theological college in Hanover, visited to talk and to pray. Sometimes too many friends or ac-quaintances came calling. A nurse made a sign for Jane's door: *Limit Visits to Ten Minutes Please.*

One Sunday morning at four A.M. the telephone rang beside my bed at the Days Inn. It was our doctor in New London telling me that my mother was suffering congestive heart failure again. In half an hour I stood beside my mother, gasping in Emergency at the New London Hospital, only an elevator ride away from her room. Lucy's eyes were wild, a rabbit caught in a trap, and it was excruciating to hear her rasped breathing and her moans, but she was responding to medication and it looked as if she would pull through. Gradually, with cannulae carrying oxygen into her nose, her breathing became calmer, and her eyes no longer jerked and snapped. I sat with her for an hour or so, until the staff moved her from Emergency to an ordinary hospital room, and she slept. Then I drove north again, along Route 89 to the turnoff for the Days Inn and the hospital. At six o'clock I entered the sleeping Jane's room carrying the leather tote of work. When I had secured the *Globe* and coffee, I returned to her side as she was stirring awake in the blue February morning. I told her about the adventures of the night. We agreed that henceforth I would visit my mother every day instead of every other.

As February progressed Jane's bloodwork showed that she was responding to treatment. Chemotherapy was destroying bone marrow, healthy and cancerous cells together. She became neutropenic, with a diminished immune system, vulnerable to infection—but we could expect her marrow to grow back, at first without discernible leukemia. She would enter remission—weak, thin, and bald—and take physical therapy. Sometimes the masseuse Briane Pinkson rubbed her into momentary contentment. Sometimes Jane and I walked around the floor, past nurses' pods and racks full of johnnies, blankets, unused pumps, and syringes. "Thirty laps equal one mile." One morning it was snowing thickly when I arrived at six, and Jane was awake and restless. She used a walker as we ventured outside the village of hospital rooms and nurses' pods, few people about, toward the revolving door that led outside. Like an animal Jane sniffed the fresh cold air of the world.

It was extraordinary how, after only two weeks, life had become IV poles and venous catheters and constant nausea. Earlier, we had survived my colon cancer, operation and recovery, followed by metastasis to the liver, operation and gradual recovery complicated by chemotherapy. My approaches to death had brought us closer than we had ever been, a closeness that came to seem like identity. With leukemia there was no event like eight hours on the surgeon's table, from which recovery might follow a predictable if uncertain curve. Leukemia was a dreary continuous landscape of drips, injections, and pills; sleeplessness and long sleep; nausea until there was nothing more to vomit. We sat in a small room with a big window, and we became ourselves a small room bounded by a door and a window, obsessed to remain together in life.

As we talked each day about losses and recovery, Jane fretted about her hair. When I knew her first she was twenty-two with short straight sensible hair. A year or two later, after we started dating, she let it grow long. She was in her thirties when she began to curl it, and came into her middle-aged comeliness led by her abundant erotic helmet of hair with its white streak, like a hairdresser's streak, over her forehead. With the strong bones of her face—cheekbones and chin—and her large nose, Jane's beauty was powerful. If she had been an actress you could have read her face from the second balcony. Anxious about approaching baldness, early in February, Jane decided to go by stages, and invited her hairdresser Dale to drive up from Concord and give her a shaggy short haircut. Soon after, the new haircut accumulated each morning in the shower's drain, and hair sprinkled Jane's pillow. She wrote in the plaid notebook:

> In the shower this A.M. fists full of my hair . . . Looks as if a deathly battle between two minks had occurred.

Wanting to get it over with, she arranged for the barber from the hospital's fourth floor to shave her head. The young man had never shaved a woman's head before, and trembled as he cut and clipped it away. Suddenly my wife was as bald as Michael Jordan. I admired the shape of her bald head, and caressed it continually, but nothing reconciled Jane to her baldness. Dale drove up from Concord with a selection of wigs, and Jane picked one that looked like her interim haircut. Dale took it back to Concord to streak it. Mostly Jane's head stayed naked, in the hospital. The wig was for visitors.

(Over the fifteen months, stubble grew out from time to time, only to vanish under further assault of chemotherapy and radiation. In Seattle, January and February 1995, poisons receding as the new marrow functioned, fuzz started on her bald skull and slowly and softly extended. An archipelago of white stubble forecast the streak. "My hair will save me," said Jane. "My hair will lead the way.")

By Valentine's Day of 1994 it looked good for Jane's remission. From L. L. Bean she had ordered me a green cotton sweater, dialing the 800 number from her hospital bed and using her Visa. Unable to present her with candy, wine, flowers, or dinner, I bought her a supermarket tabloid which announced that doctors had revived President Lincoln's body, and that he had lived for eighteen seconds. I found a Mahler CD done by Ozawa and the Boston Symphony; she listened to it three times a day, a supportable distraction. Music was such a passion for Jane. At BSO rehearsals, to which we bused ourselves three or four times a year, it was enthralling to sit beside her and feel the ecstasy breathe from her body. I am musically stupid—but I took in the music by attending to Jane.

In the plaid notebook I read, after her death, notes for poems that will never be written:

> Dr. looks at my fingernail, presses it, drops the hand like a woman feeling yard goods . . . Up walking for two nights, trying not to cry . . . My body and soul and mind are much more firmly attached to the world than I knew. My little army has closed ranks . . . Back of hand suddenly huge bump. On Heparin. They give me platelets . . . Lie down. Lie down on the bed. Trust God, and be where you are . . .

One day as we walked the circle together we met our old friend Betty, skinny as a sparrow and bald as a sparrow's egg. She house-sat for us in the winters when our house lacked central heat. Our first ten years at Eagle Pond, if we left home in the winter, we hired someone to tend the stoves. Betty was young and pretty, a carpenter whose partner, an older woman, sat by her side in the hospital as I sat by Jane's. Betty had a solid tumor, responding to treatment, and she was hospitalized now for an infection ancillary to her cancer. She and Jane fell upon each other with greed, sisters in cancer, and over the weeks we four developed a kinship—two old, two diminishing young.

The plaid notebook:

> Bone marrow down to almost nothing. Weak and breathless, but still eating, walking, *trying* . . . Spasms of esophagus and gut pain. Dr. Solow found me standing over the dressing table and holding my gut and crying when he came to see me mid-day. I felt trapped by the pain . . . Kate [a nurse] shaving my legs and putting cream on me. I felt as though Mother Teresa was taking care of me . . . What looked like a bird corpse hanging on the flowering crab: a sunflower head! All day slow deep powder snow. Severe gastric pain for forty-eight hours. Put on Caroline's poet shirt and slept upright with the radio on . . . Now it is time for me to lie down—lie down in trust, and be where I am . . .

Jane felt strongly the systems of friendship and love that reached toward her. Because she was depressive she had not always credited the love that her friends felt for her. Her friends telephoned, they visited when they could, they sent gifts: Alice Mattison found pretty scarves from Italy; Joyce Peseroff mailed a bathrobe with teapots printed on it; Caroline Finkelstein sent the poet shirt, later a blue-striped flannel nightgown. When forbidden flowers arrived we distributed them to the sills of nurses' pods. We did not know Garrison Keillor, but he heard about Jane's illness and sent her half a dozen Lake Wobegon tapes. We heard regularly from Wendell and Tanya Berry, from Galway Kinnell and Bobbie Bristol, from Bert Hornback, from Liam Rector and Tree Swenson. Friends talked with each other about Jane's condition, and consulted with others who did not know Jane. After her death, I heard stories: One man suffered constant advice about Jane from an advocate of naturopathic medicine. Friend X, convinced by her doctors that Jane would die, attempted to so persuade Friend Y, who believed with passionate certainly that Jane would live; they hung up on each other. Many telephoners were annoyed with me for refusing to hand Jane the phone, which I withheld only at Jane's entreaty. Some letters made me angry because they assured me that everything was going to turn out fine. The writers knew no such thing; they just wanted to change the subject, and there was no other subject. By and large, women are better than men at acknowledging dread and fear. Eighty percent of women are more clear or open than men in expressing grief or dread. Many men, and some women, deny possible or probable death. Under our circumstances, anybody's cheerfulness was acutely depressing.

As the weeks wore on I held together because I could focus entirely on Jane. I did not have to go to an office or meet a class. I could be with her fourteen hours a day, twenty-four if she needed me. A couple of years earlier I had suffered from vertigo—a trivial but debilitating affliction of the inner ear, causing staggering and nausea, that visits old men and women—but only on rare occasions, maybe three times a year. While Jane was sick, and for two or three months after her death, I had these attacks as often as once a day. In the middle of a night at the Days Inn I dreamed dizziness and woke with the room spinning. There was nothing to do but lie still and try to nap it away. I telephoned the nurses' station to tell Jane that I would be late. Otherwise, my health was good. I continued checkups on my own cancer, dreading that I might get sick and be unable to care for Jane; my reports remained clean.

Every morning the doctors made rounds and Jane's room filled with a hematologist, at least one nurse, a pharmacist, one or two medical students, one or two residents. I saved questions for them, keeping a list because Jane in her weakness could not remember: a new pain, a mark on her skin, a possible side effect. Early on, one morning the crew spent an hour telling us our future, their plan for treating Jane's leukemia, a protocol for a forty-six-year-old woman with ALL. Even after remission, without further chemo the leukemia would return. After two years of drugs, maybe it would stay away. The protocol specified a sequence of chemicals, their frequency and virulence declining toward the end. About four weeks after discharge in remission, Jane would receive the "first intensification," a booster of chemotherapy. Something different was planned for four weeks after that—the second intensification—and so on. Sometimes for an intensification she would need to return to a hospital bed, infused with something disabling. Sometimes the clinic could infuse her as an outpatient; sometimes a visiting nurse could give her a shot at home; sometimes she could merely take pills. One intensification, months away, would require radiation to Jane's skull. During this briefing, Jane and I first heard about bone marrow transplants for leukemia, apparently a drastic procedure but something that might be required to save her life.

At Dartmouth-Hitchcock, four hematologists each had his or

her specialty, and each took turns doing rounds among the hospital beds or attending in the clinic. Jane's principal doctor would be Letha Mills. The most regular attention came from nurses, and the Bubble nurses were uniformly caring and intelligent. A friend wrote me early in Jane's illness, trying to assign me a distracting task, "Tell me about the grumpiest nurse." There was no grumpy nurse. They rushed, they were harried, they dealt quickly and continuously through twelve-hour shifts with sick patients who were not always rational. They needed also to attend to caregivers like me, prone to interrupt their routine urgencies with an immediate, particular necessity.

No one medical ever minced words with us; no one condescended or minimized danger. Mary Roach was the nurse who was the best explainer of all. She had the talent to speak with careful clarity, and her mercies did not end with her articulate intelligence. When we first heard about Jane's protocol and its intensifications we were battered by the quantity of information. Confused, we asked questions of Mary after the doctors left. Mary found us a protocol for a past ALL patient, photocopied it, and left it with us as an example. As Mary talked us through the sample, she gave explanations of chemical or medical processes and procedures in language that even technophobic right-brained poets could follow. She spoke behind her transparent-framed glasses, with her cap of gray hair, in sentences that were comprehensible, without jargon or acronyms, words neat and precise without pedantry—and all the time, as she spoke, steady tears rolled down her cheeks.

From the plaid notebook:

The nurses remind me of Special Collection librarians the way they guard me . . . I dreamed last night that I was in a contest to see who can be the laziest person around—who can call for things from bed . . . First normal crap for three weeks. The simple pleasures of the poor . . . The docs say I may go home next Wednesday—in five days! Terror and delight in almost equal proportions . . .

The Grandmother Poem

Jane Jennifer Kenyon was born on May 23, 1947, in Ann Arbor, Michigan. Her father played the piano for a living. Reuel Kenyon (1904–1982) grew up the son of a butcher, and his mother was the fierce Methodist grandmother of Jane's poems. When he was only fourteen, he played for fraternity dances at the University of Michigan. After high school, he studied architecture, more his passion than music was, but could not afford to take a degree. Instead he sailed to Europe, where he spent the 1920s playing *le jazz hot* in Paris and on the Lido; he recorded hundreds of sides in these years, with Lud Gluskin et Son Jazz. (A discophile presented Jane with an LP after her father's death; we listened to young Reuel's barrelhouse left hand.) He returned to the United States as the Depression began, when his father was dying. Then he toured with big bands like Eugene Goldkette's, living out of a suitcase, playing dance halls one night in Cleveland and the next in Akron. In 1930 he jammed with Bix Beiderbecke in Walled Lake, Michigan, a wild Prohibition town north of Detroit. His first marriage was childless and ended in divorce. During the war he was performing with a dance band at a hotel in downtown Detroit, where he met Jane's mother Polly, who played cocktail piano and sang in the hotel's bar.

Pauline Miller (1913–1995) grew up in Winnetka, Illinois, the daughter of a minister who later left the church and with her mother drifted to California. At eighteen Polly began singing in

Chicago nightclubs, some with underworld connections. Her first marriage also ended in divorce. When Polly was eighty I asked her what her first husband had done, and she looked proud as she told me, "He was a professional gambler." As a young woman she traveled through the Midwest and East, singing with bands or to her own accompaniment. In glamour photographs from her professional career, she looks like Jane after Jane turned beautiful in her forties. When Polly married Reuel and bore children, she stopped singing and became a seamstress, intent on her new profession— its learning, its finesse, its equipment. Polly gave dressmaking lessons, the French Couture Method, in a fabric store in downtown Ann Arbor. Prosperous women visited the house on Newport Road for alterations, and for new dresses that Polly designed and executed.

The house was small and eccentric, perched on the outskirts of Ann Arbor. Newport Road was a dirt lane then, and opposite their house was a working farm. As a child Jane loved to tag after the farm wife as she tended to sheep and chickens. Until she was nine Jane went to the one-room Foster School, across the Huron River and north of their house. In several poems she recorded her displeasure in her one-room school. She attended a middle school nearer the city, as the city was extending itself to take over the countryside. Newport Road turned into pavement. The farm across the road stopped being a farm, and new houses sprouted like milkweed in the fields, replacing milkweed.

The Kenyon house was the domain of freelancers. Reuel gave piano lessons, worked a few hours a week ordering sheet music for an Ann Arbor bookstore, ran the local branch of the musicians' union, and played the piano—in bars, for weddings, with a Dixieland band called the Bollweevils, and at the Elks Club. When I knew him, from his late sixties until he took sick and died at sev-

enty-seven, he played weekends at a club north of Detroit. Jane
and her brother (two years older, also Reuel) had to be quiet on
weekends because the piano player slept late. Weekdays, sometimes they needed to stay out of the way when seamstressing
clients dropped by for an appointment. Life in the Kenyon house
was free, maybe scattery, a daily improvisation with little sense of
completion. Reuel was successful as a musician but would have
preferred design; he entered architectural competitions and won
honorable mentions. Sometimes he made pencil sketches of objects around the house. Jane speaks in a poem of her father's rendering of her stroller, a pencil drawing that hangs on the wall of
her study. There was something withheld or unfinished in the
house's endeavors, as if it would be dangerous to give yourself
wholly over to any one ambition. Reuel loved to read—his Lewis
Mumford collection was vast—and the house was crowded with
books, but in many of them a bookmark, halfway through, showed
where Reuel stopped reading.

There were memorable pleasures to the life on Newport
Road. Apart from professional associations, the family was virtually self-contained. The four Kenyons gardened together, caring
for their wild acre. They cooked and ate and punned together. Few
friends visited. What mattered most in this house was music and
objects of beauty. They treasured few things but they were handsome ones, china and furniture, drawings on the walls and LPs on
the hi-fi. When Jane went to bed as a child, she slept over music
and drifted to sleep hearing Debussy, Ives, Chopin, and Copland.
Making a living was always a secondary matter on Newport Road.
Neither parent was shrewd with money, and Polly was famous for
charging her clients too little.

In middle school, Jane found poetry when she read Witter
Bynner's translations from the Chinese, *The Jade Mountain*. The

aesthetic of the image remained with her forever. At first poetry was only one of the arts she loved and practiced. Like her brother she drew pictures, and Jane sang with a chorale. From the age of fifteen she worked to save money. She cleaned house one day a week, which she loathed. She baby-sat, and worked in John Leidy's gift shop in downtown Ann Arbor, the source of some of the house's prettiest things. Using her savings, at eighteen she toured Europe—Germany, England, Ireland—as one of the young singers of the Michigan Chorale. She worked at Leidy's part-time through high school into college, full-time through the year and a half when she dropped out, and part-time when she returned to the university. She borrowed money for tuition, and worked to pay it back. When we were first married, and living in Ann Arbor, she worked for the Early Modern English Dictionary, a project of linguists in the university's English department. She stopped working only when we moved to New Hampshire.

Jane never enjoyed school, except for some literature classes, English and French. One high school English teacher filled her with love for Shakespeare and left her with hundreds of memorized lines. When she first entered the University of Michigan she quickly flunked a science class and left school. Often depressed, undiagnosed and unmedicated for many years, she felt that she lived at the periphery of things. As an adolescent Jane had acne, wore thick myopic glasses that disguised her beautiful bone structure, and tended toward fat. Grown-up Jane liked to weigh a hundred and twenty-eight (at five foot six) and felt gross when she went to a hundred and thirty-four. In high school she had weighed as much as a hundred and sixty-five pounds.

When she returned to the university, she majored in French. Spring term of 1969, Jane took my course "An Introduction to Poetry for Non–English Majors." It was a class I loved to teach, in which I could evangelize—"Come to poetry!"—with enthusiasm, but that year was a bad one for me. My first wife and I had separated in 1967, and the divorce was final on Valentine's Day 1969—the same day I underwent general anesthesia to remove a spermatocele from my left testicle. A month later I had my gallbladder out and missed two weeks of classes. I think I taught well despite the miseries, but I never made Jane's acquaintance among the hundred and forty students. The following summer, Jane applied for admission to my fall class in writing poetry, then the only such class at the university. Annually, about fifty people submitted their work, and I picked the ten or twelve students whose work I liked best. Jane's manuscript included "The Needle," as yet untitled, which is reprinted in *Otherwise* and resembles her later, best work. Among the poems that she submitted, it stood out. Once I had read it—in August of 1969, summer of astronauts on the moon, summer for me of bourbon and lonely misery—Jane Kenyon's name went on the list of students accepted for English 429 that I posted on my office door. The rest of our lives—a twenty-three-year marriage, Eagle Pond Farm, and many poems—derived from "The Needle," which she wrote when she was nineteen, about visiting her sick grandmother. Every young poet writes a grandmother poem; Jane's was not generic.

That poetry workshop was the best of a dozen I taught during my years at Michigan. The students, who ranged from sophomores to graduate students, were smart, funny, lively, talented, outrageous, and agreeable. We met one long evening every week in the big living room of the old farmhouse I rented, cramped between newer houses on South University Avenue. We drank a case or two of beer and argued about poems. For the first few meetings I held the floor—talking about student work and about poems from an anthology—to establish criteria and provide vocabulary.

Before long the students took over direction of this class, in high hilarious seriousness, praising and blaming. They loved and assaulted each other, using critical terms like "shit," caring for poetry not diplomacy. Jane's voice was prominent. The teacher became peripheral, maybe an adjudicator, frequently shouted down. For the last class meeting, I brought in things of my own that I was working on, and the class tore my drafts to bits and pieces, turning my own standards back on me. After the class ended, it continued to meet in student rooms once a week for two and a half years without my presence. On rare occasions I was invited to a session.

There were no stars in that class but a cluster of bright, irreverent people who loved poetry. Jane is the one who developed, persisted, and produced the best work. Teachers become familiar with good students who take off in other directions. Two of these poets became lawyers, one hosts an NPR talk show, another edits a newspaper. (Several have continued to write poems and have published books.) Eventually, Jane wrote the poems of *Otherwise*, but no one could say that *Otherwise* was implicit in 1969 in the work of the twenty-two-year-old witty woman with short straight hair, a handsome figure, and a military vocabulary. So much in our lives depends on chance. Jane, who was seldom happy in groups, was happy in this group of student poets. She charmed and argued, swore and praised and denounced, laughed and teased with the rest of them. She made long friendships in that class, and in conference with me she was natural and easy. She never made me feel like an institution—but apparently I was terrifying enough at first. After Jane's death, I read a notebook from her undergraduate years that contains a sentence she wrote before English 429 started meeting. My house was near her co-op, and she wrote a note: "When I found out Donald Hall lives 3 houses away I felt like I did when I found that Dublin was a Viking stronghold or when I tried to catch the goldfish and found that the water was too cold to support life."

When term was over, Jane came to office hours with new work, and I saw her socially with other members of the class or at poetry readings. I enjoyed her for her brains and humor, her kindness and support for others. She had a number of boyfriends or lovers but only Bill—I'll call him—was serious. Jane was fond of him, but he wanted to marry her and Jane was skeptical. She compromised, and in June of 1970 moved in with Bill. I saw little of her while they lived together. She was practice-teaching in the autumn, toward a certificate. "Mrs. Canyon" loathed practice-teaching, and her relationship with Bill deteriorated. She felt angry all the time, she told me later, and exercised her rage on Bill. Then Bill started seeing someone else. As 1970 drew to a close, I heard from Jane's friends that she was moving out of the ménage and had taken a room in another co-op. Although it was she who did the breaking off, she felt miserable over what she perceived as her failure. I called her up and asked her to supper in January 1971. Unhappy myself, I worried for Jane, whom I knew to be vulnerable. When we ate supper that night she talked about nothing but Bill. (I countered with my own complaints.) We continued to see each other, about once a week, and for a while the subjects remained the same. Jane spoke of needing psychotherapy. Through friends in the field, I helped her find a smart Freudian, whom she visited two or three times a week, cheap enough because he was still a student. Therapy did not cure her depression but helped her identify feelings (telling love from rage, for instance) so that she could attempt the deliberate life. Whenever we saw each other she stayed overnight. We were not passionate or committed lovers but comforts to each other—and in 1971 if a couple had dinner together they tended to have breakfast together. I continued to date other women, and made sure that Jane knew it. If she saw anyone else I did not know about it, nor would I have minded. After two or three months, one night a week became two nights a week, and we spoke less frequently of other people.

Meantime we were both writing poems, neither of us well. Jane wrote angry poems about Bill. Receding from inadmissible reality, I wrote poems of a light and goofy fantasy. College audiences laughed when I read them aloud but the poems were evasive and trivial. In these slapdash weeks and months I looked forward to my dates with Jane but began to feel nervous, noting that increasingly I attended to one woman, as old loves sloughed off, got married, or moved to Oregon. Neither Jane nor I said "I love you." Maybe both of us feared that "love" was a synonym for "pain"—and we were feeling only pleasure together, light pleasure. We laughed together; we spoke of poems; we fretted over our friends.

In summer Jane sunbathed at a municipal pool and wore minidresses that showed off her tanned legs. Always when I parked at her co-op, to pick her up for a date, I watched her walk from the front door before I could get out of the car. (We remained promptness freaks, something in common.) Then I signed a contract to write a biography—never completed; a long story—that required my presence in Los Angeles. In the summer of 1971 when I flew west for a month, it was Jane I took out the night before leaving. We exchanged letters; we talked on the telephone. I missed her; she missed me. When I flew home, Jane and I had supper the day I landed.

We saw each other not only alone but in company. My children liked her. I took her to middle-aged cocktail parties. We had picnics and played volleyball in Delhi Park outside Ann Arbor with the young scholars and writers of Michigan's Society of Fellows and with poets from Jane's old workshop. We began to see each other three nights a week, sometimes four. Therefore, I worried about what would become of us. It would hurt to stop seeing each other—yet obviously we couldn't remain together because I was nineteen years older. Actuaries had Jane outliving me by twenty-five years. One night we were drinking a nightcap in my living room when my mother cat entered through the cat port with a large flap of stomach skin torn open and hanging down, red meat showing. Horrified, we packed her into the car and drove to a veterinarian who stayed open at night. The wound, though ghastly looking, was superficial. The vet knocked her out, applied antibiotics, dispensed some pills, sewed Catto up, and sent us home. We sat down again, to finish our watery drinks, with hearts still pounding. As adrenaline flowed and defenses disappeared, I found myself asking, "Do you think we ought to get married?" That night, we spoke of the issue reasonably. (We were unromantic lovers; ten years later we practiced candlelight and flowers.) We decided that we were too far apart in age; we would stay as we were. Jane was completing an M.A. in English. Maybe later she would do an M.F.A. at Iowa, but for now . . . I felt relief as we climbed the stairs.

Jane wept through her psychotherapy and began to perceive a coherence and history to her troubles. I was her confidant; intimacy became habitual. From time to time, in our evenings and early mornings together, we alluded again to the possibility of marriage and put it aside again. Then, on Christmas Day of 1971, we had a terrible fight, worse than any other fight before or after. We parted shaken, trembling, uncertain when or if we would see each other again. After twelve or fourteen hours apart, I felt bereft and desperate at the prospect of losing her. I telephoned and discovered that she felt as I did. When I picked her up, her face was wretched with fatigue. "Maybe we *should* get married," I said. Jane nodded, and we embraced without speaking. Surely the dread of separation has accounted for more than one engagement, and doubtless there are better reasons for getting married—but all marriages start in ignorance and many from need; what matters is what you do after you marry. We set the date for April 17, 1972, when my son Andrew would be home on school vacation. We told friends. My Ann Arbor contemporaries were surprised, and I don't think they gave us much of a chance. Who could blame them?

We went ahead, although I was assailed with misgivings and I am sure that Jane was. It was a relief to concentrate on one woman—but did I love her? Was *this* what I wanted for the rest of my life? She was so young, twenty-four. (I was so old, forty-three.) Suppose she stopped writing poetry? Poetry was what brought us together, and Jane's commitment to the art burned at her center, but would it endure? Would she remain a poet and prevail? One night I was regretting that as a poet she would be Jane Hall. The moment I said so, we looked at each other with the same thought: In 1972, it was no longer obligatory for a woman to lose her name, so Jane Kenyon remained Jane Kenyon.

We were anxious, but before the wedding we were distracted by a crazy adventure: We flew to Florida and I tried out—as it were—for the Pittsburgh Pirates, despite my age, my two hundred and fifty pounds, my unspeakable conditioning, and my stunning athletic incompetence. (There is an account of this caper in *Fathers Playing Catch with Sons*.) Two or three times players addressed Jane as "Mrs. Hall," and she was unresponsive. When we returned I was bruised, half crippled, and exalted. We continued to make wedding arrangements as the date inexorably approached. The day before the wedding we had lunch together at a downtown bar—pale, shaky, hardly speaking. We were married by a judge at city hall in the company of my children, Jane's parents,

Jane's brother Reuel, and her old roommate Dawn, who later married Reuel. Our families had posed no problems. Neither Polly nor Reuel spoke against the marriage. My children, just-eighteen and almost-thirteen, had known Jane for more than a year, from picnics and volleyball games and suppers. After the brief ceremony, we settled in to champagne and lobster at the Gandy Dancer.

School was over soon, and Jane and I flew to New York for a short holiday or honeymoon, her first visit to the city. We stayed at the Plaza and hired a horse and buggy to rattle through Central Park. Shortly after New York we flew to Los Angeles, where I put in some work on the biography. Everything was novel, and a little frightening. We quarreled rarely; we were careful or cautious with each other. I remembered fifteen years of a marriage that ended in failure; the failure of Jane's six months with Bill still weighed on her. We investigated the miraculous notion that people could live together and be courteous, remain wary of the other's feelings.

From Michigan, we drove east with my children to see my grandmother and my mother, first in New Hampshire where Kate was ninety-four, and then at my mother's Connecticut house. Jane loved the family farm, the old Cape sprawled backward into Ragged Mountain, white clapboard and green shutters. In the living room an unplayable piano heaped with family pictures. The beds were too swaybacked for comfortable couple-sleep, but the house carried for Jane profounder comforts, with its warren of little rooms and doors, its low ceilings, its long side porch, its iron stoves and low set-tubs covered with oilcloth, its prospect of Mount Kearsarge, Eagle Pond, and the Blackwater River.

This place had been the Eden of my childhood. My grandmother Kate kept sheep and chickens until she was in her nineties but was now increasingly senile. The Glenwood kitchen range had been fitted with kerosene and Kate would turn the burners so high that they scorched the ceiling. Kate obsessed about certain subjects, like a minor dispute with a neighbor over boundaries. She returned to these worries endlessly, repeating the same questions. When I visited with my new wife, Kate addressed the mystery of her grandson's divorce and second marriage. Ever since Jane and I had married in April, my mother Lucy had answered Kate's multiple questions by multiplying simplifications, hoping to solve Kate's worry by providing a quick, false explanation. Kate had to hear it from me. I suffered her interrogations in the dining room—Lucy, Jane, and my children sat in the living room next door, so that my children were liable to hear her—as she asked me in a loud whisper, "Now, *the other one* didn't take care of you? But *this one* takes care of you?" I said *hush hush* and rapidly nodded my head. A few months later, further into dementia, Kate entered the Peabody Home in Franklin.

The autumn of 1972 I took leave without pay for a term, and Jane and I spent a month in England. I interviewed people for the biography. In the spring term I taught again, and we undertook further adventures. In June I rode twenty-six miles in a hot-air balloon. Jane took photographs of the ascent, then followed the flight south into Ohio where we landed digging up a farmer's field. In that second summer of our marriage, we stayed at the farm with my mother and visited my grandmother at the Peabody Home. The weather was perfect and Jane and I went exploring by foot and by car. Both of us preferred country to city. Ann Arbor was dinner parties and cocktail parties on weekends, "come on over after the game." When Jane and I gave obligatory reciprocal parties, we panicked. When the doorbell rang, and new guests arrived who had to be introduced, each of us ran away so the other could misremember the names of friends. There were two routes from the front of the house to the kitchen in the rear. More than

once Jane and I almost knocked each other down, running by opposite paths from the challenge of the doorbell to the back of the
house. We had dear friends in Ann Arbor, but if a gathering was
larger than two couples, overpopulation impeded the pleasures of
friendship. It was the life I had grown accustomed to over a dozen
years. While my first marriage was ending, party weekends provided a refuge. Now, with Jane leading the way, I looked for another kind of existence—which would more closely resemble the
ways of an only child who had wanted to write poems and who
cherished summers on the farm.

The next academic year I had a Guggenheim to work on the
biography. Again I took time off, and again Jane and I went to
England, for pleasure, plays, and interviews. But now the project
failed, when the widow of my subject detested a partial draft and
withdrew from our agreement. I apologized to the Guggenheim
Foundation and looked around for something else to undertake.
In March I did a poetry reading in Florida and visited my old Pi-
rate teammates in Bradenton, where they stretched and practiced
for the new season. I missed the nation of baseball that I had
briefly explored. When Dock Ellis hinted about a Dock Ellis book,
I foresaw hanging around the game and being paid for it. Our
agents took over and I signed a contract. Jane and I followed the
Pirates—and entered an African-American universe—while she
took photographs and I made notes toward *Dock Ellis in the
Country of Baseball.*

That summer, before another visit to New Hampshire, we
drove around the flat Michigan countryside among horse farms,
thinking about moving from the city. Jane said, "It's silly to look at
farmhouses here when there's the house in New Hampshire."
When I heard her words I was thrilled, although her suggestion
made no sense on the face of it. How could I commute from New

Hampshire to classes at Michigan? She spoke out of love and need, not out of a practical plan. Growing up, I had wanted to live where my grandparents lived but in my twenties I discarded the daydream. Now in one sentence Jane rehabilitated my old desire. If we took over the farm, we would buy not inherit. Neither of my aunts, Caroline and Nan, had money saved up for old age. My mother had a moderate income from my father's estate, but she was spending capital to keep her mother in the Peabody Home. The three sisters decided to mortgage the farm, in order to support Kate in her senescence, and then to sell it after her death. I set about to discover if I could afford to buy the place. I arranged to have the land surveyed, first time since 1865. When the surveyor reported that the farm included one hundred and fifty-two acres, I hired a real estate agent to look the place over and set a price. The house had no central heat, no insulation, and no storm windows; it did have a bathroom, cold and grungy but a bathroom; it had unreliable electricity and a noisy telephone. The agent priced the bundle (in 1974) at ninety thousand dollars. I consulted our Ann Arbor lawyer, who advised me about finances. It seemed possible that the fantasy of childhood could become the reality of middle age.

Although my mother had power of attorney, and although Kate would never leave the Peabody Home, no one wanted to complete the transaction while she was alive. I would give my mother a mortgage of thirty thousand dollars, to pay for the Peabody Home, a sum that would later become the down payment. My lawyer told me I could afford to borrow the money, but I had a better notion. When I was twenty-one, my grandfather and grandmother gave me a sixty-five-acre farm across from their land on New Canada Road. It was not a gift of monetary significance but an act of piety; they knew how much I loved the land, and the old Elder Morrill place—where my grandfather for decades had pastured his young cattle—was growing up and could no longer sustain heifers. The Morrill farm had been abandoned during the Great War, and my grandfather had bought it with maple syrup money. The old house collapsed into its cellar hole as the pasture became a pine forest; my grandfather sold the softwood to help with his daughters' college tuitions. In twenty years, he calculated, I could sell off the pine again.

A year after he gave me the land, he had another idea. Adjacent to my sixty-five acres was another abandoned farm, thirty-five acres owned by my skinflint cousin Jesse Johnson, who had sold off the timber. Every spring when he paid eight dollars in property taxes, Jesse whined about it. My grandfather said, "I think Jesse would sell it cheap." "How cheap?" "Maybe fifty dollars." Put together with the Morrill place it would give me a hundred acres. I had fifty dollars in the bank and liked the notion of extending and rounding off my acreage. "You mean just before taxes?" I said. "No," said my grandfather. "Just after."

Jesse sold me the farm for fifty dollars in 1951. Year by year my taxes rose, maybe reaching as high as twenty dollars. At some point in the 1960s, a letter arrived for me in Ann Arbor with an urgent appeal to buy my hundred acres. A rich man had bought the land adjacent to my property. I refused, not wishing to sell my grandparents' gift. And I disliked the putative buyer. The rich McGuff (he was not McGuff but he was rich) had done something that displeased me. He was known in the neighborhood for his condescensions; he told funny stories about the natives, and enjoyed reporting that he had outsmarted them. My grandfather had died leaving Kate four hundred acres and no cash. At some point in her eighties my grandmother sold McGuff two hundred and fifty acres at ten dollars an acre. She thought she made a killing.

Because he knew what he was doing, McGuff persuaded Kate's three daughters and two sons-in-law to sign a paper giving approval to the sale. (Our local Republican congressman, a lawyer from New London, assisted in this endeavor.) My mother and Kate's other heirs signed the paper because Kate was fierce, proud, and delighted with her financial acumen. Not to sign the paper would be to doubt her shrewdness.

When I needed thirty thousand dollars cash for the mortgage/down payment, in the summer of 1974, I remembered McGuff's inordinate lust for my land. I would be willing to sell my grandparents' gift to buy my grandparents' house. A real estate man told me that my hundred acres might go for as much as eight or ten thousand dollars. With malice aforethought, on the summer visit to New Hampshire I dropped a note to McGuff saying that I was thinking about putting my acreage on the market. It seemed only courteous, I disingenuously allowed, to let him know. The note no sooner reached his house than his black Porsche zapped into our U-shaped drive. McGuff sat in the living room, for the first time since he had swindled my grandmother, and offered me five thousand dollars for the land. I told him that I wanted more. After three seconds of thought he offered me eight thousand. I told him I knew it was probably ridiculous but I was going to list it at thirty thousand dollars. He laughed and shook his head and laughed some more and wiped his eyes and offered twelve thousand. I repeated that I knew I was being silly but in fact that very day I was going to list the land for sale at thirty thousand dollars. He sighed rapidly, three times, and agreed to pay me thirty thousand dollars. My grandmother was avenged.

Jane and I could look forward to owning the farm after my grandmother died. Freud says somewhere—it doesn't sound like Freud—that an adult's greatest bliss is the fulfillment of a dream from childhood. My mother and her sisters were delighted by the notion of succession: the same family continuous in the same house since 1865. No one was happier than Jane, and if her family regretted our potential exodus from Michigan they concealed it well. Because I published a textbook that began to sell, Jane and I could think about taking a year's leave without pay, the academic year of 1975–76. We decided to stay for a year in my grandmother's house, visiting my grandmother at the Peabody Home. I applied for leave and received it.

In the remaining summer of 1974 Jane and I traveled with the Pirates, talking with ballplayers late into the night and spending considerable time in the Los Angeles neighborhood where Dock grew up, visiting at length with his mother and his sisters, with old mentor coaches, and with friends Dock had run the streets with. Back in Ann Arbor the fall began an onset of poetry for me, the best things I had done for a long time. "Kicking the Leaves" anticipated a permanent move to New Hampshire that my consciousness did not acknowledge. All year as I unknowingly taught my last terms at Michigan, Jane and I looked forward to the New Hampshire year coming up. That summer of 1975 we drove to the farm dragging a U-Haul behind us, bringing comfortable chairs, a TV, bushels of manuscript, and winter clothes. My grandmother, who had not spoken for many months, began to have difficulty breathing: congestive heart failure. The great vessel of affection and endurance lay dying at last, old body shutting down. My mother, my aunts, and I took turns at Kate's bedside. We stood beside her for her last breath, my mother rubbing her head and I holding her hand. Walton Chadwick, who had buried my grandfather Wesley twenty years before, took Kate's body to New London. Daughters and grandson picked out a casket, pine covered with gray fabric, and the neighborhood attended calling hours for a last look at Kate Keneston Wells, who had played the organ at the South Danbury Christian Church for seventy-eight years, from the age of fourteen until she was ninety-two. We buried her beside Wesley, next to her parents and siblings in the Proctor graveyard. The Reverend Jones, whom my grandmother had admired when he preached at the church, improvised a prayer in which he said that Kate in heaven would keep on "growing . . . and growing . . . and growing . . ."

My mother left for her Connecticut house, September flared, and Jane and I began our lives.

Terror and Delight

On Thursday, February 24, 1994, Jane was discharged from Dartmouth-Hitchcock in remission from leukemia. Polly stepped onto the porch as we drove into the U-shaped driveway, and Gus bounded out to greet the familiar car, sniffing Jane, singing and dancing. I helped Jane back to our bed, unloaded the car, and began unpacking. It was almost as if ordinary life could resume. I set her boom box at its usual perch on the dresser beside her bed, CDs next to it. Because she would need often to stay in bed, in her weakness—and further chemo would begin in a month—I ordered a phone jack for the bedroom. Jane could speak with friends and family while she was resting. Polly stayed with us at first, helping Jane clean her Hickman, sitting with her while I shopped and did errands. As soon as Jane felt more vigorous, Polly moved back to her flat. She enjoyed her privacy; she respected ours. When she stayed with us, sleeping in the parlor/guest room, sometimes Jane and I retreated to our bedroom to hug and weep. Polly did not appear in the doorway to ask if there was something she could do.

Jane came home sick but hopeful and with surprising energy. Some of her energy was dogmatic or insistent, reminding me of times when she was manic. Prednisone is a steroid with remarkable and mysterious properties. It is anti-inflammatory and it is chemotherapy for leukemia. But each time Jane took a heavy course of prednisone it brought side effects, maybe in conjunction with other drugs, that affected her mind—mania, delusion, delirium, even psychosis. Now it promoted the Battle of the Microwave. For years we had been the only house on Route 4 without a microwave oven, and now Jane wanted one. It made sense. Jane was in no shape to cook, and at eighty Polly had largely retired from cooking. I could cook, and did, but a microwave would save time and energy; and I could quickly heat up Stouffer's macaroni and cheese. I bought the smallest microwave I could find, and Jane and I had a rare and prodigious fight over where to put it. Jane wanted it over the electric stove, which placed it directly in my line of vision, toward the kitchen, from my habitual blue chair in the living room. In my sightline, it would replace an elegant Marisol *Paris Review* poster. The microwave was ugly and I was determined to set it elsewhere. I was stubborn and adamant, tricky in argument and dogmatic. (It is possible that the most helpful and kindly of husbands was freaked out and irritable.) Usually we remained mild in our disagreements or quarrels; this time we were heated. Jane won, and the bloodshed was minimal, but Jane in her prednisone mood reported great warfare. In the plaid notebook she wrote: "Perko fighting really dirty." She told Philippa that we almost got a divorce over the microwave. A year later, back from Seattle after the bone marrow transplant, hopeful and cautious, Jane was telling someone of my daily attentions and said, "There was never a cross word between us." There almost wasn't.

Prednisone altered not only Jane's mood but her figure. The drug reduces muscle mass, and her legs became twigs. Prednisone puffs out the face and the upper body. She looked in the mirror at her wide bald head, feeling repelled and repellent. "I am Telly Savalas." Several times we made love, but when Jane felt ugly her desire diminished. Lovemaking was not up to standard, and at her suggestion we stopped trying. Decent days were followed by set-backs, with sudden necessities to drive to Emergency and check out a new symptom. Jane took Percocet or morphine for pain, with resulting constipation, with resulting laxatives. The plaid notebook:

> Bliss at the beauty of the house, though it is messy. Over-whelmed by having to think my way through cleaning wound, flushing catheters, keeping meds straight. Still happy to be home . . .
>
> March 2—the nadir . . . intractable pain . . . I've been off my drugs [psychotropics] for almost a month. I am not protected now . . . Guts opening again with massage and Senekot . . . Total exhaustion. Can't even talk on phone. Fuddled by Percocet. We switch to Motrin. Pain Pain Pain. . . . Perky helped me with impossible mail: "I'm a composer who has set 'Let Evening Come.' The concert is next Thursday. May I have your permission?" . . . Snow up to dining room windows in back . . . Still can't read . . .
>
> March 3—panic after dinner trip to ER . . . Terror and boredom . . . home at midnight. Shaking uncontrollably . . .

Every day Jane cleaned the wound where her Hickman entered. The hole was high on her chest, above her breasts, slightly off center. Every day Jane pulled yesterday's dressing off—a plastic covering called Duoderm that protected the gauze and held it in place—and the gauze that fitted around the tube extruding from the wound. With Q-tips and an antiseptic she scrubbed at the edges of the hole, studying the site in a mirror that stood angled on the table's top. She moved slowly and carefully, concentrated. She spread antiseptic around the wound's edge, then covered it with new gauze, sliced to fit around the tube, then patted new Duoderm in place. She flushed the Hickman's three ports with heparin, keeping them clear—they tended to occlude—for blood-drawing or for infusions on our visits to the clinic. Twice a week we drove there for bloodwork, which sometimes showed that Jane needed a transfusion of red blood cells or platelets. We always had questions: a new pain, a new symptom, a new pattern of nausea. At home, my children paid us visits bringing the grandchildren. My daughter's eldest daughter, Allison, who would turn six in the summer, found it upsetting to look at Jane—plump-faced, pale, and wigged in a rocking chair.

Every day I left Jane and drove to New London to sit for half an hour by my mother's bedside. There were times when Lucy was so deaf that I talked to her by writing on a pad; at times we could speak at a normal volume. When Jane's blood counts rose, and she was no longer so vulnerable to infections, she visited Lucy as well, wearing a mask through the public area at Clough Extended Care, wearing her wig. Lucy's room burgeoned with family photographs and cookies that Maine cousins mailed to her. My mother's one complaint was the establishment's food. One day she spoke with wistful longing about how she would love a piece of apple pie. I bought her a slice at a family restaurant nearby and watched as she ate it with a plastic fork from a plastic plate, ninety years old, dying, barely able to walk with her arthritis, with pale piercing blue eyes and seamed face transformed by the rapture of gummy apple pie.

When Lucy had recently suffered an episode of congestive heart failure, she was exhausted and could do nothing, not read nor listen to the radio. But there were good times. Once as I arrived she was sitting in her chair sewing nylon scrubbers—the busywork of an old lady brought up to suffer no idle moments; her mother in her nineties stitched potholders for sale at the church fair. Beside her was Willa Cather's *My Ántonia*, which she had been reading with rapt attention. Often she could manage to read nothing more than the large-print *Reader's Digest*, which I fetched her from the hospital library upstairs. She read large-type Agatha Christies, and claimed that old age was a blessing: She could read the same mystery twice in two weeks, having forgotten the plot.

Only last August we had brought her from Connecticut to New London Hospital, fifteen miles from our house. Four months earlier she had turned ninety at her house in Hamden. Jane and I were visiting for her birthday—we drove from New Hampshire to see Lucy once a month—and my children surprised her by arriving at noon with their five children, aged one to four. Lucy's spirits were remarkably sanguine despite her age and afflictions, and we took photographs of four generations. After an hour, I could see Lucy's fatigue rising like shadows at night. I chased my children and grandchildren away so that she could take a nap. Her mind was fine but not her body. She could hobble to the toilet with its raised plastic extension; she could hobble to the kitchen nearby. Jane and I were present for two episodes of congestive heart failure, which were desperate to endure or observe as she panted in panic, largely unable to breathe. She would dial 911 and the medics would arrive, give her a shot, fix cannulae in her nose, and take her to Yale–New Haven Hospital. When an attack occurred and we were not present, her neighbor across the street, Bob McIntosh, would call us in New Hampshire and we would drive down. As she spent a week in the hospital recovering, Jane and I would drive back to New Hampshire, pack up, return to Connecticut, bring her from hospital to house, and stay with her for a week or ten days after the attack. Jane would make soup and freeze it, or turkey meatballs.

We performed this pattern maybe ten times. A month after

her ninetieth birthday in April, she was hospitalized again; again in June; then again late in July. We brought her home in August of 1993 and were still with her two days later when she had to dial 911 again. This attack convinced her that she had to leave her house, where she had wanted to die. Always, when she talked with us after recovering from an attack, she would wish she had not dialed 911, but the panic was too great. Her eyes rolled in her head, she made terrible noises, and death would not come, only terror. Years before, she had said that she would someday leave her house for the Peabody Home, where her mother Kate died—but that time never came. By August of 1993 she was too sick to enter the Peabody Home, so I found her a place at a facility attached to New London Hospital. When she had an attack, nurses could wheel her into the hospital's Emergency.

At the Clough Extended Care Center, unhappily removed from her house, Lucy underwent times of lethargy and depression. I knew, she knew, everyone knew that she could not live long. She wanted it to be over with. Yet when I visited her daily, her face lit up. Her sixty-five-year-old child performed a daily connection to the vanishing life of affection. Philippa drove up from Concord with Allison and Abigail. With the ninety-years-younger Abigail, my mother played hand-slap on the rails of her bed. Andrew and his wife Natalie drove from Belmont, outside Boston, with three more great-grandchildren, always aware that one visit would be the last. After an episode of congestive heart, she was tired and confused. One day in March when Jane was too sick to visit my mother, I went alone and returned to tell Jane that it was an unhappy visit. Lucy tended to disguise her feelings upward, stiff upper lip, but on this day she felt too horrid to fake it. She wanted to die. She scarcely gazed in my eyes but mumbled disconsolately, and yet she didn't want me to leave after my usual half hour. I stayed longer, but became anxious over Jane and left. When I told Jane how bad my mother felt, Jane decided immediately that we would pay Lucy a surprise visit after supper. We ate supper with Polly, then drove to New London and walked in Lucy's door. I remember her old head turning wearily toward us, then its look of purest joy to see us arrive unexpectedly.

The first intensification was set for March 22, when Jane would spend the night in the hospital because the new drug might cause an allergic reaction. Naively we assumed that these boosters would simply guarantee Jane's continuing remission. In fact, each of them involved a new assault on her marrow and her immune system, more neutropenia, more side effects. It was on this visit that we heard the bad news from our doctors. Jane wrote about it in the plaid notebook:

> Tuesday March 22. We learn from Dr. Mills that they want a bone marrow transplant ASAP because of the Philadelphia chromosome markers, which make a relapse much more likely. So we're after R. [her brother Reuel] today for blood to send to Dedham, where they make a culture with my blood to determine compatibility . . . Shock. I thought I was putting myself back together, and now I must start over . . . I've had a lumbar puncture and four or five other things: 2 hornet stings in the arm. I'll learn to inject myself today, and get away mid to late afternoon . . . Perky shattered. I just want to get going.

A condition first identified in Philadelphia in 1960, the Philadelphia chromosome, present in certain leukemic cells, causes a peculiar fragmentation, and these cells cannot be destroyed by chemotherapy and radiation. Eventually they will overcome any remission. Such cells seem to hide when under assault, then reappear months or a year or two later. As I discovered after Jane's death, when I was shown her karyotypes in an electron microscope photograph, the fragmentation of certain chromosomes within her cancer cells was even greater than the usual Ph fragmentation—and therefore Jane's prognosis was particularly poor. She needed a bone marrow transplant, called a BMT. The donor's blood must match the recipient's HLA antigens or the new marrow will be incompatible with its host. The new marrow must first engraft, inside host bones, and then produce new blood. The most likely matches come from relatives, and we set out to investigate Jane's brother as a possible match. A laboratory can test for a marrow match by examining the prospective donor's blood, and the Red Cross in Michigan arranged to draw Reuel's blood. Brothers and sisters match one time in four. We knew that finding an unrelated donor—marrow from someone anonymous, searched through the National Marrow Donor Program—was a chancy business.

For Jane and me, the discovery of the Philadelphia chromosome was devastating. It was the day on which I first clearly foresaw Jane dying. We knew that a BMT was agonizing—all around us in the Bubble were people undergoing autologous BMTs, in which a patient's own marrow is harvested, saved, and returned— but the mind must make room for what it may not avoid. We learned that Hitchcock did only autologous transplants—with Jane's acute lymphoblastic leukemia, her own marrow would not work—and that therefore we would have to find another hospital. I walked the corridors weeping. Nurses and doctors and a social worker stopped to hug me. In two weeks we had more bad news: Only four of Reuel's antigens matched. Jane's chance for life depended on finding a nonrelated donor from the donor bank, which kept on file a record of potential donors—then two hundred thousand—largely collected during drives conducted in areas where someone was looking for a match. Before we could try for a donor, we needed to choose a hospital that would oversee the search. I wrote the Minneapolis office of the National Marrow Donor Program and received its catalog of hospitals.

Jane's projected transplant was almost a new variety. The first nonrelated transplant took place in 1979. Only recently had nonrelated transplants extended to people in their forties—the older you are, the poorer your chances—and there were few hospitals that had much experience of such a procedure. I read the catalog from start to finish over an anxious week. We preferred a Boston hospital, to stay close to house and family. Brigham and Women's by the end of 1993 had done thirty-four nonrelated BMTs, and Dana-Farber thirty-two. These figures compared well with New York hospitals. We made an appointment at Brigham and Women's to discuss the possibility of a BMT. We feared that maybe *no* hospital would accept her for transplant, even if we found a match, because Jane's age and the virulence of her disease made her an especially difficult case. It was isolating to think how few people had undergone what we hoped Jane would undergo. I kept reading the catalog of hospitals that performed BMTs. Halfway through the list, I thought that we would go to the Twin Cities: The University of Minnesota had done two hundred and thirty nonrelated transplants. The list of possible hospitals was alphabetical by state, and when I got to Washington I found that the Fred Hutchinson Cancer Research Center in Seattle had done more than six hundred nonrelated transplants. When I spoke of this discovery to Letha, she perked up. She had worked at the Hutch, and I learned that the man who developed the bone marrow transplant—E. Donnall Thomas, who won a Nobel for his work—was a founder of the Hutch. It was the place for hard cases, and Jane was a hard case. We canceled our appointment in Boston and negotiated with the Hutch about overseeing the search.

We could only say that we *hoped* to go to Seattle—and the alternative was death in New Hampshire. In the donor program archives, the computer could quickly discover, there were no samples that matched Jane in all six antigens, but many of the donors were listed for only four antigens. (Two other antigens are more complex and expensive to type.) The Bone Marrow Donor Program began retesting people who matched at four, to look for a full match. They summoned six or ten at a time to draw more blood. We waited, aware that scientists in Seattle and elsewhere were searching for possible matches. We were lucky that it seemed worthwhile to search. Only a year earlier, Jane would not have been considered for a transplant. At the Hutch, now, there was a new protocol for a person of Jane's age with Jane's disease.

The day after the first intensification, with no allergic reaction to the new drug, Jane was discharged and I brought her home, where Polly had installed herself again during our overnight absence. Jane was tired and weak, and I told her I would drive her home to bed, then return to see my mother. But our drive home would take us close to my mother, and Jane insisted on stopping briefly to see her. Soon Jane would be neutropenic again, from the latest insult to her marrow, which would make a later visit more dangerous. We spent twenty good minutes with my mother, and we did not regret it. At eight the next morning my doctor Don Clark telephoned again. He didn't think my mother would make it this time. When I arrived, I saw Don Clark sitting in the hallway writing notes. He caught my eye and shook his head. On her bed Lucy lay dead at last, one month short of ninety-one, pale and still twisted with her struggle. I felt relief along with loss; I would no longer divide my attention. For a while I sat beside the old body, then drove home to the house where she had been born, then telephoned my children, her sister Nan's husband Dick, cousins, and friends. From Lucy's longhand notes I wrote an obituary. To Chadwick's I brought a pretty caftan for her to wear in the box, and picked a dark Vermont hardwood coffin with strong handles and brass decorations. When I picked out the coffin I asked if Chadwick's offered a two-for-one sale.

The next day Jane insisted on coming with me to empty my mother's room. Lucy's possessions resided mostly at the Connecticut house, which we had put on the market only weeks before, so it was no great task to clean out the room. Lucy's memorial service in our South Danbury Christian Church—which she had attended from infancy into old age—took place on the Monday after her death, a week after the first intensification. Jane was vulnerable to infection, advised to avoid contact with groups of people, but there was no keeping her from the service. We sat with Polly in the pew that Lucy's grandparents, Ben and Lucy Keneston, had bought in 1867. The gathering was aged, many women who had known Lucy when she was a big girl and they were little. Lucy's body would remain in New London, not to be buried until Jane felt well enough to travel to the Whitneyville Cemetery of Hamden, Connecticut, where my mother would lie beside my father, 1903–1955.

The day after the service, Jane woke vomiting and continued to vomit all day with unusual intensity. She vomited fourteen times. When she had retched and gagged and throbbed and nothing was left to come up, she let me drive her to the New London Hospital. It was unthinkable to subject her to an hour in the car, to go to Emergency at Hitchcock. (I didn't think of calling an ambulance.) I drove her to the clinic where Dr. Foote had examined her two months before, next to the extended care center where my mother had just died. Doctors put Jane in a hospital bed and eventually, by an intravenous infusion through her Hickman, controlled her spasms of vomiting. Nurses took her temperature and discovered a fever, but an x-ray revealed no source of infection. New London doctors consulted hematologists at Hitchcock, who wanted to admit her to the Bubble—but there were no beds. Tomorrow they would find a bed.

That night I slept a few hours back home, and in the morning loaded the car for Hitchcock and the Days Inn. Polly moved back into our house as I joined Jane in New London to wait for the ambulance. At four in the afternoon, Hitchcock found Jane a bed, not in the Bubble but on the same floor, in a ward that the hematology crew could walk to. In the new room Jane was examined, her temperature still high but the source of the infection elusive. It looked like pneumonia, and her blood-oxygen numbers kept dropping, but nothing showed in her lungs. A week after my mother died with cannulae carrying oxygen to her nose, my wife lay in a hospital bed outfitted with cannulae. Every time I returned to Jane from the cafeteria, I turned left when I came from the elevator, in the direction of the Bubble, instead of right where Jane occupied room 150. We longed for the comfort of our familiar nurses. One time as I mistakenly approached the Bubble I saw a woman rush out of the glass doors, her face shattered with tears, followed by a social worker I recognized who put her arm around the distraught new widow and led her to a cubicle. When I entered Jane's room, where she lay white and weak, I did not tell her what I had seen. In a little while a nurse told us that a bed had become available in the Bubble.

Then an x-ray revealed a spot in Jane's lung, doubtless the source of fever, but x-rays do not reveal the nature of an infection:

viral? bacterial? fungal? Treatment would differ. Thus it was that on Easter Day of 1994 Jane underwent a bronchoscopy, a procedure in which a surgeon inserts a device through the mouth into the lungs, peers through a camera to look at lung tissue, and biopsies a snippet for the laboratory. The patient receives not general anesthesia but a drug like Versed or Demerol that bestows amnesia. I worried for Jane, who was not stoical. The drugs worked. As they wheeled her back into the room after an hour and a half on Easter afternoon, she was alarmed, wide-eyed, saying, "They didn't do it! I don't know why!" But they had done it, looked into her lungs and clipped off a sample while the amnesiac fulfilled its function. Jane the lover of music forgot the procedure but remembered the surgeon's genealogical provenance. When she told me there had been no bronchoscopy, she added with excitement, "The surgeon was Gustav Mahler's great-grandson!"

It took a while for laboratory examination to name Jane's disease. When I returned to her room the next morning, nurses and doctors were smiling, anxiety lifted. The lab had reported on Jane's disease, and the doctors were confident that they could treat it. She had PCP, *Pneumocystis carinii* pneumonia, which strikes patients with depressed immune systems—notably victims of ALL or AIDS. Bactrim usually overcomes the disease. Jane would also need to go back on prednisone. Research with AIDS patients showed that prednisone prevented PCP's scar tissue, which would diminish lung capacity. Bactrim took effect and Jane's color returned as her blood-oxygen numbers rose, and the cannulae left her nostrils.

It was two weeks after my mother's memorial service before Jane could come home, weaker than before. We left the hospital in the morning, had our lunch at home, and took a nap, our old routine, but I woke with a nightmare after a few minutes: I was at

Chadwick's. Calling hours were over, Jane lay in the coffin, and I was pulling rings off her dead fingers. I wrote the dream down in a notebook (and never wrote in the notebook again), giving the date of April 11. It was April 11, one year later, when we found out that Jane would die.

Jane came home tapering her latest prednisone. This time the drug left her not manic but agitated. She felt continually as if she were driving and had just missed a collision: the jolt of adrenaline, the rapidly beating heart. As we lowered the dosage she became calm, and for moments felt almost normal. One morning she told me how she had sleepily let the dog out, fed the cat, and walked to the bathroom to wash her face. "Then in the mirror I saw the bald woman with leukemia."

We had put my mother's house on the market shortly before she died and it sold quickly. It was a six-room mock Tudor, to which my family moved when I was eight in 1936. I left Hamden in 1944 to go to prep school, and had been a part-time visitor for fifty years, with small affection for the structure, the neighborhood, or the middle-middle culture of Spring Glen and Ardmore Street. Still, Ardmore Street was where I grew up; it was where my father and I played catch outside and ping-pong in the cellar; it was where my father died and where my mother cared for my grandmother Kate during the winters of twenty years; it was where Lucy turned into an old lady surviving on a recliner in the sunroom. Papers were passed. The new owners would move into the house on May 1, and the house needed to be empty of furniture and broom clean. Meantime it was crammed with the accumulations of fifty-eight years. I was anxious: When could I clear out my mother's house, and how could I do it? My children would meet me there, to choose furniture and rugs for the larger houses they would one day move to. Only Saturday or Sunday would be practical. Polly would stay with Jane, but I could scarcely bear to leave her. Suppose something happened? A drive to Emergency? As Jane improved in small but discernible increments, we settled on Saturday, April 23, by coincidence my mother's birthday, a year after the celebration of her ninetieth. I left Jane at five A.M. for one more trip to Ardmore Street, and arrived at nine. Andrew and Natalie in one car, and Philippa in another, would arrive at ten. It was impossible to think of dismantling this house in a few hours, four floors of accumulation from 1936 to 1994. Attic and cellar were full, disused things put away in case they might come in handy, or because of reluctance to part with old acquaintance. In a little room on the fourth floor were books and magazines and ancient manuscripts of my own, including a novel I wrote at seventeen. At first I scurried from floor to floor and room to room, undone by the task, not knowing where to begin. There were five thousand books; there were four chests of drawers with each drawer stuffed full; there were closets of clothing on every floor; the kitchen drawers were full. In one drawer I recognized a utensil that my mother had told me came from a bridal shower in Franklin, New Hampshire, in 1927.

I brought boxes, I brought lists, I brought rolls of stickers in different colors that we could fix to the furniture for the moving vans—red for my daughter's house, blue for my son's, yellow for the few pieces that would come to Eagle Pond. When my children arrived, we wandered through the six desolate rooms, cellar, and attic. Alternately, they chose beds, desks, bureaus, and chairs. My mother had designated a few pieces. When we had done with the big things we started on the small. My mother over ninety years had collected little but acquired much. She loved her fancy teacups and her Royal Doulton figurines. At times in her eighties she dreaded that her beloved objects might sell for a nickel in a yard sale. With kindness both my daughter and daughter-in-law claimed to take pleasure in the figurines; now we wrapped them in paper, boxed them, and set red and blue disks on the boxes. We wrapped silver—nobody wants to polish silver—and crystal and teacups. After four hours of intense and exhausting labeling and wrapping, my children left to return to their children.

And the house remained full of objects undesignated and untouched and undiscovered. I had a thousand decisions to make—mostly to bag small decorative objects for hauling to the dump. At two in the afternoon every surface I looked at was still covered. I put a few small things into boxes to carry home in the car—an Eskimo sculpture and a Florentine box that I had given my mother, a good Oriental rug. Then I carried white plastic bags in my left hand and with my right hand swept my mother's lifetime of possessions into sacks for the dump—decades of used-up life: Christmas presents and souvenirs of travel, decorative coasters, pretty perfume bottles dry for forty years, doilies in tatting and lace, *Walden*, leather boxes, letter openers, candlesticks, a sewing bag, bad paintings, audiotapes, snapshots of my father at college, a framed picture from the ninetieth birthday. I swept glasses and miniature ugly mugs into one bag and another and another. I filled twenty-seven bags. I threw away caftans and dresses and pantsuits. I threw away the fancy green-and-gold dress she bought when we took her to Bermuda for her eightieth birthday. When I thought I was through with one room I found another shelf or an unopened drawer or closet stuffed full. There was no time to arrange for a yard sale. I felt crazier and crazier, manic with destruction and discard. As I was about to toss a cut-glass tumbler into the bag of junk, I stopped: It was stained red at the top, and script on the side read *Lucy 1905*—an object of her second birthday. The tumbler went into a box to return to the farm it had started from.

At six I quit, drove north, stopped for supper, and got home at ten-thirty. With Jane and Polly both asleep, I sat in my chair with a beer looking over the day's mail. All night I dreamt shallow unkempt disturbing dreams of haste and waste, highways and fire. When I woke I felt hung over. All Sunday I was black-hearted and could not keep from staring at *our* things, objects that we had given each other: Staffordshire dogs and cricketers, wood engravings, a terra-cotta Etruscan woman, an Indian miniature of Shiva and Parvati.

The minimal visit to the clinic began with blood-drawing on the first floor. Then we took an elevator to the Hematology-Oncology Clinic, or Hem/Onc, where we waited for an hour while the lab checked Jane's blood. Sometimes Jane had an infusion, part of the second intensification, which was easier than the first had been. Sometimes she had methotrexate injected into her spine. Sometimes a nurse tapped into her pelvis to remove bone marrow for a biopsy. Often Jane, tired and weak, lay in an infusion room bed, eyes closed, to wait for the results of bloodwork, even if no procedure was scheduled. A nurse would take vital signs; Letha Mills's assistant, a nurse practitioner named Diane Stearns, would visit and ask how Jane had been doing. I kept notes in my Day-Timer: "Ask Letha or Diane: When do we finish the prednisone taper? / Results from the Biopsy? / Any word from the Bone Marrow folks? / Why do Jane's feet hurt? / Is the red mark on her chest an infection? / When she vomits after taking a pill, and takes another, is there danger of overdosing?" I was a nuisance; no one ever made me feel like a nuisance. Diane would closet herself with Letha; they would consult the laboratory results, and return together to Jane's bedside. If Jane's red cells or platelets were low, and she needed a transfusion, I telephoned Polly: "Jane's getting two units. We'll be four hours or so." Letha would answer questions: "We can't be sure when the next intensification will start because we have to watch the blood counts. The sore feet are a vincristine neuropathy. No word yet on a match for the marrow."

As May progressed and turned into June, Jane felt stronger. Green started up in the hayfield, the ice and snow finally gone, and we had some sunny warm days. It was the best patch in the fifteen months of leukemia, and Jane could work a little. Climbing to her study on the second floor, which had been Jane's joy for almost twenty years, was a grave satisfaction. Its windows admitted light from the south and the west, illuminating books and papers everywhere, a broad desk stacked with work, and an IBM Selectric II. Pictures covered the walls, and letters in frames from *The New Yorker*, the Guggenheim Foundation, and Billy Martin. There was a big reproduction of *The Daughters of Edward D. Boit* and photographs of Jane's family. There was an old small desk from her childhood house. There was a wall of bookshelves, over which she hung a portrait of Reggie Jackson by Tom Clark, and three paintings by her friend Loa Winter. Near the door was the small decorative tin-and-iron woodstove we found in the back chamber when we moved here. When we added central heat after ten years of woodstoves, we heated downstairs only, so Jane built a fire every morning, even on summer days when it was damp and chilly. The end of May, beginning of June in 1994, she used a quartz heater for her short visits to her desk. For three weeks Jane mounted the stairs each day to her workplace. She labored at poems on good days for as long as half an hour, and in this brief interlude of mental energy she revised the twenty new poems of *Otherwise*. Late in 1992 and throughout 1993, she had enjoyed a prolific time, writing "Happiness," "Reading Aloud to My Father," "Prognosis," "Afternoon at MacDowell," and "Dutch Interiors." Now she had the strength to budge them the final inch into completion. On warm days, she even managed to spend fifteen or twenty minutes outside among her beloved flowers, frustrated because she could do so little. She came inside to bed, her fingers grubby with dirt.

My mother's body remained at Chadwick's. As Jane's improvement sustained itself through the mild second intensification, as she survived neutropenia without infection and could safely endure the presence of others, we planned my mother's burial for Saturday, June 12. My children and their spouses would make the trip. Chadwick's arranged with the Whitneyville church for a minister and a hole in the graveyard beside my father. Marion and Charlie brought Lucy down in the back of their camper as Jane and I drove again down I-91 from Vermont to Massachusetts and Connecticut, through the Connecticut Valley alongside the river. A young couple now lived in the Ardmore Street house with their baby, and Jane and I stayed at a motel that was especially ugly. The room was brown, "the color of shit and death," Jane said.

Up at six, I prospected for a newspaper and could not keep from checking out the graveyard. No hole. I cultivate anxiety; I took a look again at nine-thirty and was gratified to see a backhoe laboring. We met at the gravesite at eleven. Marion and Charlie had erected a little canopy against the sun, and set out folding chairs. Jane sat down, and so did eighty-year-old women and men who had been my mother's friends. There were neighbors from many decades, old Brock-Hall workers, my Aunt Norma who was widow of my father's younger brother Art, her son and a grandson. Many people came forward and introduced themselves—faces I recognized from their middle age, now altered into antiquity— whom I introduced to Jane and my children and each other. We stood and sat in the pale sun chatting about Lucy and my father Don and old times. Then a woman in pastoral robes, a minister from the Whitneyville church, approached us and introduced herself. During the brief service, my mind played a slapstick tape of Lucy and Don meeting in heaven, aged as they were at their deaths—the nervous black-haired man of fifty-two and the bent crone of ninety.

When it was done, Andrew dropped a handful of cookies into his grandmother's grave. She had been a prodigious supplier of cookies. Jane said that she was up to lunch. It was not quite noon as the funeral party drove in separate cars to a Red Lobster across from Hamden High School, where I had survived 1942–44. Waitresses fixed us a big table, and the party of nine mourners chatted happily. After lunch Jane and I drove north, the journey we had made so many times, Jane resting and sleeping beside me. We passed Connecticut's long collapsing tobacco sheds and the hills of western Massachusetts, motoring alongside the Connecticut River in Vermont to exit 7 and across the private toll bridge into New Hampshire and another hour of Route 11 until we pulled into our driveway.

Animals Inside the House

LEAVING Ann Arbor in 1976 for our permanent move to Eagle Pond, we packed dishes into barrels and books into boxes. Tons of books fit into a big U-Haul truck. I weighed the truck and found I had space for more. I added seventeen years of manuscript and correspondence and weighed the truck again; my papers amounted to a ton and a half, which led me to speculate about a library archive. I drove alone, two long days to the farm, and hired help unloading. The bookshelves were not ready, so the toolshed and the barn filled with boxes of books. We had left behind at the farm our second car, the old Saab, which I drove back to farewell parties in Michigan. We said goodbye to many friends after many years, but our eagerness to establish ourselves at Eagle Pond outweighed regret. The movers came to empty our house, and Jane and I drove separately under Lake Erie through Ohio, Pennsylvania, northern New York, and Vermont to New Hampshire. We drove through the United States, instead of taking the shortcut through Canada, because we brought three cats with us.

When we were married we had fourteen: briefly, an accident of overlapping litters. By the time we undertook New Hampshire, transporting them back and forth the first year, the cast had settled down to three. We kept this troika for another eight years. Jane had grown up with cats and doted on them. There were no dogs in her life until she discovered Gus, halfway through our twenty New Hampshire years. In the landscape of Jane's poems, for all her hills and lilies, animals get much attention. She reveled in the relative tranquility of pets and farm animals, as well as in their quirky habits and attentions, and she looked to animals for models or symbols. When we drove past a herd of Holsteins—placid on the grass, standing together under a tree during a storm—Jane vowed that after her death she would return to the earth as a cow.

The two elder cats were Ann Arbor strays who had attached themselves to my house when I was single and lonely. Mio was senior, red and enormous, long as any cat I've ever seen, and fat: thirty pounds. His character was phlegmatic, his hobby sleeping, and he provided continuous amusement. In turn, we gave him a generous food allowance, sewage disposal, petting, and praise. Mio's sleep was ponderous and tangible. When he was taking a serious nap, we could cover him with pillows, blankets, or encyclopedias without causing him disturbance. He slept all night in our bed, under the covers. So did at least one other cat every night, sometimes all three, and invariably they slept on Jane's side of the bed. If they made it difficult for me to turn over or straighten out, I gave them a shove. No shove was gentle enough for Jane, and for years she slept crooked, adapting herself to feline space. During the day, if Mio was missing from his accustomed sunny places, we would find him under the covers of our made bed—an enormous hillock, a carbuncle pushing up the quilt. We called him The Lump.

Catto was the old mother, tiny and calico and fierce. She was a great hunter and defender of her young, a doughty intelligent female of vast endurance. When I was single, and Catto had a litter of kittens, I placed them with my students. I was unprincipled enough, when the last kittens of the litter were slow to go, to bring them with me to class in a cat carrier and display them on the podium while I lectured about *Ulysses:* FREE KITTENS. For ninety minutes, kittens tumbled and played as I glossed Leopold Bloom, and when I finished lecturing they went quickly. Our third cat Arabella was Mio and Catto's daughter, a kitten we kept after Jane and I married, from Catto's next-to-last litter. Arabella inherited size from her father and calico coloring from her mother, but by a misadventure in early youth her character was blighted; she lived in perpetual dissatisfaction—dour, depressive, needy, never quite good enough. She was the Whiner Cat. She had been the comely kitten we could not part with, playful and lively, cavorting with her mother, who lavished on her the ultimate attentions of love. Overnight, after three months, Catto abandoned her, paying no attention to her formerly doted-on daughter except to hiss at her and bat her with brutal blows. Poor Arabella was desolate, receiving total rejection when she had become accustomed to tenderness. As we discovered soon enough, Catto was pregnant again, and her brain chemistry had enforced an immediate terrible weaning by violence. The chemistry never altered, even after Catto's new kittens had left the house. (We became responsible and fixed our cats.) Arabella pursued her mother's remembered esteem for ten years, receiving nothing in return but loathing.

In Ann Arbor the cats had roamed free, but outside Eagle Pond Farm pickups did sixty on Route 4. As a boy in the 1940s I had buried countless barn cats, victims of Model A's. The three Michigan cats adjusted to kitty litter and an indoor rural life. They were a continuity in the midst of our great change; only our cats and our books repeated Ann Arbor at Eagle Pond Farm. As Jane and I began to live in isolation, our attention to the cats increased. In Jane's early poems, cats put on makeup and dream of being worshiped in ancient Egypt. Childless as a couple, we made the cats our children. My own kids came for visits only. The cats were permanent residents, whom we fed, exclaimed about, petted, de-flea'd, and fretted over. Jane especially spoke of them as children, and worried. She felt anxiety over whatever or whomever she loved. To children or grandchildren, to an RD man, and lastly to her nurses, she was wont to exclaim, "Your color's not good today. Are you all right?" She was capable of discerning pallor even under a cat's fur, and our animals visited the veterinarian more often than most people's animals. When Catto and Mio turned old and sick, she nursed them as she nursed her dying father. In conversation with her friends, as in her poems, cats were a constant subject. At Christmas people gave Jane cat presents—three different door-stop cats, a cat nightlight, cat dishtowels, oven mitts and place-mats in the shape of cats. Among her chief loves it would be difficult to make hierarchy, but cats were major, in advance of secondary passions like baseball, birds, and theater. Cats belonged with flowers, church, poetry, climbing Kearsarge, me, and music.

For seven or eight years our cat family remained intact and thriving. Then Catto developed cancer in a leg. A tumor was removed, then returned, and Catto became a three-legged cat, a tripod with one limb up front. She never appeared to notice, fierce as ever, still bent on brutalizing her bewildered middle-aged daughter. Mio grew slower and more ponderous, spent more days as well as nights as The Lump. Then there was a flash of red fur in the barn, and we found that a young red male lived there, presumably dining on bats. He turned up early in the autumn. Summer people, going home after Labor Day, habitually abandon cats near hospitable-looking houses. We tried to approach him, kitty-kitty, but he ran away when we came near. Then Jane left out some food, and more food, and in a day or two I looked out the window to see her carrying our new cat into our house.

We called him Amos, after the prophet, for no good reason.

He was the most magnificent cat we ever had, beautiful and affectionate and funny. Red fur stuck out between his toes; Jane spoke of his feathers. He was a great leaper, like an NBA guard, and startled us by jumping five feet from floor to bookcase top on impulse and without strain. When he wanted to pass from one room to another, he tried turning a doorknob and occasionally succeeded. Jane and I would sit in the living room, the only people in the house, watching the front hall doorknob turn. Amos loved to lie upside down on our laps, head stretched down between our knees, four limbs splayed out, long hair (white underside) standing up straight. We were not even required to scratch his stomach.

Spring of 1984 Jane went through a manic episode. When she was manic, which happened rarely, her personality altered. She knew what she wanted and was forceful in pursuing her desires. She stopped seeing into everybody else's insides, and it was only when she was manic that she said anything insensitive to anyone around her. When she was manic my feelings got hurt. She was not angry at me, or trying to be mean, but she had no notion of how something she said might strike another person. And she was no longer hypochondriacal about the creatures she loved. No one's pallor frightened her. Amos began to look sluggish. He walked stiffly. He slept more than he normally did, and took to spending long hours behind books in my study, where it was difficult to find him. He was the missing Amos. He had a history of bladder infections, and therefore a history of Jane whisking him off to the vet's. Worrying over cat health was Jane's territory, which is why that spring I was slow to take him to the vet. When I finally did he was almost dead, and he died in a few days of liver malfunction. If Jane's fretfulness had not been in temporary abeyance, there might have been a ponderous sixteen-year-old feather-pawed Amos living in this house when Jane died.

We picked him up sealed in a box with plastic tape, and dug a hole on the hill next to the barn which would become the cat graveyard. We buried him, putting his food bowl in the grave with him, his beautiful silky hair gone dull with his illness. Not long after, it was the elderly Catto's turn, as the cancer advanced and took her. She lay near Amos. Then Mio had trouble breathing, eating, or even moving. In his evident discomfort we didn't want to disturb him. Our vet motorcycled to our house with a lethal needle, and Mio died lying in the sun of our back garden. He occupied a large hole near Catto and Amos. Arabella was dowager queen, and lingered until 1988. She had the bed to herself, and seemed briefly cheerful to have survived her parents. Then her life was ruined, yet again, as we brought into the house first a dog and then a kitten. Gus the new dog offended Arabella, but Ada the kitten offended her more. Arabella was haughty and spiteful, pretended to ignore the other animals, and walked with her head high and her tail elevated—but her affectation of dignity was ineffective. Until her death a year later, when she joined her parents under the hill, it was clear that Arabella felt cheated and deprived again, weaned by the world one final time.

Jane was such a cat lover, I had assumed we would concentrate on cats forever, but in a major life change, Jane became doggish. When she visited her friend Alice Mattison, she petted Alice's dogs. Then her friend Joyce Peseroff acquired Duncan, a West Highland terrier. Visiting Joyce, Jane met Duncan and her heart went soft. She began to think *dog,* and decided that a dog was essential to Perkins's health. I spent my day alternating between a sitting position, for writing, and full lateral recline for reading. Jane took walks and sometimes I went with her, but often I needed (I thought) to finish a piece for a magazine deadline. Jane decided that if I had a dog to walk, I would have to walk.

As she developed these notions, Jane encountered an amiable and available dog. Acquaintances of ours were landlords who allowed no pets in an apartment they let. Tenants moved in, with a temporary dog, and while they worked all day they tied up their young dog on a snowdrift outside; if they left him inside he chewed on boots and they beat him. The landlord gave notice to the tenants: Get rid of the dog or leave. Hearing the story, Jane offered to take him. Actually, Jane asked if we could have *her*, because the landlady speaking of the dog used female pronouns. When we drove to pick up our dog—I grew up with dogs—we decided that her name would be Ada. When the landlady asked us what we would name the dog, we told her, and she shook her head rapidly from side to side, repeating, "But she's a he, she's a he, she's a he!" On the way home in the car with our new animal, Ada turned into Augustus. My father's mother was an Augusta, but I think the name had another provenance: I had been reading Gibbon, and I was full of ancient Rome. Augustus quickly became Gus or Gussie, like ten billion other dogs.

He was midsize, forty pounds, part golden, part sheepdog, with a sheepdog's handsome nose. He was beautiful, and heard himself called beautiful day and night from the moment he entered our house and our lives. He was trained, we were told. We brought him into the house, took him off the leash, and he began his shy exploration. Finding an open patch in the parlor, he immediately assumed the posture of defecation. "No! No!" two voices screamed, and he stopped, and resumed outside on the leash. Never again in our house did he express his nervousness in such a fashion.

Thus the poetry dog arrived at Eagle Pond, and Jane's poems left cats behind. She entered her dog period, which continued as long as she wrote. So many of her poems have Gus in them, receptacle for every feeling. Since dogs do little else but eat, piss, shit, and *feel*, they are useful vehicles. Gus entered my poems also, and when I wrote poem-letters to Jane after her death, I kept her informed about Gus. Jane and Gus loved each other eagerly. When Gus rolled in carrion, Jane took him into the bathtub. Summers we hosed him down outside, using bottles of hotel shampoo. He became another site for Jane's phobias and hypochondrias. When we took him with us to the shore of Eagle Pond on summer afternoons, Gus developed an obsession with rocks. He would dig them out of moss, or wade into the water and duck his head to lift them from the bottom, paddle with them to shore, and chew on them— growling and nudging them to make them seem to run away. Clearly they were some animal he was programmed to catch. He chewed stone relentlessly and with audible grinding enthusiasm. Jane fretted over his teeth, and took him to the vet for oral examination, and prevailed upon Philippa's husband Jerry, who is a dentist, for inspection and diagnosis.

Not long after Gus's arrival we decided to add a kitten to the mix. Old Arabella was failing and in a snit about Gus's presence. (Gus was respectful of her, maybe frightened by her hissing; Gus was a wimp.) Our vet moonlighted as an adoption agency for unwanted pets. Thus we learned of a female kitten, black and white and two months old, available in Newport where the house's new baby had proved allergic to cats. As we drove back with the tiny kitten Ada—a female name was available—I remarked that she would surely be frightened of Gus, and we could expect her to hide for a few days. When we brought her inside and set her down, Gus approached to inspect her, and Ada leapt from the floor and attached herself to his muzzle in fierce assault. Her claws dug in and Gus yelped. Ada dropped off but continued to menace him. Gus knew his place and bowed before her wild supremacy.

Ada was *wild.* She climbed curtains. She climbed cabinets and investigated. She ate cut flowers and potted plants. Jane constantly admonished her, chasing her from counters and keeping her off stoves and out of her cooking. "Wicked cat!" was an epithet frequently repeated, even when Ada was calm and submitting to a caress. Jane adopted and sustained a moral contrast between the children: Ada was a devil of mischief and wickedness, female subject to constant reproof, always without affect or response; Gus was noble and sympathetic, put-upon heroic son, whose sibling gave him no peace. Of course I objected that Jane enacted the bad mother's preference of son over daughter, contrary to feminist principles, but my sensible criticism remained without issue.

Meantime Gus and Ada did not understand each other but found each other indispensable. Gus cared first for Jane and second for me, with Ada a close third. For Ada there was no second object of affection, no third. When we took Gus with us down to my mother's house, breaking them apart for two or three days, on our return Ada paid no attention to Jane or me but tagged after Gus's every move, and groomed him endlessly. Ada's interest in humans was negligible, except when she was hungry. She was a little cat, in part Maine coon cat, and polydigital—seven toes up front, six in back. She disdained being held, and scooted as soon as she could, but sometimes at night would leap onto my lap. She put her forepaws high on my chest, leaned forward, and licked my nose. Her principal hobby besides Gus was mice. Without claws, well fed, she was not an avid hunter—but she enjoyed sport and cruelty. In autumn and winter we were regularly gifted with small corpses, forever deposited in the same place, usually at night but sometimes with visible pride by day. I wore slippers in the house, while Jane enjoyed padding about barefoot when she woke in the morning. I came to recognize a special aborted shriek when Jane had stepped on a dead body.

Ada and Gus took naps together, cat curled inside the curved sleeping dog-body. Continually, they extended cross-purpose play-time. Ada groomed Gus's muzzle, assiduously washing him. Gus believed she was proposing mock warfare, and detached her from his jaws to pretend-bite or pretend-snap at Ada. He was clearly careful, and I never heard her screech as she did if I stepped on her tail. Often she turned from her grooming to battle, standing on her hind legs, batting at his face with her paws. Sometimes he stalked her, like a boxer looking for an opening, making little rushes and starts. She retreated, retreated—and leapt furiously at his head. Sometimes she hit an eye, and Gus would make a wounded sound and back off, looking aggrieved. More often she detached herself, pretending terror in the manner of cats, hiding away under a footstool, only to leap out at him a moment later when he dropped his guard. Sometimes Gus stopped playing when he noticed that human beings were watching in amuse-ment—how many nights Jane and I watched and laughed—for he was more interested in human response than in feline admiration. Whenever Ada had enough, it was easy for her to squeeze into a small space, behind the sofa perhaps, and take time out. But al-most always the play ended in a brief exhibition. The play excited whatever remained of Gus's truncated sexuality, and he tried to hump Ada, who at first appeared to enjoy the suggestion, raising her rump—and then removed herself. At this denouement, Jane always remarked upon Gus's "triumph of hope over reality."

So it was, animals inside the house. For the watchful dead, it must have been shocking—the sight of four-footed furry creatures *inside*. Back before Route 4 killed pets, my grandfather kept dogs.

They helped him in the summer when he climbed to fetch the cattle for milking, but their companionship mattered more than their utility. My mother remembered Hunter and Trip from the first years of the century, and remembered finding Hunter's body in an abandoned gristmill, where he had taken himself to die. Never did a dog enter the house, nor a cat, except as temporary mouse exterminator. Always there were squads of barn cats, essential to control the rats that accumulated in the vicinity of grain. When my grandfather and I fished at twilight on Eagle Pond, we caught bony perch and fed them to the barn cats. Milking, my grandfather would angle a Holstein teat and squirt a stream of hot milk into the gaping jaws of a kitten waiting for a treat. There was a mother cat, nameless, who endured for most of my childhood, bearing litter after litter. Her dugs hung down to the barn floor. Route 4 took care of overpopulation, and regularly in my summers on the farm I found young cats dead in the ditch. I dug holes and buried them.

Gus's grief over Jane resembled mine and was companionable; even Ada seemed to notice. Gus lived five years, increasingly infirm. In 1999 I brought the animals with me when I spent three months in Manhattan, on the twelfth floor of an apartment house at the corner of Bleecker and LaGuardia. When I let Gus out of his box in his new environment, he immediately squatted on the red rug, as he had squatted in the parlor when he was a year old. He never did get the hang of elevators. I did not enjoy scooping poop, which is not required on New Hampshire's dirt roads. It was a nervous time for Gus—so many people! so many dogs!—but he sniffed on Bleecker and LaGuardia with the enthusiasm of a miser inheriting gold mines. On the whole, Ada didn't seem to notice a change. Gus was there; she had brought with her her system of affect.

Back at the farm, walking with me in the graveyard, Gus became stiffer and stiffer: the hindquarters, as usual. Then came the day he could not step up the porch stairs. I let it go on too long, until the night he could not stand but scrambled his legs frog-fashion to move a few inches at a time. I carried him to the vet's, and sat on the floor scratching his ears as the needle entered a paw. A few days later I picked up his ashes and scattered him on Jane's grave, as I had promised Jane I would do. He was seventeen. Ada lived two years longer, reaching eighteen; then she rejoined Gus as more ashes on Jane's grave.

The Village Saved Destroyed

JUNE 21, 1994, Jane entered the Bubble for another intensification, a weeklong infusion of high-dose Ara-C, or cytarabine. She entered the hospital walking and strong, after the three relatively good weeks when she worked on poems, pulled weeds, and helped bury my mother. When I brought her home a week later she used a walker; she was broken and never mended. Weakness, bone pain, neuropathies, delirium, and daily vomiting were not results of her disease but of its treatment. I thought of the American major who reportedly told Peter Arnett, after an assault on Ben Tre in Vietnam, "We had to destroy the village in order to save it." The analogy is false, because Jane's despoilers were not ironic majors but doctors trying to keep her alive. All the same, the village of Jane was razed again and again—bamboo huts burned down, market napalmed, oxen machine-gunned, wells polluted with blood and offal. After old grasses started to rise again in the fields—surviving villagers creeping back, cleaning wells and rebuilding structures—one day the helicopters rattled and boomed again.

On Jane's skull the fuzz of hair, which had begun to grow, fell out again. She lost weight and muscle. I watched her sink; she watched herself sink. The mind needed constantly to remind itself: This is not dying-dying; we suffer *this* dying to avoid *that* dying. When we came home, we had missed the brilliant height of the peonies. Jane's huge white border by the porch stopped traffic every June. We returned in time for the old roses—tiny, frail, single; pink, white, and pink-white—that had bloomed here for my grandparents and great-grandparents. We settled down for summer, but there was no summer as there had been no spring and as there would be no fall or winter. The days were endlessly the same in the way that the ocean is the same although it moves without pausing. The ocean differs when there is fog or when the sun is out, when a packing case or a patch of seaweed floats by, but differences only intensify the daily nightly sameness. When you are so sick, there is nothing wherever you look that is not sickness. A friend visits and it is a strain even to acknowledge her presence; love is good but it is painful to feel unresponsive to love. Everyone wants to help but no one can give the help that would help.

July Fourth is Andover's big yearly holiday, beginning with a Lions Club breakfast in the school, continuing with a flea market, a parade of horses and fire engines and marching bands and old cars, pony-pulling and softball, supper, a midway, and fireworks. Most years, Jane and I went midday for the flea market, the parade, a sausage sandwich (Andover Snowmobile Club), and outstanding strawberry shortcake from the women of the Andover Service Club. This Independence Day I attended for half an hour in the morning while Polly helped Jane take a shower and clean her Hickman. Drying Jane's back after her shower, Polly discovered hundreds of tiny red freckles. I called Letha Mills, at home on the Fourth with her three small boys, who told us to drive to Emergency. The anteroom was full, the hospital understaffed on a holiday and crowded with firecracker burns. The marks on Jane's skin were petechiae, little hemorrhages that indicate lack of platelets in the blood. She needed two units of platelets transfused into her bloodstream. The resident told us that after the transfusion Jane would be admitted to the Bubble again. I telephoned

Polly to assemble our hospital gear, and on the way home I stopped at the Days Inn and made a reservation. But when I drove into our driveway an hour later, Polly stood on the porch shaking her head. Just after I left, the resident had contacted Dr. Kritz, the hematologist covering on July Fourth, who told him that the hospital would be the worst place for Jane, so subject now to infection. Jane should come home. I turned around, drove back, canceled the Days Inn, and arrived as Jane's infusion completed itself. We went to bed exhausted at ten P.M. without fireworks. The next day, we left the house at seven to drive back to the clinic for scheduled bloodwork. The petechiae faded away.

As potential marrow donors were examined, ten by ten, a match failed to turn up. I telephoned Seattle every few days to ask about progress, although I understood that they would let us know if they had good news. Polly continued to help us, moving back and forth between her flat and our house, although pain in her back began to bother her. Later in July, a series of spots or blisters turned up on Jane's skin. They were not petechiae. I telephoned Letha Mills, who told us to come to Emergency again. From the description, Letha felt sure Jane had herpes zoster, or shingles, which often strikes cancer patients or others with depressed immune systems. Jane spent another week in the Bubble, treated with acyclovir. Still later in July, after returning from the newest intensification, Jane woke early in the morning with her eyes burning. A telephone call, and I drove her back again. It was a medical error by the physician who had sent us home, the only physician's error during her illness. Jane should have been taking steroid eye drops after this treatment, but they had not been prescribed. Now an ophthalmologist treated her and stopped the burning, avoiding permanent damage, but her eyes had to be bandaged for eight hours. The doctor taped white gauze over her eyeballs and I wheeled her to the parking lot, lidded white like a marble statue. I maneuvered her into the front seat of the Honda, drove her home, and led her through the house to bed.

Then, in a week or two, Jane saw her father, who had been dead for thirteen years. Quickly she corrected herself. The next day she thought that her brother and his family were staying down the road in our cottage, where they usually resided when they visited us late in August. "They ought to be stirring soon," she said in the morning. When I told her that they were not there, she agreed, but then she asked me if I knew where Amos was, because she hadn't see him lately; our cat had died nine years before. Every time I corrected her, she felt something like shame for her mistake. For the caregiver, mental episodes are especially terrifying: The sick loved body suddenly has an alien mind. But I tried not to be alarmed. I knew that Jane was taking morphine—MS Contin—to numb the pain of her vincristine neuropathies, and I remembered how Jane's father, taking codeine, had similar illusions or delusions. We had a clinic appointment on Monday, when I could tell Letha about these misapprehensions, but on Sunday morning at ten I saw Jane rushing to finish cleaning her Hickman, obviously in great haste, and asked her why she was hurrying. She reminded me that it was always at ten on Sunday mornings that we watched Johnny Carson.

When I telephoned Letha I used the word "dementia," which she corrected to "delirium," and we drove back to the Bubble for another week. They took away morphine; they stopped the current intensification. They wanted Jane to have an MRI of her skull, but the narrowness of the MRI's cocoon activated a panicky phobia in Jane. When the delirium stopped and it was safe to take Versed, her doctors doped her up and she managed to endure the MRI, on condition that I remain with her all the time. They

MRIed her skull for thirty minutes, and two days later MRIed her spine for an hour. I sat with her in the magnetic field, all metal removed from my pockets lest it fly into the machine. I watched the digital seconds flash on the machine, hearing frequent crashes and booms, inhabiting the set of a science-fiction movie as disembodied voices pitched from the control room. I sat with my eyes fixed upon the narrow tray that slid my wife up and down.

Whatever symptoms caused Jane's readmission to the Bubble, her Hitchcock doctors attended to other symptoms as well. Her neuropathies remained painful, and on this visit Letha Mills, being prudent, arranged for examination by a neurologist. The most painful track moved down her right leg. An eminent neurologist put Jane through the usual paces. She was able to touch her forefinger to her nose and to accomplish the other tricks that neurology has us perform. He found no reason to believe that Jane was compromised in a new and different way, and said something cheerful, and—in the hearty manner of a buddy slapping his pal on the back—pounded Jane's right leg, so that she leapt in the bed and cried out. The doctor exited with embarrassed apologies—while Jane and I laughed. It was slapstick worthy of Mel Brooks. There weren't many things to laugh about.

Both of us preferred home, but there was comfort in the Bubble. In the Bubble, when something new turned up—an especially savage bout of diarrhea, emesis of a new color or texture, blisters running a new line on Jane's back—we could press a button and receive professional opinion and response. At home, as unlicensed and ignorant caregiver, I needed to describe symptoms over the telephone; or I needed to pack suffering Jane into the seat beside me and aim the car north for an hour.

Back home, I kept up my job as cook. Jane held to a vegetarian diet except on rare poultry occasions. Polly's high blood pressure precluded salt. Night after night I served up ripe tomatoes and fresh corn on the cob, with strong old Cabot cheese for protein: glorious, but a touch repetitive. When Loa Winter on the telephone asked, "Isn't there something I could *do?*" I blurted out, "A saltless, meatless casserole." Then my daughter called. Almost as soon as I hung up, Loa swung into the driveway with baskets: vegetarian lasagna, portobello mushrooms in garlic and oil, a walnut cake. Then my daughter pulled up with fifteen quarts of a bulky meatless chili made with bulgur, and two days later arrived with a gallon of Spanish rice that was sharp and nutty. The big freezer in the shed creaked with its burden. To make room, I emptied out old stuff, a major archeological dig: there were spaghetti sauces dated 1982 and 1986, soups from the old world, rolls and squash/turkey/gravy from an ancient Thanksgiving. Jane laughed until she wept—but asked me never to tell, perfidious Perkins— when I found bicentennial stew, neatly dated 1976.

One day late in August Philippa visited us with Abigail and Allison. Allison did not leave the car because she could not bear to look at Jane. As Abigail and the grown-ups sat in the living room, the telephone rang. I jumped to answer it. When the caller identified herself as from the Fred Hutchinson Cancer Research Center in Seattle my heart zinged. I heard the words we had yearned for since March: They had found a donor marrow, mismatched at one antigen, that might work for Jane. The linkages looked good. The Hutch wanted us to fly to Seattle late in September for a bone marrow transplant early in October. Holding the phone away from my mouth, I shouted toward the living room: "They've found a donor! We're going to Seattle!" Joy erupted from the women of the next room. The Hutch was mailing us information and informing Dartmouth-Hitchcock. I hung up and ran into the room where everyone was weeping. I hugged Jane, hugged Polly and Philippa.

Then I ran out to the car and told Allison, who knew what we were looking for. I told her that we would bring Jane back whole and healthy, and that Jane would play with her again, making clothespin dolls and putting on shows. She burst into tears.

When you have wished for something with intensity, and it happens, your first reaction is overwhelming: *All problems are solved.* Soon enough I remembered, as Jane remembered: After we arrived in Seattle, the Hutch would spend a week making more tests; she could still be rejected for the transplant. Then there would be weeks in the hospital, first to destroy all vestiges of her own marrow, then to infuse the donor's, then to wait for the new marrow to engraft and produce. We knew: People die during the first hundred days of a BMT. Although we would fly to Seattle together, a month later I might bring Jane home in a box—after the new marrow failed to engraft; after an unstoppable infection with no immune system; after liver failure when the new marrow attacked its stranger-body. If she could last the first hundred days, her chances for survival would leap forward.

But now our concentration shifted from the immediacy of Jane to the immediacy of Polly—for she had taken her backache to a doctor, who had x-rayed and found a spot on her lung, which *could* be pneumonia: ultrasound, CT scan, more x-rays, more ultrasound. With maddening slowness, tests and procedures moved toward the conclusion: Polly had lung cancer (she had stopped smoking fifty years earlier), which was inoperable because it had entered her ribs. It was on one side only, and peripheral, and because she was eighty years old, the tumor might grow slowly. Taking chemotherapy in combination with radiation, she might live for a year, maybe two. We planned; we decided: When Jane and I flew to Seattle for the BMT, we would take Polly with us and she would begin her treatment there. I made reservations for three with USAir, Manchester, New Hampshire, to Seattle, Washington. I looked at Seattle maps and read descriptions of apartments. It was imperative that there be a washer and dryer inside the apartment. By telephone I rented a place big enough for three. I negotiated with Polly's doctors to transfer her treatment cross-country. I talked with radiation oncologists in Seattle; they talked with their counterparts in Hanover. I would rent a car so I could drive Polly across town for radiation while Jane was in the hospital. Polly's first University of Washington appointment was on the calendar. I would hand-carry her x-rays on the plane and deliver them when she began treatment.

We planned; we packed. We returned to the clinic for blood-work, for prophylaxis against PCP, and for methotrexate injected into the spine. Jane had a bone marrow biopsy on September 14, and we did not return to the clinic until the twentieth, which was my sixty-sixth birthday. When Letha sat with us in the consultation room, I began to tell her where our Seattle apartment was; because she had trained at the Hutch, I thought she might recognize the street name. She cut me off as if she were impatient. The bone marrow biopsy showed that Jane's leukemia had returned, blasts in her marrow for the first time since February. Her leukemia was in residence again, remission remitted. The virulence or aggression of her cancer cells, with the Philadelphia chromosome, gave its testimony. Letha had already talked with the Hutch, which would put off harvesting the donor's bone marrow for one month while Hitchcock tried to reinstate Jane's remission. Tomorrow morning we would move into the Bubble again, for at least three weeks. If we achieved a second remission, we could fly to Seattle late in October for a transplant early in November.

In the consultation room I babbled like a spoiled child about airplanes and apartments and appointments for Polly's radiation that would need cancellation. Polly could delay treatment no longer and must begin chemotherapy and radiation in New Hampshire. Consulting with Letha, I made another plan. Polly would be treated in New Hampshire while we went to Seattle. When Polly responded—maybe by December she would have recovered from the pains and fatigue of radiation and chemo—she would fly to Seattle and join us in our apartment. Back home, I canceled airplane and apartment and rental car and Polly's Seattle appointments. I could not make new reservations because we didn't know when—or if—Jane would enter remission again. This time, Hitchcock would infuse two chemicals it had not used before, because the old ones had caused so much trouble. I arranged for Polly to begin New Hampshire treatment. With Jane back in the Bubble, Polly needed chemo and radiation five days a week. The radiation unit at Hitchcock was still at the site of the old hospital, four miles away. I needed to be with Jane. We could have moved Polly into the Days Inn but she wanted to stay at the farm while we returned to Hitchcock—still answering the telephone and attending to Gus and Ada. Again I telephoned the friends and neighbors who had said, "Is there is anything we can *do?*"

Someone picked Polly up every day at the farm at one o'clock and drove her to the front door of Hitchcock, where I met her with a wheelchair and took her to the infusion room, where she lay for an hour as cisplatin dripped into her blood. I sat beside Polly until the infusion was complete, then pushed her to the north elevator, descended to the Bubble, and wheeled her to Jane. Mother visited daughter for ten minutes. At four o'clock I pushed Polly's chair to the driveway in front of the north entrance, where her day's driver—having poked around in Hanover for two hours—drove her to the old hospital for radiation, then home.

If Jane did not go into remission she would die; if she did not go into remission soon, we would lose the contracted bone marrow. After a week or ten days, another bone marrow biopsy showed nothing at all—which was a good sign; the poisons had killed marrow and therefore cancer cells. While we waited for her marrow to return, with its leukemia in remission, I made new reservations, two seats this time, to fly from Manchester to Seattle on Sunday, October 23, scheduling our return for February 24 after the hundred days. We found a woman from a nearby town to house-sit and help Polly in our absence. I rented a flat for Jane and me in a Seattle apartment house near the Hutch and its clinic that serve BMT patients. If Polly joined us I would get a bigger place in the same building. I arranged for a volunteer to meet us at the airport and drive us to the apartment.

We waited, day after day. Friends kept each other in touch. Caroline, who had visited the farm in May for a couple of hours, drove up from Cape Cod to visit Jane in the hospital and to eat a quick supper with me at a Chinese restaurant in Lebanon. I ate at the same restaurant with Wendell and Tanya Berry after they saw Jane briefly. One day toward the end of Jane's treatment, as I pushed Polly's wheelchair to Jane's room, I saw nurses and residents gathered, the pharmacist, a social worker, Letha and Diane. They rolled into Jane's room a wheeled cart lush with cake and cookies and shrimp and crudités and pop and soda water. The staff was giving us a going-away party for our trip to Seattle; it was good to understand their confidence. Kate MacKay presented us with a blank book she had filled with photographs of all our helpers—blood collectors, room moppers, nurses, hematologists— to which she added facetious commentary. "This is for you to take to Seattle," said Kate, "so that you don't forget us." Jane could eat little, but her spirit gorged itself. Night nurses and staff finished off the party food from the cart where it stood outside Jane's door.

Four days before our scheduled flight, Jane had a bone marrow biopsy and was discharged. We drove home to a flurry of packing without knowing for sure that we would leave. Two days later Diane Stearns telephoned: Jane was in remission; the Hutch was ready for us. Polly rejoiced that her daughter was back on track for hope; but Polly's throat and chest burned from radiation, she ate and drank little, the cisplatin fatigued her, and she lost weight. It was appalling to leave her behind, but Jane's chance was now or never. None of us doubted what we must do. The morning we left for Seattle, I took pictures of mother and daughter, arm in arm in our yard among drifts of red-orange maple leaves, Jane wearing one of her floppy hats over her baldness, Polly looking frail and small.

The Third Thing

BACK IN 1976 AND 1977, when we first moved to New
Hampshire, friends visited to check us out. Many worried
that we had made a hasty or imprudent decision to give up teaching and to reside in the old house heated by wood on Route 4 with
the railroad running between it and Eagle Pond. Ann Arbor
friends paid visits, as did my poet friends: Louis Simpson, Robert
and Carol Bly, Galway Kinnell. It was good for Jane to talk poetry
with the old boys, and on one of these early visits Robert Bly
pointed her in the direction of Akhmatova—who provided Jane an
important change of direction. Reading over Jane's current
poems, he said, "You need a master." "I don't want a master," she
said. "I want a mistress." "Akhmatova," he said. "Go to Akhmatova."
Later Bly and Simpson collaborated in acquiring for Jane the best
translator to work with—the Russian literary scholar Vera San-
domirsky Dunham, who lived near Louis on Long Island. Jane
spent five years immersed in the work of a great lyric poet, ex-
panding her own command of poetry in the struggle to represent
Akhmatova. Bly's advice, she felt, led her to the most crucial concentration of her writing life.

If anyone had asked Jane and me, "Which was the best year of
your lives together?" we could have agreed on an answer: "The one
we remember least." There were sorrowful years of disease and
death, cancer and depression and mania. There were years remembered for adventure: a trip to China and Japan, two trips to

India; years when my children married; years when the grandchildren were born; years of triumph as Jane began her public life in poetry: her first book, her first poem in *The New Yorker*, the Graywolf Press publishing subsequent books, an NEA, a Guggenheim. But the best moment of our lives was one repeated day of quiet and work. Not everyone understood. Visitors, especially from New York, would spend a weekend with us and say as they left: "It's really pretty here" ("in Vermont," many added), "with your house, the pond, the hills, but . . . but . . . *what do you do?*"

What we did: We got up early in the morning. I brought Jane coffee in bed. She walked the dog as I started writing, then climbed the stairs to work at her own desk on her own poems and on Akhmatova. We had lunch. We lay down together. We rose and worked at secondary things. I read aloud to Jane; we played scoreless ping-pong; we read the mail; we worked again. We ate supper, talked, read books sitting across from each other in the living room, and went to sleep. If we were lucky the phone didn't ring all day. In January Jane dreamed of flowers, planning expansion and refinement of the garden. From late March into October she spent hours digging, applying fifty-year-old Holstein manure from under the barn, planting, transplanting, and weeding. Sometimes I went off for two nights to read my poems, essential to the economy, and Jane wrote a poem called "Alone for a Week." Later Jane flew away for readings and I loathed being the one left behind. (I filled out coupons from magazines and ordered useless objects.) We traveled south sometimes in cold weather: to Key West in December, a February week in Barbados, to Florida during baseball's spring training, to Bermuda. Rarely we flew to England or Italy for two weeks. Three hundred and thirty days a year, we inhabited this old house and the same day's adventurous routine.

What we did: love. We did not spend our days gazing into

each other's eyes. We did that gazing when we made love or when one of us was in trouble, but most of the time our gazes met and entwined as they looked at a third thing. Third things are essential to marriages, objects or practices or habits or arts or institutions or games or human beings that provide a site of joint rapture or contentment. Each member of a couple is separate; the two come together in double attention. Lovemaking is not a third thing but two-in-one. John Keats can be a third thing, or the BSO, or Dutch interiors, or checkers. For many couples, children are a third thing. Jane and I had our cats and dog to fuss and exclaim over— and later five grandchildren. We had our summer afternoons at the pond, which for ten years made a third thing. After nap we loaded up books and blankets and walked across Route 4 and the old railroad to the steep slippery bank that led down to our private beach on Eagle Pond. Soft moss underfoot sent little red flowers up. Ghost birches leaned over water with wild strawberry plants growing under them. Over our heads white pine reared high, and oaks that warned us of summer's end late in August by dropping green metallic acorns. Sometimes a mink scooted among ferns. After we acquired Gus he joined the pond ecstasy, chewing on stones. Jane dozed in the sun as I sat in the shade reading and occasionally taking a note in a blank book. From time to time we swam and dried in the heat. Then, one summer, leakage from the Danbury landfill turned the pond orange. It stank. The water was not hazardous but it was ruined. A few years later the pond came back but we seldom returned to our afternoons there. Sometimes you lose a third thing.

The South Danbury Christian Church became large in our lives. We were both deacons and Jane was treasurer for a dozen years, utter miscasting and a source of annual anxiety when the treasurer's report was due. I collected the offering; Jane counted and banked it. Once a month she prepared communion and I distributed it. For the church fair we both cooked and I helped with the auction. Besides the church itself, building and community, there was Christianity, the Gospels, and the works of theologians and mystics. Typically we divided our attentions: I read Meister Eckhart while Jane studied Julian of Norwich. I read the Old Testament aloud to her, and the New. If it wasn't the Bible, I was reading aloud late Henry James, or Mark Twain or Edith Wharton or Wordsworth's *Prelude.* Reading aloud was a daily connection. When I first pronounced *The Ambassadors,* Jane had never read it, and I peeked at her flabbergasted face as the boat bearing Chad and Mme. de Vionnet rounded the bend toward Lambert Strether. Three years later, when I had acquired a New York Edition, she asked me to read her *The Ambassadors* again. Late James is the best prose for reading aloud. Saying one of his interminable sentences, the voice must drop pitch every time he interrupts his syntax with periphrasis, and drop again when periphrasis interrupts periphrasis, and again, and then step the pitch up, like climbing stairs in the dark, until the original tone concludes the sentence. One's larynx could write a doctoral dissertation on James's syntax.

Literature in general was a constant. Often at the end of the day Jane would speak about what she had been reading, her latest intense and obsessive absorption in an author: Keats for two years, Chekhov, Elizabeth Bishop. In reading and in everything else, we made clear boundaries, dividing our literary territories. I did not go back to Keats until she had done with him. By and large Jane read intensively while I read extensively. Like a male, I lusted to *acquire* all the great books of the world and add them to my life list. One day I would realize: I've never read Darwin! Adam Smith! Gibbon! Gibbon became an obsession with me, then his sources, then all ancient history, then all narrative history. For a few years I concentrated on Henry Adams, even reading six massive volumes of letters.

But there was also ping-pong. When we added a new bedroom—turning the old master bedroom into a bathroom and laundry—we extended the rootcellar enough to set a ping-pong table into it, and for years we played every afternoon. Jane was assiduous, determined, vicious, and her reach was not so wide as mine. When she couldn't reach a shot I called her "Stubbsy," and her next slam would smash me in the groin, rage combined with harmlessness. We rallied half an hour without keeping score. Another trait we shared was hating to lose.

Through bouts of ping-pong and Henry James and the church, we kept to one innovation: With rare exceptions, we remained aware of each other's feelings. It took me half my life, more than half, to discover with Jane's guidance that two people could live together and remain kind. When one of us felt grumpy we both shut up until it went away. We did not give in to sarcasm. Once every three years we had a fight—the way some couples fight three times a day—and because fights were few the aftermath of a fight was a dreadful gloom. "We have done harm," said Jane in a poem after a quarrel. What was *that* fight about? I wonder if she remembered, a month after writing the poem.

Of course: The third thing that brought us together, and shone at the center of our lives and our house, was poetry—both our love for the art and the passion and frustration of trying to write it. When we moved to the farm, away from teaching and Jane's family, we threw ourselves into the life of writing poetry as if we jumped from a bridge and swam to survive. I kept the earliest hours of the day for poetry. Jane worked on poems virtually every day; there were dry spells. In the first years of our marriage, I sometimes feared that she would find the project of poetry intimidating, and withdraw or give up or diminish the intensity of her commitment. I remember talking with her one morning early in New Hampshire, maybe in 1976, when the burden felt too heavy. She talked of her singing with the Michigan Chorale, as if music were something she might turn to. She spoke of drawing as another art she could perform, and showed me an old pencil rendering she had made, acorns I think, meticulous and well made and nothing more. She was saying, "I don't *have* to give myself to poetry"—and I knew enough not to argue. However, from year to year she gave more of herself to her art. When she studied Keats, she read all his poems, all his letters, the best three or four biographies; then she read and reread the poems and the letters again. No one will find in her poems clear fingerprints of John Keats, but Jane's ear became more luscious with her love for Keats; her lines became more dense, rifts loaded with ore. Coming from a family for whom ambition was dangerous, in which work was best taken lightly, it was not easy for Jane to wager her life on one number. She lived with someone who had made that choice, but also with someone nineteen years older who wrote all day and published frequently. Her first book of poems came out as I published my fifth. I could have been an inhibitor as easily as I was an encourager—if she had not been brave and stubborn. I watched in gratified pleasure as her poems became better and better. From being promising she became accomplished and professional; then—with the later poems of *The Boat of Quiet Hours,* with "Twilight: After Haying," with "Briefly It Enters," with "Things"—she turned into the extraordinary and permanent poet of *Otherwise.*

People asked us—people still ask me—about competition between us. We never spoke of it, but it had to be there—and it remained benign. When Jane wrote a poem that dazzled me, I wanted to write a poem that would dazzle her. Boundaries helped.

We belonged to different generations. Through Jane I got to be friends with poets of her generation, as she did with my friends born in the 1920s. We avoided situations that would subject us to comparison. During the first years of our marriage, when Jane was just beginning to publish, we were asked several times to read our poems together. The people who asked us knew and respected Jane's poems, but the occasions turned ghastly. Once we were introduced by someone we had just met who was happy to welcome Joan Kenyon. Always someone, generally a male English professor, managed to let us know that it was *sweet* that Jane wrote poems too. One head of a department asked her if she felt *dwarfed*. When Jane was condescended to she was furious, and it was only on these occasions that we felt anything unpleasant between us. Jane decided that we would no longer read together.

When places asked us both to read, we agreed to come but stipulated that we read separately, maybe a day apart. Late in the 1980s, after reading on different days at a university, we did a joint question-and-answer session with writing students. Three quarters of the questions addressed Jane, not me, and afterward she said, "Perkins, I think we can read together now." So, in our last years together, we did many joint readings. When two poets read on the same program, the first reader is the warm-up band, the second the featured act. We read in fifteen-minute segments, ABAB, and switched A and B positions with each reading. In 1993 we read on a Friday in Trivandrum, at the southern tip of India, and three days later in Hanover, New Hampshire. Exhausted as we were, we remembered who had gone first thousands of miles away.

There were days when each of us received word from the same magazine; the same editor had taken a poem by one of us just as he/she rejected the other of us. One of us felt constrained in pleasure. The need for boundaries even extended to style. As Jane's work got better and better—and readers noticed—my language departed from its old habits and veered away from the kind of lyric that Jane was writing, toward irony and an apothegmatic style. My diction became more Latinate and polysyllabic, as well as syntactically complex. I was reading Gibbon, learning to use vocabulary and sentence structure as engines of discrimination. Unconsciously, I was choosing to be as unlike Jane as I could be. Still, her poetry influenced and enhanced my own. Her stubborn and unflagging commitment turned its power upon me and exhorted me. My poems got better in this house. When my *Old and New Poems* came out in 1990, the positive reviews included something like this sentence: "Hall began publishing early . . . but it was not until he left his teaching job and returned to the family farm in New Hampshire with his second wife Jane Kenyon that . . ." I published *Kicking the Leaves* in 1978 when Jane published *From Room to Room.* It was eight years before we published our next books: her *Boat of Quiet Hours,* my *Happy Man.* (When I told Jane my title, her reaction was true Jane: "Sounds too depressed.") I had also been working on drafts of *The One Day,* maybe my best book. Then Jane wrote *Let Evening Come, Constance,* and the twenty late poems that begin *Otherwise.* Two years after her death, a review of Jane began with a sentence I had been expecting. It was uttered in respect, without a sneer, and said that for years we had known of Jane Kenyon as Donald Hall's wife but from now on we will know of Donald Hall as Jane Kenyon's husband.

We did not show each other early drafts. (It's a bad habit. The comments of another become attached to the words of a poem, steering it or preventing it from following its own way.) But when we had worked over a poem in solitude for a long time, our first reader was the other. I felt anxious about showing Jane new poems, and often invented reasons for delay. Usually, each of us saved up three or four poems before showing them to the other. One day I would say, "I left some stuff on your footstool," or Jane would tell me, "Perkins, there are some things on your desk." Waiting for a response, each of us already knew some of what the other would say. If ever I repeated a word—a habit acquired from Yeats—I knew that Jane would cross it out. Whenever she used verbal auxiliaries, she knew I would simplify, and "it was raining" would become "it rained." By and large we ignored the predicted advice, which we had already heard in our heads and dismissed. Jane kept her work clear of dead metaphor, knowing my crankiness on the subject, and she would exult when she found one in my drafts: "Perkins! Here's a dead metaphor!" These encounters were important but not easy. Sometimes we turned polite with each other: "Oh, really! I thought that was the best part . . ." (*False laugh.*) Jane told others—people questioned us about how we worked together—that I approached her holding a sheaf of her new poems, saying, "These are going to be *good!*" To which she would say, "*Going* to be, eh?" She told people that she would climb back to her study, carrying the poems covered with my illegible comments, thinking, "Perkins just doesn't get it. And then," she would continue, "I'd do everything he said."

Neither of us did everything the other said. Reading *Otherwise* I find words I wanted her to change, and sometimes I still think I was right. But we helped each other greatly. She saved me a thousand gaffes, cut my wordiness and straightened out my syntax. She seldom told me that anything was *good.* "This is almost done," she'd say, "but you've got to do this in two lines not three." Or, "You've brought this a long way, Perkins"—without telling me if I had brought it to a good place. Sometimes her praise expressed its own limits. "You've taken this as far as the intellect can take it."

When she said, "It's finished. Don't change a word," I would ask, "But is it any *good?* Do you *like* it?" I pined for her praise, and seldom got it. I remember one evening in 1992 when we sat in the living room and she read through the manuscript of *The Museum of Clear Ideas,* written when I was most in Gibbon's thrall. Earlier she had seen only a few poems at a time, and she had not been enthusiastic. I watched her dark face as she turned the pages. Finally she looked over at me and tears started from her eyes. "Perkins, I don't *like* it!" Tears came to my eyes too, and I said, rapidly, "That's okay. That's okay." (That book was anti-Jane in its manner, or most of it was, dependent on syntax and irony, a little like Augustan poetry, rather than on images.) When we looked over one another's work, it was essential that we never lie to each other. Even when Jane was depressed, I never praised a poem unless I meant it; I never withheld blame. If either of us had felt that the other was pulling punches, it would have ruined what was so essential to our house.

We were each other's readers but we could not be each other's only readers. I mostly consulted friends and editors by mail, poets from my generation and poets Jane's age and even younger. Jane worked regularly, the last dozen years of her life, with Joyce Peseroff and Alice Mattison. The three came together for a two-day workshop three or four times a year. When we lived in Ann Arbor we knew Joyce because she was a fellow in the Michigan Society of Fellows. As Jane and I left Ann Arbor for New Hampshire, Joyce returned to Massachusetts and married, living only two hours away. Joyce and Jane started up a poetry magazine called *Green House.* Both of them found editing and publishing more taxing than they had expected, and this quarterly printed six issues in three years. It is a smart idea for young poets to edit. An editor becomes seriously in touch with the poetic moment. Finding fault with other work, you find the same faults in your own, product of the same moment. You work hard to make good judgments and sometimes you fail: A poem you returned is printed elsewhere and looks good; the wonderful poem you accepted with enthusiasm six months ago reveals itself an embarrassment in print. If you make such mistakes, doesn't every editor? You learn to take editors less seriously—so that neither acceptance nor rejection seems crucial or authoritative.

In 1977 Joyce published her first book of poems, *The Hardness Scale,* with Alice James Books in Cambridge. With the same publisher, Jane's *From Room to Room* followed a year later. Part of the cooperative arrangement was that each poet worked in the office once a week—and Joyce and Jane saw more of each other. Then Alice James published Alice Mattison's first book—a collection of poems—and Alice became Joyce's and Jane's friend. Their workshop meetings started in January 1982. Alice was writing stories as well as poems, then stories and a novel, then more stories, more novels. The three of them worked wonderfully together, each supplying things that the other lacked. They fought, they laughed, they rewrote and cut and rearranged. Jane would return from a workshop exhausted yet unable to keep away from her desk, working with wild excitement to follow suggestions. The three women were not only being literary critics for one another. Each had grown up knowing that it was not permitted for females to be as aggressive as males, and all were ambitious in their art, and encouraged one another in their ambitions. I felt close to Alice and Joyce, my friends as well as Jane's, but I did not stick my nose into their deliberations. If I had tried to, I would have lost a nose. Even when they met at our house, I was careful to stay apart. They met often at Joyce's in Massachusetts, because it was halfway between Jane and Alice. They met in New Haven at Alice's.

The three also saw each other two by two. Alice lived four miles from my mother's Hamden house. When Jane and I visited my mother, in her eighties, Jane and Alice took walks together and talked about husbands and literature. When my mother recovered after a hospital stay, and we helped her out, Jane and Alice spent time with each other. Sometimes Alice alone visited us in New Hampshire by train and bus. Joyce and Jane met for lunches at the Mall of New Hampshire for friendship and literature. This three-part friendship was essential to Jane's poetry.

Meantime we lived in the house of poetry, which was also the house of love and grief; the house of solitude and art; the house of Jane's depression and my cancers and Jane's leukemia. When someone died whom we loved, we went back to the poets of grief and outrage, as far back as *Gilgamesh;* often I read aloud Henry King's "The Exequy," written in the seventeenth century after the death of his young wife. Poetry gives the griever not release from grief but companionship in grief. Poetry embodies the complexity of feelings at their most intense and entangled, and therefore offers (over centuries, or over no time at all) the company of tears. As I sat beside Jane in her pain and weakness, I wrote about pain and weakness. Once in Hitchcock I noticed that the leaves were turning. I realized that I had not noticed that leaves had come to the trees. It was a year without seasons, a year without punctuation. I began to write "Without" to embody the sensations of lives under dreary, monotonous assault. After I had drafted it many times, I read it aloud to Jane. "That's it, Perkins," she said. "You've got it. That's it." Even in this poem written at her mortal bedside there was companionship.

Pill Hill

ALBERT HOPKINS drove us to the Manchester Airport—
October 23, 1994—unloaded us, and saw us to the USAir
boarding gate. The plane was on time. We boarded, took our luxurious first-class seats—and something went wrong with the equipment, as airlines like to call airplanes. We filed off and sat morose
on uncomfortable chairs, Jane pale and huddled, until the flight
was canceled. In the old life, travel upsets had inevitably left me
panicky and demanding, but death minimizes hangnails. At my
entreaty, USAir approached United, which broke its rules to put us
on a flight to Seattle through O'Hare, and we arrived only two
hours later than we had expected. We flew coach, it was uncomfortable, and it worked.

Our flat was bedroom, living room with fold-out sofa, big
chair, small tables, television set, kitchen and bathroom, washer-
dryer in the hallway. The place was shabby, gimcrack, clean. While
Jane rested on the big bed, I strolled out to explore the neighborhood, establishments mostly closed late Sunday afternoon. We
were living on Seattle's First Hill, rising steeply from downtown
and Puget Sound, nicknamed Pill Hill for its doctors' offices, for its
hospitals and clinics and imaging centers. On Madison one block
up was a Payless drugstore, a bagel shop, five restaurants and a
pizza place, a bookstore, banks with cash machines, a Korean grocery, and two Starbucks. I bought coffee, bread, peanut butter,
frozen macaroni and cheese, milk, juice. Returning, I asked Jane if

she could manage a pizza for supper; we ate watching the news. I watched football for a while before joining Jane in bed.

Seattle was entirely new—and in our four months we never lived there. I felt affection for the city I never quite inhabited as I spent four months gazing from the eleventh floor of the hospital, cherishing especially the lighted grid of winter nights. In Seattle there is a great bookstore called Elliott Bay; we never entered its doors. We lived in an apartment on a street of the city but our only address was leukemia. We woke and ate breakfast and showered in leukemia. We walked around the block, keeping up strength, in leukemia's neighborhood. We slept in leukemia all night, tossing and turning with unsettling dreams.

The next morning, Monday, was fair and warm and we walked to find the clinic, where Jane had her first appointment the following day. We would visit the clinic first for testing before the BMT, afterward for weekly appointments with the attending physician and the nutritionist, for infusions of platelets and red blood cells, for help with pain. We found the Hutch's clinic crowded with bald men and women carrying pumps to infuse themselves, with puffy red faces and feet that clearly pained them, some using walkers or wheelchairs. We saw what we would be. As we left that first day, we observed however something else: A woman approached the receptionist to say goodbye; she was leaving tomorrow. She was sick, sick, sick—but she was hopeful and going home.

I put off picking up a rental car because I was anxious about finding my way in a strange city. From our apartment we walked and found Keena's, a good place for lunch one block up on Madison. Jane ate borscht while I chewed on a Hebrew National knockwurst. I walked a mile to a supermarket on Broadway and took a taxi home with four bags of groceries. I took a cab downtown to a recommended department store and returned with a boom box and a VCR, storing the boxes in a closet so that, when we left Seattle, I could ship them back to New Hampshire. I bought Jane CDs of Mahler ("The surgeon was Gustav Mahler's great-grandson!") and Ives; back in New Hampshire Polly picked out a dozen favorites and put them in the mail. On Tuesday the tests began, and continued almost daily, tests that established benchmarks against which, after the BMT, changes would be measured: pulmonary function, conditions of skin and mouth and vagina. Post-BMT, her body would show signs of GVHD, which is graft-versus-host disease; the new marrow tries to reject the body it occupies. Her mouth would be assaulted by radiation before the transplant. There were usually troubles with blood flow from the vagina. We spent an hour with our social worker Winona, and an hour with the Hutch's psychologist Dr. Devney. Because the Hutch had done so many transplants, Dr. Devney had records for thirty-five manic-depressives with BMTs. No drug normally used for depression—not tricyclics nor MAO inhibitors nor serotonin-based drugs—could be used after transplants; all had been known to suppress blood counts after BMTs.

Besides these appointments, there were classes or gatherings for prospective BMTs and their attendant caregivers. Jane and I sat in a small classroom with other pairs—mothers with daughters and daughters with mothers, sisters together, brothers together, two other married couples. One of our first teachers was Percy, a chaplain to the Hutch, who had himself undergone a BMT ten years earlier. It was encouraging to see him healthy. I learned that, as Jane approached discharge, I would attend pump class, to learn how to program pumps in our apartment and infuse Jane with water, food, and drugs. My technophobia covered its eyes. When we heard that Jane would be unable to manage her own medications, we felt skeptical: Intelligent medical people tend to be gloomy in their predictions, so that later you may feel encouraged.

Every day in the clinic, that week before admission, we saw men and women and children after their BMTs. They grew long cyclosporine hair on their swollen faces. They carried bottles of water against their dry and painful mouths. These figures shuffled on sore feet to sit blankly waiting on chairs for their names to be called. On these days we walked the four blocks from apartment to clinic, but these people were not capable of walking four blocks. Each day we strolled home in silence. In a clinic interview, our momentary chief physician shook his head from side to side as he read laboratory reports from the latest bone marrow biopsy. "All those blasts!" he said, looking discouraged. Jane's mood plunged; so recently we had heard of a second remission. We were told that Jane would enter an LAF room, for laminar air flow, which isolates patients in a sterile cocoon separated from the human and bacterial world by a thick curtain of plastic. I would see Jane through a wavery transparent curtain, and I could not touch her except while wearing the heavy gloves that poked through the curtain. There were no LAF rooms in the Hutch proper, but in the adjacent Swedish Hospital the Hutch maintained floors for many BMTs. In the past, LAF had been commonplace for BMTs—half of the rooms at the Hutch were originally LAF—but now this isolation was rarely employed. From Jane's medical records, which I read after her death:

> Forty-seven-year-old woman with ALL in relapse here for bone marrow transplantation with one antigen mismatched unrelated donor. This raises her risk of GVHD to a very high level. Therefore, she will be placed in a laminar air flow room.

Everyone speaking to us of LAF sounded tentative, and emphasized that it could be terminated at any moment. The staff was
aware of Jane's bipolarity:

> Manic-Depressive Illness. The patient has known history of
> manic-depressive illness and laminar air flow with the iso-
> lation required may be very difficult for this patient. If this
> proves to be the case, LAF will be DC'd [discontinued] as it
> is only of marginal benefit.

For some patients, we were told, the isolation was intolerable, and
for others LAF felt cozy. A clinic nurse asked us if we would like to
have a look at an LAF room, and we paid our first visit to the
eleventh floor of Swedish Hospital, seeing a bald man living behind plastic in one half of a large room, beside an immense high
window looking down on Puget Sound. The arrangement did not
appear intolerable. I could sit beside her all day long, outside the
plastic but not three feet from Jane's body.

Each day when we visited the clinic, we pulled the day's
schedule from the "Jane Kenyon" file among the patients' mail-
boxes. Years ago, Jane had been told that she might be allergic to
penicillin, and the Hutch had to know for sure. We spent two
hours with an allergist and determined that Jane was not allergic
to penicillin. Jane's constant emesis suggested the possibility of a
duodenal ulcer. In another clinic Jane underwent an endoscopy, in
which one's mouth is propped open while a tube with a small camera is lowered through the throat into the relevant areas. I
watched Jane's insides in color. She did not have an ulcer. Whenever possible I stayed with Jane during her procedures. Because
Jane had suffered so much from neuropathies, the Hutch made an
appointment with a neurologist at the Virginia Mason Clinic. The
neurologist was a woman, and when she arrived to examine Jane,

I departed for twenty minutes on an errand. When I returned Jane was sobbing, as the doctor finished examining her. She had cried uncontrollably after I had left her.

We took lunch at Keena's every day. We saw no one. We came to Seattle bristling with addresses and telephone numbers: old friends, acquaintances, the children or in-laws of friends and acquaintances. We telephoned no one in Seattle, wanting only each other's company, long hours of embrace, small walks in the neighborhood, *MacNeil/Lehrer* on the tube, and videos of Ken Burns's *Baseball*. We talked twice a day with Polly. We found a shoe store and bought Jane oversize sneakers—for sore feet—and dark blue boiled-wool slipper scuffs made in Germany. I picked up the rental car, to shop for groceries and to drive Jane to the clinic post-BMT. The day before Jane would enter Swedish, we took an automobile excursion. On a map I noted that Madison Avenue, one block up from our apartment, would take us directly east to Madison Park, on the shore of Lake Washington. I could not get lost. I drove to the shore, parked, and we walked together in the soft wet November air. That night, we hiked a short way down one of Seattle's prodigious hills to eat Greek food in a dark bar. The night of November 8 was our last together before the separation of the hospital. I dozed and woke, dozed and woke. I remember turning in bed to snuggle against Jane sleeping—curling my knees behind her curled knees, pressing against her bottom, my head against her shoulder. This position of utter comfort, making the spoons, is cold comfort when you realize that you might never make the spoons again.

We were due to register for admission late in the afternoon, between four and five. Waiting in the apartment was intolerable, and not even Ken Burns could distract us. I wrote nothing that day and Jane could not listen to me read. There was nothing to do but feel the tension build. When we registered early, we made our-selves more waiting—but now we waited *inside* the hospital where we would live or die, not sitting in the flat looking at the clock that edged toward the point of departure. In the hospital we entered another kind of time, outside daily living, inside the hollow of live-or-die, in the palace of the capital city in the country of leukemia.

We watched a crew conducting its thorough sterilization of her room. Every surface, every cranny—the isolated half—was meticulously swabbed down, outfitted with sterile equipment like needles and swabs, and swabbed down again, the cleaners wearing sterile uniforms and masks. It would be hours before it was ready, and it would be hours before Jane would be fitted to enter the en-closure. She would need to undergo a sterile bath, two nurses working over the surfaces and apertures of her body. It would be late at night before she would enter room 1112. The number be-guiled me. Anarithmetic, I use numbers as magic and control. Our apartment on Spring Street was 1314.

Having introduced ourselves at the nurses' station, we waited in a consultation room a few yards down the hall—a room with which we became wholly familiar in our eleventh-floor routines. It was a long narrow room, oddly constructed as a facet of Swedish Hospital's twisted shape. At a wide end stood an exercise bicycle. Along the internal wall, as the room extended and narrowed, were a sofa and two chairs—but the beauty of the room was its tall row of windows giving us downtown Seattle, the southern end of Puget Sound, and highways heading south toward Tacoma. Much later, when Jane could walk again, we exercised by circling the floor—Jane on my arm, Jane with a walker, Jane pushing a wheelchair. Often we paused to rest in this room, looking out on a scene differ-ent from what we saw from Jane's window on the opposite side of the floor. Often we walked at dusk, at the end of day watching the slow budging of taillights heading south to home in the early dark of November, December, and January.

Tomorrow her physicians would begin to infuse Cytoxan, or cyclophosphamide, which was potent enough to destroy her. (Several months later, at the Dana-Farber Cancer Institute, the *Boston Globe* health columnist Betsy Lehman was killed by a mistaken overdose of Cytoxan.) Her treatment would last two days; she would feel the assault. Then she would have a day off before she underwent total body irradiation. Then, with marrow and all fast-growing cells burned away, her bones would be emptied out and ready for the new marrow. As we waited this afternoon we had occasional visitors. A tall charge nurse with a gruff voice told us again about the LAF bath, a few hours off. Nurses or social workers entered with forms to fill out, asking questions Jane had already answered half a dozen times. We were told that Dr. Cheever (a distant relative of the writer John Cheever, he told me) would be with us as soon as he could manage. He would be our attending physician for the rest of November. The position of AP on the floor rotates, something like once a month. APs do morning rounds and remain present as problems arise all day long—crises, deaths.

This afternoon we mostly sat alone on the sofa, holding hands and hugging, which we would not be able to do tomorrow. The clock ticked toward separation. We watched the darkness grow heavier, revealing the lights of ferries crossing the sound. We were mostly alone, high in the air of a hospital on a hill, suspended behind a wall of glass, waiting to be done to. We napped in snatches. We spoke little. I left Jane to find my way to the cafeteria and a quick supper. I cannot remember if Jane ate supper; maybe she wasn't supposed to. Hours passed before Dr. Cheever entered with a nurse and a clipboard. We sat with him in our narrow high room, its lights turned on and Seattle shut away. Dr. Cheever went over everything again, telling us what to expect—mouth pain was first on everyone's list—and the routines of LAF. He told us when we could look for encouraging figures in Jane's bloodwork, and asked the old questions again: medical history, allergies. He made the necessary warnings. His notes:

> The requirement for high-dose chemotherapy and radiation therapy to eradicate the relapsed ALL was emphasized. The general toxicities of chemo-radio therapy were discussed. The need for post-transplant immunosuppression and antiviral therapies were reviewed. The problem of increased GVHD from the one antigen mismatched unrelated transplant as well as marrow rejection from T-cell depletion were specifically mentioned. The patient and her husband seemed to have an excellent appreciation for both the problems and prospects of BMT.

(Could medicine exist without the passive voice?) When Dr. Cheever finished, 1112 was ready, and two nurses prepared to administer the LAF bath, which would take more than an hour—after which Jane, suited up as if for a spacewalk, skin permitted to touch nothing unsterile, would be wheeled into 1112 and cross the threshold into isolation. As she departed for her bath, Jane asked me to leave, to return to the apartment. She knew that she could telephone and I would come to her side. I kissed Jane goodbye and walked back to Spring Street.

The next morning when I woke—every morning when I woke—I hurried through wake-up chores to return to her bedside. I started the coffee, shot insulin, drank a cup while eating breakfast and thermosed the rest. I packed my tote with books and manuscript and bought a newspaper on my way. When I swung into the room I saw Jane stretched out in bed—but I saw her as if through water. A thick transparent plastic curtain reached from floor to ceiling. Her face and body looked wavery. I stuck my arms into the clear plastic sleeves that reached toward her chest and dangled thick plastic gloves. I wiggled my fingers into the gloves, held her hand, and patted her shoulder.

At the foot of her bed the curtain stopped, and there were two feet of open space, a white line on the floor marking the border between my germy world and her sterile one. A fan blew its antibiotic wall along this open space. I could stand at the line, twist my head, and see Jane more clearly. Because the plastic was thick, and because the fan made a racket, it was hard for Jane and me to talk. I shouted to ask about her night. She shouted back. Later that morning we discovered how to hold a conversation. On her side of the wall was a sterile telephone, on my side its bacterial sibling. Sitting side by side, while LAF endured, we talked by telephone.

Already Cytoxan flowed by pump through her Hickman into her bloodstream. Next to Jane's bed, on my side of the curtain, rose a little aluminum forest of IV poles bearing various Abbott pumps. Because different chemicals required different pumps, and because she was often infused by more than one device at a time, the technical forest bristled; once I counted eleven pumps. She could not eat. Cytoxan nauseated her. She needed hyperalimentation, also called TPN or intravenous feeding, for many hours a day, and when she was not having TPN, she was being hydrated. Besides the Cytoxan, she was taking drugs to reduce side effects like nausea and anxiety. There were also drugs for pain, including morphine, and drugs to help her sleep. Much medicine came through her Hickman, but there were also pills, which she found it difficult to keep down. A nurse wearing gloves dropped the pills into a sterile cup on Jane's sterile table. The nurses were adept at manipulating plastic arms and fingers, their petrochemical armor. Wearing the thick gloves, they flushed her lines with heparin and saline, hooked and unhooked her, took her blood pressure and her pulse, and listened through a transplastic stethoscope to her heart.

A large and formidable-appearing nurse introduced herself, Jane's charge nurse during the day, Aurora Brandvold, who continued our education in the politics and policy of LAF. Several times a day someone suited up in sterile gear to enter Jane's zone— a nurse, a resident fellow—to examine her firsthand. I was allowed to suit up and visit once a day. Suiting up was difficult, and if one did it incorrectly, one might import bacteria. At first I did not dare do it. This morning I watched Aurora go through the procedure, her movements brisk with practice. She put on a mask—not the ordinary clean mask that one wore even if one approached the open patch between zones, but something rigorously sterile wrapped in paper that, one had to remember, could be contaminated on the outside. She unwrapped and adjusted a floppy sterile hat to cover her hair. She undid a package of paper boots and tumbled them on sterile paper that lay across the white line. She worked herself into a long flowing blue paper gown, following a procedure for securing it that prevented her skin from touching the gown's outside. She put on sterile gloves—not the ordinary latex gloves that lay in boxes everywhere, but special thick sterile gloves wrapped protectively. Masked, capped, gowned, and gloved, Aurora pulled on paper booties and stepped across the line.

When I finally found the courage to do so, I could touch Jane's whole sore body through her layers of protection, and sit beside her bed on the recliner she occasionally moved to. Through the mask I could talk almost normally, and though I could not hug her as we wished—we were still cocooned—I could caress the shape of her limbs and torso under the covers. Jane relieved my gloom by telling me that I looked like a huge blue condom.

This first morning, I set my thermos of coffee, Seattle paper, book, and manuscript beside my recliner. For Jane I dialed Polly at Eagle Pond Farm, and later telephoned my children and a few friends—telling them Jane was settled in, passing around the new telephone number. I spoke with the nurses about sterilizing clothes for Jane; she hated to wear a johnny. I could send three items a day to be sterilized, and it would take three days for them to return. Jane and I discussed what we would sterilize first. She wanted her white slippers, she wanted sweats. I walked back to the apartment and loaded up, bringing also the boom box and some CDs, to see if Jane could hear music through the screen and over the noise of the fan. You couldn't sterilize a boom box. And Jane's hairy white slippers defied sterilization. I sent off sweats and un-derpants, and tomorrow maybe I would do a brassiere and more sweats. When clothes returned wrapped tightly in double sheets of thick paper, the trick was to open the package without touching the cloth and dump the sterilized garments over the line into Jane's chamber, where she could pick them up with sterile fingers.

With the noise and the swathed curtain, Jane's music came through distorted. After a few days of thought and negotiation, I bought a long-lined hard-plastic earphone, which could be swabbed sterile, and plugged it into the boom box. Wearing gloves, I fed the sterile line with its earpiece through the curtain. By the time I solved the problem, Jane was too sick to enjoy the Boston Symphony.

Separation became harder as Jane became sicker. Cytoxan drove her into extremes of nausea, stomach pain, and fatigue. Mouth pain began, as Cytoxan killed the quick-growing cells of her mouth and digestive tract. The fuzz on her skull fell out and her whole body was hairless again. Sometimes she felt anxious as well as hurtful, and I was less able to help—to rub her back, to comfort by close presence—than I had been in New Hampshire. There was no shower in her sterile nest. With difficulty Jane gave herself a sponge bath every day, and always felt grubby. There was no toilet, and she pulled herself out of bed to use a commode. I guarded the door for her privacy, but otherwise there was little I could do for her: I read her letters over the telephone. A letter arrived from her publisher's new editor, proposing that, when Jane felt well enough to work on it, Graywolf would publish a new-and-selected volume of Jane's poems. Insofar as any news could be cheerful, this was cheerful news. It would be a good way to ease herself back into poetry as she got better. It was also cheerful to hear that Bill Moyers's program about us, *A Life Together,* had won an Emmy as a documentary.

Hayden Carruth continued to write Jane a letter every week, looking out his window in northern New York State to describe squirrels and snowfall. Other friends telephoned and wrote. I dialed Polly morning and night, and Jane picked up after Polly answered. Both women worked to sound better than they felt. I told callers the latest. "Jane ate a spoonful of oatmeal today." "Jane did half an hour of PT." When I had delivered the day's bulletin, I asked Jane if she had the strength to talk to Andrew or Alice, Philippa or Caroline, Joyce or Liam. I was guard dog. "Three minutes," I would bark.

While we were in LAF I learned how to turn off the irritating complaints of a pump ("Air in Line," "Infusion Complete") and alert a nurse to finish the job. I was present for medical rounds, to ask questions that Jane might in her weakness and fatigue forget to ask. Once a day a room cleaner (sometimes two at once) would suit up and spend an hour wiping down Jane's antibiotic isolation. One was a tiny nimble young woman who squatted and leapt, bright with unstoppable energy. Another was Marie from Martinique, whom Jane enjoyed for her cheer and grace. Our first resident fellow was a burly young doctor from Chicago, East Indian in extraction, who nearly burst through his LAF clothes as he entered the zone to examine Jane. With Cytoxan, then with total body irradiation, or TBI, Jane's vital signs, her heart in particular, needed close attention. Young physical therapists suited up and put Jane through stretches and mild exercises. *The New Yorker* arrived with Jane's poem "Prognosis." Readers who knew of Jane's illness assumed she wrote about her own disease, but the poem was about my prognosis after my cancer of 1992. (Jane took a while to finish a poem.) I showed the poem to our nurse Aurora, who copied and posted it. I pointed it out to Dr. Cheever in the corridor and he read it, nodding his head. "Ominous," he said.

Over the two days of Cytoxan, Jane dimmed like a light with the rheostat turned down a millimeter an hour; she diminished to the faint glow of a filament. She found it difficult to shuffle a few feet to her commode or her recliner. When Dr. Cheever visited, hearing reports from nurses and fellow, studying bloodwork numbers, he congratulated us; things were just as they should be. Jane looked at him blankly. After the two Cytoxan days and a day off, it was time for TBI. For eleven half-hour sessions, Jane lay on a gurney in an underground room while radiation invisibly, without noise and without smell, poured itself into her body. No one could stay alongside her in this room walled with lead. Before the first session I was allowed to accompany her and inspect the room when the radiation was not yet spewing forth. The stretcher lay poised between two machines, painted cheerfully, that resembled large potbellied stoves. The walls and ceiling were bright also, like the kindergarten of a tony day school. Children lay in this room as well as adults. Once in the elevator I met a young woman, rising from the depths to the tenth pediatric-oncology floor, who had just left her screaming two-year-old strapped to the gurney. At least Jane knew why she was doing what she was doing. It was as if she capped Chernobyl with her body.

For Jane to depart 1112's LAF for TBI, she needed to suit up as I suited up to enter her room. A gray-haired nurse with a wheelchair stood beside the white line directing her painful and clumsy motions. When Jane sat in the wheelchair, or when she lay down for radiation, her skin touched nothing but sterile clothing. Capped and masked, gloved and gowned, she was wheeled away and wheeled back an hour later. By the last day she began to feel further pain as her mouth and throat worsened, and the pain became steadily more intense over the next two weeks. Like Cytoxan, radiation kills fast-growing cells. The destruction of the gastrointestinal tract is unavoidable; slowly, new cells grow back.

One night as I sat alone in our apartment the telephone rang. It was Jane, suddenly overcome with panic and dread. Could I come over? Quickly I packed for the night, expecting to doze on the recliner beside her, and walked into her room twelve minutes later. Through plastic sleeves and heavy gloves I touched and rubbed her. She told me that she had already felt less anxious when she knew I was coming. After an hour she persuaded me to go home again, both of us leaning intently toward the immediate future: In two days, Jane's new marrow would arrive by courier.

The Soul's Bliss and Suffering

JANE FELT that she had been born with her bipolar mood disorder, described and embodied in her poem "Having It Out with Melancholy," the disease inherited from her father. When I first knew her, and when we were first married, I noticed her moods especially when she was dark. In her first book of poems, finished when she was thirty, she wrote from bleakness and in elation. Many times during our early marriage, she was energetic and horny and high, noisy and humorous. More often she was withdrawn and private, brooding and sad. Becoming Christian, she found a site for both extremes in the dark of Maundy Thursday and the elevation of Easter sunrise. When she was low I might attempt to comfort her, as she did me in my bad times, and sometimes comfort or loving helped, but there were times I could not reach her, times she was beyond my help. At these times I learned not to fuss at her; I did not ask, "Was it something I said?" (During years of psychotherapy, before I knew Jane, I learned that I was not responsible for everything around me.) She also knew when to stay close and when to withdraw; mostly we let the other be. But nothing is simple: By temperament, I am on the move, eager (as Jane said) for "the next thing, the next thing." Often she sank into speechless discontent while I remained energetic, depressive wedded to hypomanic.

When something in the real world hurt or upset us, we told the other, but not always at first. After receiving an upsetting letter or telephone call, I waited until I had talked it over inside myself. I remember Jane asking, "Did you get something bad in the mail?" when she saw my distressed face. Sometimes I learned about Jane's depressed or even suicidal feelings only when I read a poem months afterward. The double and separate psychiatric help we had received was useful in our marriage by letting us understand that each carried burdens that the other could do nothing about. This separateness, in the usual way of the psyche, helped bring us together.

In 1981 Jane volunteered to become a hospice worker, a good idea for a chronic depressive, who is forced away from inward-gazing misery. She took training, and one of the exercises was keeping a journal of her training. I found it two years after her death, when I dismantled her workroom and sorted through her papers. Thinking over her mood history at that time, she spoke of a depression after the end of her "first marriage." She put quotation marks around the reference to six months of cohabitation with her boyfriend before she and I dated. Jane had just finished hospice training, prepared to take on her first case, when her mother called from Ann Arbor to say that her father had terminal lung cancer. (He had stopped smoking decades earlier, when the children were born, but he made his living playing the piano in bars dense with smoke.) Like his daughter, Reuel Kenyon was cancer-prone. In 1970 a surgeon had removed cancerous polyps from his colon. A few years later it was cancer of the thyroid, again surgically removed. His lung cancer was inoperable. Because Jane and I were writers with portable work, we were able to drop everything, load up the car, leave the key with neighbors who would feed the cats, and drive to Ann Arbor.

Jane's first hospice patient was her father. She stayed with him all but a few weeks of the six months it took him to die, and I was present most of the time. Polly and Jane and I took turns staying up all night, because the codeine made Reuel delirious. He was apt to rise at midnight, shave, and start dressing, having remembered a crucial appointment downtown. Whoever was on duty would talk Reuel down, persuade him it was two A.M., and get him back to bed. He took radiation for a while, but it pained him and it would only extend his life, not save it. Polly and Jane and Reuel together decided to stop the treatment. Jane and I slept in the small bedroom upstairs that had been hers as a girl. She wrote little at the time but later made poems about her father's illness and death. I wrote every day, down in the cool cellar at the bench where Reuel had worked over architectural drawings. In October, when he was confined to a facility for the terminally ill, I flew home. Jane was with Reuel when he died, later in the month. He had asked that half his ashes be spread on their Ann Arbor land and half in Eagle Pond; the next summer his family gathered by Eagle Pond.

Back in New Hampshire, heavy with his death, Jane one afternoon received a letter with the Washington return address of the National Endowment for the Arts. Annually, the NEA had sent Jane a form letter saying that the competition had been intense this year, and that they were sorry to inform her that . . . This time, when I looked up from reading my own mail, I saw her staring open-mouthed at a letter, reading and rereading it because she kept thinking that she had missed a negative. Jane had won an NEA poetry fellowship. Often she had felt chagrin that she did not contribute more to the finances of our establishment. Now she said, "Perkins, I'm going to take you to England." A few days later, *Esquire* offered to send me to England in January to interview John Fowles. I asked Jane if she minded *Esquire* paying my airfare. She was tolerant. We had visited England several times since the trips early in our marriage, attending theater in London, visiting a friend of Jane's who lived in Cambridge. This 1982 trip was shadowed by the death of Jane's father, as she records in "Travel After a Death." We drove through the green fields of Dorset and Devon and Somerset while Jane's mind tormented her.

It was after we returned home that Jane's depression sank to its lowest. I remember driving to a diner in Bristol one evening for supper. After one beer Jane cried bitterly. At home she curled weeping on the sofa, and for days spent most of the time weeping in the fetal position. It was not only thoughts of her father's death that filled her weeping; she was possessed by a vast, general, engulfing sadness. I could do nothing. She did not want to be fondled or even touched. She was anxious that I not think I had upset her. Her desire to remain untouched, her outrageous sadness, had nothing to do with me. Whenever depression crushed her, she worried that I would feel that I was its source. Twice she asked doctors to reassure me that her misery had nothing to do with me.

Jane's collapse early in 1982 began a new phase of her bipolarity, new in its extremity, her congenital condition exacerbated by trauma. In "Mourning and Melancholy," Freud speaks of the similarities between grief and depression, or melancholia; depression adds self-loathing to the blackness of loss. Freud observes that often mourning turns into melancholia six months or a year after the death, and a significant number of melancholics add mania to melancholy. Maybe after prolonged or intense grief, adrenal secretions accumulate on neuroreceptors, as they do with post-traumatic stress disorder. Jane's loss of her father was hard, as a parent's death is hard—but I think that her depression issued not only from his death: She was intimately his caregiver, and watched as he lost, cell by cell, everything that he was. When Jane took anything on—like cooking a meal or having a conversation or caring for someone sick—she concentrated utterly and passionately on the single task. It was not only her father who died but the object of her concentrated care. Her care had failed to keep him alive, and at some depth of unreason it must have been her fault that he died.

That first blackest time, she gradually stopped her continual weeping. Our internist Don Clark recognized clinical depression and prescribed drugs; I'm not sure which drug he began with, but it must have been a tricyclic. The Prozac class of drugs (which didn't help Jane) was not yet available. For advice on treatment, our doctor spoke with Dr. Charles Solow, head of psychiatry at Dartmouth-Hitchcock. Later, Jane became a patient of Dr. Solow, who diagnosed her as bipolar, and she relied on him for treatment until she died. The tricyclic doxepin helped her for three years, the longest stretch without a deep trough. During these years she had her ups and downs, she was sad and she was gay, but doxepin appeared to prevent deep depression. As she inhabited a fragile comfort, she could work on her poems. When her body learned how to metabolize the drug, she needed larger doses, until it was no longer safe to increase the dose. Dr. Solow prescribed a variety of drugs, and supported her in sessions of talk. Jane was medicated for the rest of her life. She kept wanting to survive without pharmaceutical help, and in 1992 tried the experiment of going naked. A precipitate plunge returned her to medication.

Doxepin, like others, gave her a dry mouth, but the side effects were not miserable. Some drugs did nothing for her, or reduced the intensity of orgasm, or included other side effects nasty enough to disqualify them. When she was manic for three months in 1984, she took lithium, which she hated. After that year, she was never manic for long episodes. Often she dosed daily on a combination of drugs. One drug that helped was an old MAO inhibitor, Nardil, which kept her from depression for almost a year, but limited her sleep so much that she became exhausted and had to stop taking it.

Twice, when Jane's usual mild depression became monstrous, Don Clark put her into New London Hospital. She was afraid she would harm herself—and maybe she needed to remove herself from my hovering anxious presence. She thought of suicide but I never believed she would do it. I remember her rolling on the bathroom floor and banging her head—without striking a sharp edge. Sometimes driving alone she was frightened by the impulse to steer into a wall, but she drove slowly. I do not belittle her misery if I suggest that fear of physical pain helped keep her alive. She also knew with Christian conviction that she should not kill herself.

When she was mildly depressive, or rising slowly from a debilitating depression, she could write—and wrote much about depression. Lovemaking helped during mild depression. Thus, we routine-freaks made love on schedule, whether we felt like it or not; after we got started, we would feel like it. She would have two good hours of energy after a midday climax. She leapt out of bed, dressed, and got to work, cheerful for the while. Jane was spiritual but Jane was also fleshy, and sex was an uproarious joy. Sometimes when we lay down I chattered too much, in my excitement. I would hear, "Shut up and fuck, Perkins." Erotic hunger quadrupled with mania, and I remember exhaustion during the insatiable spring of 1984. Manic, she was altogether a different human being. She wrote an opera libretto, best forgotten, in two and a half days. She never asked my opinion on what we would do next; she did what she wanted and brought me along. She was happy, if bossy and insensitive—who was ordinarily wholly responsive to anybody's look or tone. When she was manic I felt suddenly married to a locomotive. This locomotive was not delusional—but it drove fast, spent money, and made quick decisions. It became imperative that she buy for herself a ring displayed at a local jeweler's. At first when Jane turned manic, I became depressed, which allowed me to understand that her depression had for years provided me with secondary gain: I could flatter myself that I was a rock, the reliable one who kept things going.

Early summer of 1984, with lithium, she came down without coming too far down. In December mania reappeared briefly, maybe for a week, and it flashed on and off for the rest of her life, often for moments or days only. Once I flew back from a poetry reading to find Jane intensely happy, in a quiet state of rapture. She told me that something extraordinary happened while I was gone. She had felt the presence of the Holy Spirit. (It was female.) Mystics are bipolar—St. John of the Cross, Gerard Manley Hopkins—and proclaim the soul's dark night as well as its bliss. Along with Jane's many poems of depression are poems of spiritual ecstasy, like "Briefly It Enters" and "Notes from the Other Side." Both poles make the globe of her late and beautiful "Happiness."

Psychiatrists have documented the high incidence of bipolarity among artists. Writers are the most bipolar—and poets more than other writers. (See "Manic-Depressive Illness and Creativity," Kay Redfield Jamison, *Scientific American,* February 1995.) Only one percent of people in general suffer from manic depression, Jamison says, and cites figures for mood disorders in artists, depending on different models of sampling, that go upward from thirty-eight percent. No one can induce a mood disorder to make poems; bipolarity is not taught in M.F.A. programs. Does the practice of the art exacerbate a tendency? Surely for the artist the disorder is creative in its manic form—excitement, confidence, the rush of energy and invention. Maybe natural selection perpetuates bipolarity because mania or hypomania benefits the whole tribe, inventing the wheel and Balzac's *Cousine Bette,* while depression harms only the depressive and those close to the depressive.

It was terrible to see her suffering, especially at its worst, black rather than blue. One Christmas, not long before her leukemia, she plunged into a terrible place. We always made much of this holiday. Jane read the Gospels through each year at Easter and at Christmas, and tended to our Advent calendar. We filled big, comical stockings for each other with chocolate Santa Clauses and shortbread and writing supplies. (Always I found something for her stocking that would make her laugh. Once in a poem, through reticence or embarrassment, she made it a thin black nightgown; really it was a teddy. Once I gave her handcuffs, although we were not given to B & D.) On the depressed Christmas, everything I gave her made her feel worse. After all, if she was ugly and stupid and wicked, my gifts only emphasized her unworthiness. After an episode of blackness, events of the bad time never quite lost their tone. The presents I gave her that Christmas went largely unused, unread, unworn.

Sometimes when her friends telephoned, I had to do the talking. I passed the message that Jane could not talk. In profound depression it is impossible to speak even with the dearest. You cannot lift yourself upright when you weigh ten thousand pounds. I remember a birthday party for a granddaughter at my daughter's house. Jane stood looking on, wretched, hardly able to speak. She was silent, there were many people, and she practiced invisibility. My daughter (on whom nothing is lost) said, "You're *miserable,* aren't you?" When Jane nodded, Philippa spoke with sympathy and left her alone. (You do not try to cheer up depressives; the worst thing you can do is to count their blessings for them.) When a visitor dropped by, sometimes Jane secluded herself in the bedroom, door closed, while I explained and tried to fill two places. Several times we had to break dates with prospective visitors. Once we called off a lengthy August visit from Jane's brother and family. Once Jane asked Alice not to visit, from a summer place in Vermont. Sometimes I drove alone down to Connecticut for the monthly trip to my mother's.

However extreme her moods, Jane was never out of her head. God never telephoned her when she was manic. In depression her phobias and hypochondria stretched reality but did not quite alter it. I remember Jane telling me in alarm that the tires on my Honda were *entirely bald;* when I checked them out, there was tread on every tire—but we would need to buy new ones soon. At some point late in the 1980s Jane fretted about a rash on her side that would not go away. I could see nothing, but I sympathized. The rash smarted and made her feel dirty, so she took baths twice a day and rubbed herself with a washcloth. Don Clark could find nothing wrong and sent her to a dermatologist, who examined her thoroughly, microscopically . . . Finally, this doctor took a deep breath (as Jane described it) and told Jane there was no rash. Maybe her skin hurt because she was washing and rubbing it so frequently? Jane drove home from the appointment without her rash, but she was not relieved. She was furious with herself, humiliated.

In 1985 Jane felt a lump high on her neck. Our doctor, who later kept me alive by attention to small symptoms, thought that the swelling was insignificant. Jane's hypochondria may have saved her ten years. When she told our doctor that she remained anxious about the lump, he arranged an appointment at Dartmouth-Hitchcock with a surgeon who specialized in throats. The surgeon told Jane that the lump had to come out, that there was a fifty percent chance of malignancy. We made a date for surgery, mid-August, and I helped push Jane's gurney to the elevator, then drove home to wait for the surgeon's telephone call. Walking up and down a hundred miles, I waited for the phone to ring. "It's cancer," said Dr. Johnson. My stomach fell from my body. I talked calmly, asking questions, and told him I would give Jane the news; it was what we had agreed on. Then the surgeon spoke reassuringly. He had removed a salivary gland that contained a mucoepidermoid carcinoma, confirmed as malignant by examination. The tumor would go to Pathology, which would determine its degree of malignancy, but the tumor was wholly encapsulated within the gland. It would not metastasize; neither chemotherapy nor radiation would be necessary.

My thirty-eight-year-old wife (I was about to turn fifty-seven) had cancer. I sat by her empty bed until an orderly wheeled her in, groggy but awake enough to ask the question: I answered. I remember her sleepy voice as she accepted the information, expressing surprise. I sat beside her as she dozed and woke until I needed to go home for the dog. Whenever she woke I told her the bad news again, and the good. In the morning she was awake and solemn, and we drove home to an ecstatic year-old Gus, separated for two days from the love of his life. Seeing and smelling Jane, Gus leapt, cavorted, sang, bounced—and flailed a paw against a small incision under her chin, pulling off a Band-Aid. It was a long weekend until Pathology reported. Our marriage had been close— living together all day, writing, so many third things—but the intensest closeness, which dread of separation sponsors, began with Jane's first malignancy. Our fears were again assuaged by the surgeon. We believed him but we were shaken. Alice Mattison has declared that Jane and I lived continually with the conviction that either was likely to die in the next five minutes.

Real successes in the outside world could raise Jane up, like her NEA or the Guggenheim fellowship that she was awarded in 1992. Much of the time during her last twelve years, Jane dropped low, she suffered, but she functioned; she wrote poems especially as she climbed out of depression. Her most direct account is "Having It Out with Melancholy." It pained her to write this poem, to expose herself, but writing the poem also helped her: It set depression out as she knew it, both depression and its joyful tentative departure. She wanted with this poem to help others who were afflicted. The first time she read it aloud, in 1991 at the Frost Place in Franconia, she paused during her reading, resisting tears. When she finished, a line of people waited to talk with her: depressives, people from the families of depressives.

Jane's mood disorder became almost a party to our marriage, always looming even in lighter times—something concentrated upon and studied. There were times when she seemed headed for electroshock therapy. And there were times when events outside her overcame the endogenous depression. Jane was depressed and lethargic in April of 1992 when my colon cancer metastasized to my liver, and her brain chemistry altered itself from depression into the high energy of anxiety and care. After I returned from the hospital, she bought a massage table and rubbed me down every day, as if she would rub the cancer out. My chances of long survival were poor, according to statistics, and Jane and I both believed I would die soon. I did chemotherapy for six months or so, a mild form painful only for a week. I remember lying in bed, fatigued with the treatment, when Jane brought me "Pharaoh" and asked me, with real concern, if I minded . . . I did not mind, nor the anticipation of my death in "Otherwise." I loved these poems. As we enjoyed the busy intensities of the next year—1993 with its book publications, travel to India, poetry readings together, Bill Moyers's television show—our conviction of my imminent death lived just under the good day's skin.

Day Zero Zero

IT GREW DARK EARLY, November 1994 in Seattle. Lunch and supper I took in the Swedish cafeteria, extending my intimacy with the phenomenon of hospital food. Swedish beat out Hitchcock, despite the absence of meatloaf Wellington. The daily meat/veggie/potato plates were varied and copious and boring and fine. Just past these ordinary offerings, a series of trays provided ethnic variety, a characteristic of Seattle not prominent in New Hampshire: knockwurst and sauerkraut; trays for assemblage into tacos; stir-fry with noodles or rice and egg rolls; Eastern combinations from Thailand to India. The large complex of Swedish, joined underground and above to the Hutch and numerous clinics with other names, afforded enormous experience in the universe of elevators. When I journeyed each morning in the rainy dark I entered the doors of a clinic and ascended three floors by a small elevator. Then I followed a corridor to a skybridge, which forked to the right, then zapped straight ahead across another street to the main floor of Swedish. I zigged, I zagged, taking frequent right turns, to find myself approaching two banks of four elevators each, SW Swedish, and rose to the eleventh floor, where I turned right, peeling off my wet gear, turned left, passed two nurses' stations, nodding to night nurses still on duty, to enter 1112. When I took lunch or supper, the SW elevators sent me down to the cafeteria level, and I walked a quarter of a mile—right, left,

left, and left again—to enter the aroma of appetite. It took me
fifteen minutes to finish my meal and return, unless I hurried.

On the elevators I watched to see which buttons my fellow
passengers pushed. If young adults pushed 10, I asked them about
their children. The notion of two-year-olds with BMTs was too
wretched to consider—except that two-year-olds most of the time
recover from leukemia. When a passenger pushed the button for
the eleventh floor, I met another adult's caregiver. I told everyone
about my wife and heard stories about their charges. My only distraction during Jane's long illness and the first years of mourning
consisted of putting her illness and death, and my grief, into
words—in conversation or on the page. When I wrote or talked
about leukemia and death it was almost as if I were doing something.

Rarely, during LAF, could I do something useful for Jane. On
a Friday during Cytoxan, just before TBI, Jane dropped her glasses
inside her isolation, breaking the frames. From the onset of treatment she had been unable to wear her contact lenses—dry eyeballs—and without her glasses she could see little, neither distinct
nurses nor Seattle's skyline nor photographs of grandchildren. She
was locked in a world of fuzzy shapes, as she was locked inside the
plastic walls of LAF and the walls of pain and nausea. She kicked
the glasses out of LAF and I hastened outside to find an op-
tometrist who could supply new frames at four-thirty on a Friday
afternoon. When I brought them back, a room cleaner wiped
them down with germicide and handed them with sterile care
back into Jane's cage. Again she could watch PBS and the sunset
over Puget Sound.

A solicitous young man in a hairnet offered the patients any
food or drink they might want from the eleventh-floor kitchen for

BMT patients, who could eat only sterilized food in sterilized containers. But from November 10 or 11 until January, Jane ate virtually nothing. She drank a little. *Spécialité de la maison* of the chef on the eleventh floor was something he called Sore Mouth Drink—a few calories, and a little numbing. As well, she gargled with lidocaine, mixed half and half with salty sterile water. Take a swallow from one cup and spit it into another. Inspection of her mouth and lips occurred daily. Pain doctors came calling. Ever since diagnosis and the first assaults of chemo, doctors and nurses had asked Jane, "On a scale of one to ten, how bad is the pain?" When she had suffered with neuropathies in Hitchcock, and I witnessed her pain all day, I had been frustrated when she answered "four and a half" or "five." But she knew what she was doing. Now I heard her barely audible voice say "nine" or "nine and a half." She never said "ten."

Thursday, November 17, was the day for the transplant. Somewhere in the United States that morning a thirty-nine-year-old female (this much identity we were allowed) would undergo general anesthesia while a surgeon harvested her marrow from the large pelvic bone. As the donor woke up in the recovery room, the marrow would be sealed and placed in a cooler. Then a courier would fly with the marrow to Seattle and be driven to the Hutch. No one knew just when it would arrive, but it would not be early in the day—unless, perhaps, the harvest took place right here on Pill Hill—because of time needed for delivery. It was impossible to read or write that day. I feared for the courier—an airplane crash, a hijack, a car accident between the airport and the Hutch. Instructed by her nurse Aurora, Jane wrote a note "For the Donor" that the courier could take back to the hospital she had come from. Jane wrote on sterile paper with a sterile pencil.

Carolyn Stormer, the Seattle nurse we became closest to, went on duty at four in the afternoon, and on November 17 would set me up with a bed at bedtime. At five-thirty I dashed downstairs to supper, to be back in time for PBS news. When I returned in a quarter of an hour, I had missed the courier and her thermos. It was as if I had been buying a hot dog when Carlton Fisk hit his home run. Carolyn had brought the courier into the room with her cargo and introduced her to Jane and handed her Jane's sterile note for the donor. The courier brought a "For the Recipient," written somewhere by the woman who was donating her marrow for a stranger's life. The courier was forbidden to say where she had come from, but she could tell Jane that before she left the hospital, carrying the harvested marrow, she had talked with the donor, who was resting and sitting up in Recovery with a lame backside. The courier told Jane the donor had a history of trouble with general anesthesia but had nonetheless undertaken the harvest. The new marrow had to undergo T-cell depletion in the Hutchinson laboratory before infusion. T-cells are a concern. Residual host T-cells can cause draft rejection, and donor T-cells can cause graft-versus-host disease. On the other hand, if there are *no* T-cells, the new marrow may refuse to engraft, to take root and grow. The first fear after transplant is that the new marrow will not take. When it takes, a fear is GVHD.

Waiting that evening for the marrow's return from the lab, we watched the news together. Maybe I looked at ESPN basketball with the sound off. Carolyn, who was small and comely, rolled a bed to room 1112, and we moved the recliner outside with a note stuck to it, to reserve it for me tomorrow. (Some recliners were better than others.) Jane went to sleep. I wrote postcards, telling friends what night it was, what we were waiting for. I dozed, both of us interrupted in sleep by beeping pumps and by nurses taking vital signs. Carolyn went off at twelve, and a young pregnant nurse took over for the dead of night. In the countdown we leaned toward, the day of transplant was Day Zero. As it became November 18, Day Zero became one calendar day later than planned for, Day Zero Zero.

It was five-thirty A.M. when the bulging night nurse opened the door carrying a small plastic bag of pinkish liquid, just delivered from the laboratory with T-cells depleted. She hung it from an IV pole between my bed and Jane's, and with her plastic arms and gloves hooked it to a needle that pierced one of the ports of Jane's Hickman for infusion. The donor's marrow would enter Jane's bloodstream, find its way into the hollows of her marrowless bones, and begin (we hoped) its task of replication. Sleep was over. I sat on the edge of my bed, my face six or ten inches from the bag of pink life, studying its slow disappearance through tubes into Jane's heart. I wrote in my Day-Timer the mysterious letters and numbers on the bag's label:

> Donor Ref No: 0103–4478–6
> Recipient 926–2767
> Jane Kenyon
> collection date 11/17/94
> anticoagulant Heparin additive Media 199
> CD4 Partial CDS Depleted
> Bone Marrow Per Protocol 766.0
> Total volume: 150 milliliters

One hundred and fifty milliliters is not a cup's worth. The stared-at bag momentously diminished. Jane telephoned Alice Mattison in Connecticut to tell her what was happening. When the infusion was finished I rolled the bed away, restored my recliner, ate breakfast in the cafeteria, telephoned Polly and my children, and began another day—Day Zero Zero of the new immune system, the new possible life, extension of the old life for Jane and me; maybe a hundred days before returning home.

(One year after a BMT, if the recipient survives and the donor is agreeable, the pair may relinquish anonymity. People from opposite sides of the country or the world—maybe opposites in character, strangers with identical immune systems—may connect with each other. They may talk and visit. Some withdraw from each other in embarrassment over identity confounded with alienation. Or friendships form based on accidental replication combined with generosity. Four months after Jane died I was surprised to receive, via the Marrow Donor Program at the Hutchinson, an anonymous note addressed "To the Recipient's Family," expressing sorrow over Jane's anonymous death. Anonymously, I answered the note, "To the Donor," and at the same time asked the Hutch if I might send the donor Jane's books, necessarily revealing her name. A few weeks later the telephone rang at ten on a Sunday night, and it was the donor calling. Her name was Ronda McCormick, from Aurora, Nebraska; she was forty now, with three children. I asked her if she had been told that Jane was a poet. There was a pause. "A *poet?*" I took Ronda McCormick's address to send her Jane's poems—and the funeral program fronted with Jane's picture, and a photograph of the two of us together, and some of the printed tributes to Jane and her work that appeared after her death. Ronda McCormick wrote back a long generous letter, with family photographs and a newspaper clipping about her marrow donation. She had to go all the way to Omaha twice—early to have vials of blood drawn for further testing; later for the harvest—this woman with three children and a history of trouble with general anesthesia. She told me she was from a farm in Iowa and her husband was pastor at the Pleasant View Church in Aurora. In 1992 she was tested during a bone marrow drive, unsuccessful, to find a match for an Aurora youth. In 1994 the Red Cross told her that she was a possible match for someone, and after further examination that the match was viable. A local newspaper wrote up her donation. When the article appeared, Ronda had been told that Jane was doing well. The reporter quoted Jane's note written in LAF, "To the Donor: Thank you for your sacrifice. I will thank you in person in a year.")

We counted Day Two, Day Three, Day Four, days that distinguished themselves only by increased mouth pain. On the wall was a chart for keeping track of bloodwork—red blood cells, ANCs (absolute neutrophil counts). It would be a long time, weeks maybe, before the bloodwork revealed that the new marrow had engrafted. Regularly—Day Five, Day Six, Day Seven—a round 0 filled the ANC box. Meanwhile the plastic isolation of LAF became increasingly intolerable. Jane never felt clean. My rigmarole of dressing to enter her isolation was itself depressing. Maybe my own distress over separation influenced the doctors as much as Jane's did. The Hutch kept a sharp eye not only on its patients but also on their caregivers. Increasingly Dr. Cheever and our nurses spoke of removing Jane from LAF.

> The patient was initially placed in an LAF room as her donor marrow was T-cell depleted. The patient found the isolation required for LAF to be prohibitive psychologically. This was discussed in detail with the patient and her husband, and it was felt that as the benefit of LAF on long-term outcome is marginal and that since the patient was having significant psychological problems with LAF, this was discontinued on 11/23/94.

Jane remained in the same bed in the same room. The curtain and its steel frame swung flat against a wall, and the clattering fan went off. I washed my hands whenever I entered the room, and wore a mask when I came close to Jane, but now I could touch her; I could sit close to her; I could see her without plastic distortion. With hygienic precaution, I kissed her on the lips. We held hands. The change was miraculous, like a cure for leukemia. We could talk without using the telephone; Jane could hear Messiaen straight from the box. With help she could walk to the bathroom and take a shower sitting on a stool. She could change into clean sweats three times a day.

As mouth pain continued to mount, Jane received a morphine drips which she could supplement with a bolus. Every day she sipped a little Sore Mouth Drink. It was important to swallow; some patients stop swallowing entirely, and have to learn how to swallow again. PT had greater access to her now. Some days we walked a little in the hallway, sitting to rest halfway in the glassy room of our introduction to Jane's floor. Mostly, bathing was her greatest physical exercise. I started the shower, helped her to undress, and held on to her as she walked the few feet. While she washed I fetched a hot blanket from a supply room nearby, washing my hands before touching the fabric. All day I fetched her hot blankets.

On Thanksgiving, the family of a former BMT patient brought the courses of a turkey dinner to the tables of a caregiver's retreat on the eleventh floor. Day Twelve was the worst day, though not easy to distinguish from Day Eleven or Thirteen. Afterward, the burning diminished slightly as new cells began to replace the torn and destroyed tissue that lined Jane's mouth and throat and gastrointestinal tract. Jane tried a little food: Jell-O, soup, oatmeal. Whatever she ate she vomited. Pain still kept her awake, her sleeping potion ineffective. One weekend a new pain doctor prescribed old-fashioned barbiturates and Jane had a night's sleep. But she distrusted barbiturates and took no more.

November turned into December. It was time for Dr. Cheever to go off duty, back to the laboratory, and his successor was Dr. Kris Doney, who became the Seattle hematologist we were closest to. She had attended the University of Michigan, B.S. and M.D.; two of my old Ann Arbor friends had been her teachers in medical school. She had moved west in 1975 just as Jane and I moved east. A day or two after Dr. Cheever left the floor I took lunch at the Swedish cafeteria and looked up to see him beckoning me to sit beside him. Over lunch I found him disgruntled with the BMT as a cure for leukemia. We *had* to find another way, because the BMT was painful and difficult and—I heard underneath his words— chancy. Of course, he allowed, if the leukemia returned after a year, a patient could have a second BMT. Inwardly I shuddered at the thought and resolved not to mention this option, this *good news,* to Jane. I was missing the point—the current or undercurrent of Dr. Cheever's thoughts when he considered Jane's virulent and dogged blasts. "Of course if it comes back within the year," he concluded, "there's nothing to do."

On November 28 Jane's bloodwork chart provided the exaltation we looked for. The column for ANCs, resolutely 0 day after day, showed the figure 1. The single ANC was evidence that the new marrow was engrafting, beginning to produce a new immune system, the most significant marker in the journey of the hundred days. Soon I was required to leave Jane's side several times a week to attend pump class, and other gatherings of caregivers whose patients were headed for discharge. Caregivers were utterly necessary—our patients were helpless to help themselves, as the clinic had predicted—and we needed many lessons, to take the place of nurses. We amateur R.N.s met in the clinic, an hour or two at a time, four or five of us with a nurse to teach us. We received printed-out lists of symptoms, telephone numbers to call day or night, advice on when to consult a nurse, come to the clinic, or dial for an ambulance. We read our lists, asked questions, and heard extended descriptions. In pump class we learned how to infuse our patients with hyperalimentation and hydration and antivirals. Our teachers gave each of us a little Provider pump, a bag of water, tubing, a filter, and syringes. We learned how to remove air from bags of liquid, because pumps will not work with air in the line. We learned how to hook up tubing, fit the monitor onto the Provider, connect the filter for TPN, flush a Hickman, and protect a needle for further use. We learned to use LifeShield Protectors and Docking Stations. We learned when and how to obtain additional supplies, pharmaceutical and mechanical. Programming the pump was hardest. The technophobe sweated and trembled. I would never get it! Of course I got it. After a week or two of infusions back in our apartment—and after more instruction from a nurse who visited us there—I handled the Provider with ease, and learned to use another brand of pump and another set of chemicals. A month after discharge I felt ready to teach pump class myself.

While I fretted in pump class, while Jane struggled with pain and weakness—but her ANCs slowly increased—we talked daily with Polly in New Hampshire. She stayed at Eagle Pond Farm with our house sitter, but she did not improve. The pain grew worse and more extensive. With hope but without conviction I looked into a larger apartment in our Spring Street building, so that Polly could join us there. But then Polly was readmitted to Dartmouth-Hitchcock, subject to more tests, and her doctors discovered that the cancer had spread to her other lung. There would be no more radiation; there would be no flight to Seattle. Would she survive until we returned? I tried by telephone to get her admitted to Clough Extended Care in New London, my mother's place, but Medicare forbade it. Jane's brother and his family made plans to fly east from Michigan for Christmas.

As her ANCs slowly climbed, Jane worked at improving her physical condition. It seemed impossible that she could leave 1112, not so much to survive in our apartment as to trek back from our apartment to the clinic for bloodwork and transfusions and appointments with physicians. Then a discharge nurse, working with our Blue Cross caseworker in New Hampshire, came up with an infusion service called Caremark that would visit our apartment, do vital signs, infuse or inject anything I lacked training for, train me further, and draw blood to deliver to the clinic for analysis. This service saved Jane untold pain and discomfort.

Approaching discharge, we became more and more tense. I continued to undergo episodes of vertigo. One dark rainy morning early in December I waited for the light to change so that I could cross Madison Avenue. A bus bore down the street toward me where I waited. In a flash I thought, "I could throw myself under that bus," and almost immediately laughed out loud, saying to myself, "I didn't know I felt *that* bad!" All the way to Jane's bedside I smiled to myself over my suicidal notion, which was not strong enough to be called an impulse. I did not tell Jane. Later in the morning, I bumped into a nurse in the hallway outside Jane's room, a willowy young woman who was never Jane's nurse but who was a familiar face on the floor. She asked me how Jane was doing. I spoke about ANCs, the relief of leaving LAF, a sore mouth—to which she nodded a familiar and sympathetic head. Then she asked, as everyone did—they knew there was a secondary patient as well as a primary one—"And how are *you* doing?" I told her I was doing fine, worried about programming pumps . . . and then I laughed and told her about my bus-thought that morning, saying that maybe I was not doing *quite* so well as I thought. She did not laugh. Not long afterward, our social worker Winona dropped into Jane's room and took me walking around the floor, asking after my feelings. Not long thereafter the psychiatrist Rob Devney paid a similar call—and I understood that my anecdote, which had made me laugh, was heard without amusement and with alarm. Two years later, when I returned briefly to Seattle to revisit Jane's old helpers, Carolyn Stormer remembered hearing the story—part of a rundown of the day's events—when she arrived that afternoon for the evening shift.

Every night I took home in my tote Jane's clothes, mostly sweats and underpants, to launder them. She wore nothing else, a brassiere sometimes, but bras were tiresome and sometimes painful or awkward, because of her Hickman. Every day I brought her clean clothes. Day after day was the same day, and every day Jane's mother was dying, and Jane could have no thought of attending her. We talked daily with Polly at her Hitchcock room. By now Jane and I walked two or three times a day around 11SW. Sometimes Jane held my arm. Sometimes she pushed a wheelchair, which served a double purpose: She could lean on it, which relieved her fear of falling, and when she became too tired to continue, she could sit in the chair while I wheeled her back. Every day was a cluster of examinations and procedures. Frequently someone steered in an x-ray machine to check on Jane's lungs. With no resistance to disease and little physical action, she was always at risk of pneumonia. Two young women from PT alternated working Jane out as much as she could manage. This depressive woman—who had often wanted to be dead, who had always feared and suffered from pain more than most—struggled and strained in the hope of survival. Her desire to live, her persistence in the face of agony, astonished her.

Aurora helped to prepare me for caregiving at home with practical advice about pumps and showed me how to fix bottles of salt water for Jane's sore mouth. She coached me as I rehearsed my nursing duties in front of her eyes. At first we did not know what to make of our new attending physician, or AP, Kris Doney. Her manner was dry and ironic, and she cultivated the image of a hard-assed cynic, or HAC as she called it in medical acronym disease (MAD). True sympathy may be expressed in an ironic tone, but when your mouth is on fire you may not catch the sympathy part. When Jane was at eight-plus in mouth pain, Dr. Doney commiserated by saying, "Not the best day in your life, I suppose," which did not seem warm-hearted. But when Jane was in trouble later, with delirium or a psychotic episode, it was Kris who made time (she had no time) to sit with her calmly, to talk, to drop everything and help. Five months later it was Kris who took three days out of her life to fly twice across the country and attend Jane's funeral.

We feared leaving the safety of 11SW for the isolation of our apartment. Everyone feels that way. Babies feel that way when they are born. Later, I learned that 11SW was not so safe as I thought. I remember finding Kris Doney leaning against the nurses' station at the end of a day, utterly drawn, utterly fatigued, with dead nervous eyes and a blank white face. I said she looked tired and she stared at me; even irony failed her. I found out later that something was happening about which I knew nothing. I was so concentrated on one person and one circumstance that if the Barnum & Bailey Circus had paraded around 11SW with twenty-seven elephants and a calliope, I would not have noticed. Earlier, I had noticed the policeman. One of the patients a few doors down came from a "correctional institution," as Carolyn told us she was supposed to say. A uniformed policeman sat by the door. On this day I did not notice the plainclothesman, who was in attendance because physicians of the Hutch were under threat. A father whose son had died on the pediatric floor, just below, had sworn to vengeance and had disappeared from his house in California carrying a rifle. (He never showed up at the Hutch.) This was the day I told Kris Doney she looked tired. Again, I did not notice when Ringo Starr turned up on the floor, where his first wife was dying.

Probably we would be home for Christmas, insofar as Spring Street was home. For room 1112 I bought a foot-high plastic tree (organic trees might carry bacteria) with tiny lights and installed it by the end of Jane's bed. For the apartment I found another artificial tree, maybe a yard high, and a string of tiny white lights for it. Philippa sent ornaments that Allison and Abigail had fashioned out of paper and crayon. For Jane's return, I set the tree up on a glass table at one end of the living room, but I did not arrange the lights or hang the ornaments. Jane had always done the decorating back home, and I thought she would like to do it here, if she had strength enough. I bought another long string of tiny white lights to hang over the broad mirror opposite our bed.

Discharge date was set for the twentieth of December. Two days before, the janitor at our apartment gave the rooms a thorough cleaning, swabbing surfaces with a disinfectant. Jane's immune system was immature, and I would take her temperature twice a day. Then, a day before discharge, there was another setback. I cannot remember: Did her temperature rise a notch? Was emesis severe? The delay was devastating, and it was also relief. Then the trouble disappeared, and I would take her to Spring Street on December twenty-second. I worked to clean the clean apartment. With Scotch tape I fixed the little white Christmas lights around the bedroom mirror, imitating the arrangement that Jane had installed in our New Hampshire bedroom when she brought me home after my first cancer. I plugged them in, festive above the drab shapes and ugly furniture. Early on discharge day I parked beside the elevator in the cellar parking lot under Swedish, in a parking space marked with a wheelchair. I placed our handicapped sign so that it was visible through the windshield.

Jane was attentive, excited, apprehensive. I packed clothes and pictures, my stack of books, her boom box and CDs, and stashed them in the Toyota's trunk. A familiar nurse poked her head in and wished us well; but don't worry, she said, if you have to come back: "Everybody has to come back at least once." Jane saved her strength for the journey home. No physical therapist led her in exercise. I walked the circle of the eleventh floor alone, impatient and nervous. The routines of discharge took forever: more advice for me, lists of medications, bottles. We delayed several hours so that Jane could finish the TPN and hydration required for the day: I would not need to infuse her immediately upon our return to the apartment. Finally the wheelchair arrived, and Aurora accompanied us on the trip to the car. Jane wore a winter coat for the first time in seven weeks. We dropped down eleven floors to the main lobby and traversed more corridors until we came to the garage elevator. Jane clambered from her wheelchair into the front seat, fastened her seat belt, and we drove five minutes around Swedish, across Madison, down to Spring Street. I parked underneath our apartment, as close to the elevator as I could. I left Jane in the car and went upstairs for the walker, bringing with me the first load from the trunk. Then Jane stood up from the car, holding on to the walker, and crossed the garage to the elevator, where we pushed the button for the second floor. We spoke little. My heart pounded; Jane's heart pounded; she was as shocked as a bird coming out of its shell.

She walked into the living room and looked about her. I invited her to lie down on our bed but she wanted to sit for a moment, taking it all in: the relative normality of it, the newness of it and the oldness. While she sat I slipped into the bedroom to turn on the little lights. They would not go on! The accumulated tension of this day—these days—burst inside me, and I wailed out loud to Jane that our little lights wouldn't work! I told her what I had tried to do, to imitate the installation at Eagle Pond. She was dazed still, but tried to comfort me. I offered her water, salt water, water with lidocaine? skim milk? Any kind of fruit juice was too sharp for Jane's mouth. She sipped at some water and was ready to lie down. I fussed with the little lights and they came on. Jane said they were pretty.

Coming and Going

FOR TWENTY YEARS in New Hampshire we lived without schedules and with few deadlines, with an income from writing, with no children of our own. Jane and I might have traveled half our days, but we preferred the routines of Eagle Pond Farm, the daily solitude of writing, the connections of one with one. Therefore, our infrequent trips were memorable. Early in our marriage, we went several times to England, and flew over later to attend the wedding of Geoffrey Hill and Alice Goodman. I took pleasure in showing Jane my old places—Oxford, with my college Christ Church, and the village of Thaxted in Essex, where I spent two and a half years with my young family during my first marriage. The Thaxted I had known in 1959 and 1963 was an isolated village in East Anglia, two thousand souls and six pubs, Ron's Caff, baker, greengrocer, stores, and a shop that drew a scant line between junk and antiques. Only six citizens commuted to London thirty-five miles away, driving tortuous lanes between hedgerows to a British Railways depot. By the time I brought Jane there in 1972, motorways had come close enough so that Thaxted was on its way to becoming an exurb. Still, the great church on the hill dominated the town, high Anglican, with Greek in the liturgy uttered by a magnificent aging Communist vicar. I had studied bell ringing there. Late in the nineteenth century, the town had been taken over by a Morris/Ruskin invasion. Weavers abounded. Cecil Sharp revived Morris dancing in Thaxted. G. K. Chesterton visited. Gustav Holst lived in the village's center beside the seventeenth-century guildhall.

Jane and I stayed at the Swan and I introduced her to the village: the watchmaker, the Roman road back of the main street, pargeting on the ancient thatched row houses—and the red vicar, Father Jack Putterhill, still outrageous and magnificent in his eighties. From Thaxted in our rented car we visited Henry Moore, about whom I had written a book. We drove to Bradwell-on-Sea, on the bleak shore of the North Sea, where Romans at the time of Christ set up the fort of Othona against murderers and rapists— known as Danes—who arrived by sea from the north. Othona was the last Roman fort, abandoned by legionnaires in A.D. 400, and it was in ruins when the Celtic bishop Cedd landed there in the seventh century, bringing Christianity to the lapsed pagan tribes of the island. In the nineteenth century, a reader of the Domesday Book, investigating the location of Cedd's church, found a barn, full of hay, that was constructed of Roman brick. Hay removed, bricked-in arches of Cedd's church revealed themselves, his structure assembled from the ruins of the Roman fort. Othona remains eerie. In the distance we saw ships mothballed from World War II at anchor in the Malden Estuary. In a ditch alongside the Roman road that leads to the fort lay concrete pylons that filled the flat fields of 1940 against Hitler's expected gliders. When engineers in the same year dug trenches by the sea against German tanks, they dug up Roman seawall.

Three years later, when Jane and I moved to New Hampshire, its shallower past of place and family filled my need for historical connections. We traveled only a little. Halfway through our twenty New Hampshire years, we went to Italy. Jane had a notion that she would love this country of old paintings and modern design. We touched first on Milan and Florence, then spent a week in Rome.

We walked through the Forum and the Colosseum, through the wreckage of empire on to Renaissance palazzos and the Gucci of the moment, through parks and the Etruscan Museum, into cafés and restaurants. It was autumn for our first visit. For lunch we bought fresh bread, dolce latte, and enormous pears, which we ate sitting on the Spanish Steps. (After finishing an Italian pear one needed to return to the *pensione* for a bath.) We found the Protestant Cemetery, next to the Pyramid of Cestius, where dozens of feral Roman cats gathered and sprawled. We stood at Keats's grave and Shelley's. Elsewhere in the graveyard we found Rosa Bathurst's grave with its devastating inscription; we found the grave of Constance Fenimore Woolson, Henry James's friend who jumped to her death from a Venetian balcony, and the monuments of dozens of other nineteenth-century Italianate expatriates from America and England. We visited the room where Keats died, and lingered among the items exhibited there, Jane moony with Keats-love. A day before we left, Jane realized that it was Keats's birthday. She bought flowers and carried them to his rooms. A few years later we returned for a week in Rome and another in Florence, where we spent a morning hour in the Uffizi, and after lunch an afternoon hour gazing in the Pitti. We planned to return to Italy and never did. We planned France, Ireland, Egypt, Latin America. The solitude of Eagle Pond absorbed us—and also we took exotic trips east for the United States Information Agency, waving a poetic flag on foreign shores.

In the mid-eighties a telephone call from Washington inquired if I might be willing to visit China, perhaps Japan, the Philippines, New Zealand, Malaysia? I was invited to read poems and talk about American literature. Both of us had spoken of visiting China, but such a trip had seemed improbable. I would not go without Jane, and Jane's poems were still largely unknown, her second book not yet in print. After negotiation we worked it out that I would make the trip at the State Department's expense and that Jane would accompany me, lecturing and reading as I did, with her expenses paid after she landed on foreign soil. We negotiated not ten weeks in five countries but six weeks in two countries. In March of 1986 we flew to China for four weeks, then spent two weeks in Japan before flying home. We landed in Beijing, and from the capital visited the Great Wall and red temples. Beijing was a city of enormous steel cranes, as high-rise apartment dwellings ascended from the cramped blocks. The sense of energy, growth, and vitality was palpable; so was the drabness of costume in this political capital city, two years before Tiananmen Square. Jane and I read poems together in the ambassador's quarters with two aging Communist bureaucrats, Englishless, nodding in the front row. By train and plane we traveled to other cities: to Xi'an to visit the buried terra-cotta army, to Chengdu and Shanghai and Guangzhou and Shenyang for lectures, readings, campus visits, and meetings with societies of writers. Sometimes we did separate gigs at the same time in the same city. Shanghai was our favorite city, with its rows of poplar trees and the great seafront of the Bund.

Everywhere we encountered a cautious sense of slowly increasing freedom. On the streets, small capitalists sold oranges and dragon paintings. We talked with English speakers, students and faculty at the universities, who because of their reading knew more about bourgeois freedom than other Chinese. We talked long hours with young graduate students in love with the United States and with notions of liberty. How many demonstrated and died in Tiananmen Square? We arrived deciding not to bring up regime politics, fearing that such conversation might get someone into trouble. But the regime, overbearing like the cranes in the cities, seemed distant and removed, its oppression sporadic. Tentatively I approached the subject of the Cultural Revolution with an aging professor, suggesting that perhaps it was not all bad. With a faint smile, with facial gestures like a European's after the Second World War who had survived all horror, he corrected me: "Oh, no. It was all bad." Without passion he told stories—omitting his own troubles—about destruction of the trees along the fields, about the iconoclasm of relics. Eventually Jane and I talked to many people about the Cultural Revolution, and found only one person who defended it. She had an Oxford accent, educated in England, and gave English lessons on the radio. She had been rusticated for years, carrying bricks by hod at a construction site. She said the experience was good for her; now when she hefted canisters of propane seven floors to her room, she had use for the muscles she had acquired.

Twice we took long train rides, one of twenty-seven hours and another of eighteen, in compartments called soft sleepers that raised two bunks on each side, with straw pallets stretched out on them. At night we slept in our clothes, using a briefcase or a sweater as a pillow. By day we sat together on the lower bunk, reading sometimes, often gazing into the huge empty landscape, in the south a yellow sea blossoming with rape. Airline flights were adventurous. Always as the plane approached the landing strip the passengers stood and bustled to remove suitcases from overhead racks. In Shanghai I spent several hours with the writers' club, over lunch, while Jane talked at a teachers college. A young man next to me at lunch had just translated *Four Quartets*. His English was beautiful, and he was my interpreter. A third of the writers present had as much English as I had Chinese, and another third spoke it spottily. My host was an older writer recently rehabilitated to society. Eliot's translator told me that the host had spent five years in prison and five more years rusticated because he had praised a poet whom Mao did not like.

Usually we were met at the airport by an American representative from the consulate and by the head of the English department of the local university and sometimes its vice chancellor. At first there was considerable bowing and honoring, Herr Doktor Professor—but by the time of the banquet all formality disappeared as we told each other thigh-slapping jokes. Banquets started at five, often with another banquet on the following night with the same cast of diners—the host's banquet, then the consulate's. The fare was delicious, course after course, although we never learned to cherish sea slugs. We were warned: Don't eat much at the start—but the warning was ineffective, and we had small room for the roast duck that provided the finale. At Shenyang we ate forty versions of shau mai, sometimes called Chinese ravioli, served from the Mongolian hot pot. At first, perhaps with jet lag, Jane feared the onset of depression, but she recovered to enjoy herself, and to accomplish long and intimate conversations with alien strangers. Jane declared that the Chinese were the Italians of the East. We accepted kindness everywhere. In Xi'an a hotel porter—the job for which he had studied English at the university—came back to the hotel on his day off to put us on the right train for Guangzhou. At airports an English speaker would approach us when we looked confused, but English speakers were not conspicuous in train stations.

At night after our banquets—which ended precisely at seven, everyone standing to vanish—we walked the streets of our cities. People kept approaching us. At first I feared scams—but our interlocutors were merely practicing their English. Some conversations were memorable in reminding me of American prosperity. A man asked me if I had a bicycle. When I said I had none, he told me with evident delight about the new bicycle he had just purchased, and I realized he did not assume I owned an automobile. I carried with me a little album of photographs of our house—the long white wooden farmhouse stretched back into the hill among fields of hay, isolated among flowers and trees on abundant land—as one might carry images of children. Eagle Pond Farm is nothing grand, made and inhabited by farmers who worked with their hands sixteen hours a day. But when I showed the pictures to students at Chinese universities, they fell silent. Eagle Pond Farm seemed as spacious and sumptuous as an emperor's palace. I packed the album away.

Guangzhou was closest to Hong Kong and the West. We stayed in a hotel with an enormous lobby, big enough for a football game, decorated with an ancient bed carved out of jade. In Guangzhou—as opposed to Beijing or Mongolia—the dress was varied and comfortable, cosmopolitan and brightly colored. Shops were full, and capitalism showed itself in sidewalk restaurants and food vendors. Mongolia's Shenyang was the opposite. It was our last city before returning to Beijing and then Tokyo, and it was the most alien or exotic. We were the first American visitors that the USIA had sent to Shenyang, and we were ourselves exotic. Shenyang was a steel city and the air was made of soft coal. It had been the Russian city of Mukden for a time, and in the late 1930s a Japanese city by another name. It was Chinese in 1986, with a great cement statue of Mao opposite our hotel in the city center. In the morning we looked out our windows at three hundred people, mostly elders, doing tai chi in Mao's shadow. One graduate student of English bicycled five miles to talk with me, at some improbable hour, about the poetry of Emily Dickinson. When we prepared our lectures we had naively thought that we should speak of contemporary poetry in America—James Wright, John

Ashbery, Adrienne Rich, Allen Ginsberg—but because of politics and exchange rates, China had not read American poetry after Robert Frost and T. S. Eliot. Even Robert Lowell and Elizabeth Bishop had not arrived. We found ourselves improvising talks about T. S. Eliot and Robert Frost.

In Chengdu, where the Szechwan food was extraordinary, there was a rat in our hotel room. In Beijing we visited a park containing the thatched cottage of the poet Tu Fu (712–770) among crowds of Chinese workers on their day off, doing homage to their poet. The thatch was new. Elsewhere in China, and later in Japan, which was usually China's opposite, we visited palaces and temples billed as many centuries old, only to discover that the old building and its replacements had been destroyed many times. Continuousness was immaterial, the dates not fabrications but evidence of a different attitude toward time and change. In our last Beijing days we found entry to an antiques store and bought an old ginger jar and other relicts of the imperial past. We bought a new, elegantly lacquered chest to ship home. We bought twin ginger jars for my children. Shortly before we left Beijing and China, on Easter Sunday, the consulate found us a Methodist church for its service, and we sat with three hundred Chinese Christians, two out of the half dozen "big noses" that rose above the heads of the throng. The eight-sided church stood next to a hospital, I suppose the creation of missionaries a century before. The crowd was dressed up, in Western clothes, like an Episcopal congregation in America. Beside us a man carried a Bible that printed English alongside Chinese, and pointed out to us the readings from scripture. The supreme moment of the service was a hymn, belted out in Chinese by the choir—that great triumphalist Easter hymn "Up from the Grave He Arose!" For a moment the world seemed to center on the figure of the risen Christ.

It was late when we arrived at the Tokyo Airport, and the American cultural attaché was there to greet us. Warren Obluck hustled us through customs and onto a bus for the long ride into the city, then a cab to his apartment. We had traveled from the scattery and chaotic improvisations of a dictatorial regime into Japan's rigid capitalist democracy. We were tired, and we had little energy to devote to Japan, and were often appalled—by the passivity of our audiences and the uniform vacuous praise that followed our performances, by the nervous hurry of every moment, and by the legions of identically dressed businessmen (blue suits, white shirts, red ties) on every airplane and every train. In China, later in India, we engaged in happy argument, and people were not afraid to tell us we were mistaken. In Japan we found little candor, and a politeness desperate to avoid controversy. Toward the end of our stay, irritated by niceness, I became rude. I sat beside a surgeon, a haiku poet a little older than me and therefore the right age for the war. Over the space of a minute or two I referred to our unfortunate late hostilities, and asked a mild question or two. He did not respond in any way—it was as if I had not spoken—but the air between us flushed with a clash of cultures. Worst was the occasional bigotry toward Jane as female or young female. One dreadful morning we spent in the company of a Japanese professor of English, a translator, at his university in Tokyo. He had expected only me, which confused him, and he solved his dilemma by pretending Jane did not exist. If she asked him a question, he directed his answer to me, without looking in Jane's direction. When he toured us around his university library, he introduced only me. I would say, "And this is my wife, Jane Kenyon"—but he would omit her name a moment later when we encountered someone else.

On the other hand, we met marvelous eccentric Japanese poets, who were opposed to everything in Japan we found oppressive, and spent with them evenings of laughter, wit, irony, and argument. We visited Nara with its enormous Buddha, Hiroshima for our guilt, and Kyoto with its gardens and temples. We visited Gary Snyder's room in a monastery where he spent eight years studying Zen. On Buddha's birthday we ate vegetable tempura at a temple. And Carol Obluck got us good seats for baseball's opening day, when the Tokyo Giants defeated the Yakult Swallows.

The trips we loved most were our two visits to India, Jane and I traveling equally as poets. We flew there for a month late in 1991, and for another month—a hot September—in the last healthy year of 1993. Before our first journey, we feared India, as people tend to, and found there everything that we feared: squalor and suffering, crippled beggars, urine and feces, terrible poverty, intolerable naked human density. Yet we also found an extraordinary range of active aggressive intelligence, spirituality, tenderness, humor, and *talk*. The love of beauty was overwhelming. India is a country of flowers. With a single coin to spend, an Indian may divide it to buy one samosa and one white blossom. The saris of Indian women dazzled with iridescent silk on educated, elegant young women behind hotel desks and on countrywomen with jugs of water balanced on their heads. Driving in the country we saw women gathered on their knees scrubbing garments in a pool that looked stagnant, while gorgeous silks spread out to dry on nearby bushes. Vegetable stalls arranged splendid architectures, vegetable Taj Mahals. Jane bathed in the pervasiveness of flowers and casual beauty. When we visited a temple we were adopted by an extended Indian family, from grandparents to grandchildren, with enough collective English to hold considerable conversation. We photographed each other, we swam in benignity. In the streets we talked English, haggling with sidewalk merchants. When Jane admired a pair of shoes hanging on the outside wall of a building, and tried them on but they were small, the shoe man snatched them out of her hands, soaked them briefly, and with an instrument stretched them to Jane's size. Pillow covers at Eagle Pond glitter with little mirrors sewn into them. We danced with Ganesh.

Meantime we worked hard. India is a country of newspapers, thousands of them, four hundred in the English language, which is the lingua franca. With seventeen official languages and many more unofficial, Indians need English to talk to each other; street merchants need it to speak not only with tourists but also with Indians of different areas and different languages. In the enormous middle class, everyone speaks some English, and India is a huge market for English-language books. Almost every day on our trips, Jane and I were interviewed by journalists. These conversations were inevitably two-way, and we heard Sanskrit recited. Some interviews were arranged by USIA officials and appeared on our schedule, but we kept adding on more interviews. After one of our public appearances, a young poet, striving to make a living in journalism, would entreat us to give him an interview the following day. One morning we did three in a row, and were first interviewed at six-thirty A.M. because otherwise our schedule was full. The day often continued with a late-morning appearance—a reading, a lecture—at a university, or in an auditorium where students from several colleges could collect, followed by lunch with the departments of English. Sometimes Jane and I were able to take a nap before our next occasion, another lecture or reading followed by dinner, which was announced for eight and served at ten. We arrived back at our rooms—mostly luxurious and air conditioned, American style—at midnight. The next morning we flew to another city.

On both visits, we went to Bombay, New Delhi, and Madras. On the first visit Jane went to Bangalore while I handled Hyderabad. Then I stayed in New Delhi for a long interview and a poetry reading while Jane went overnight to Allahabad. As she left Allahabad by train the next morning, an Indian she had met the night before ran alongside her compartment to hand her a beautifully worked glasses case. (We saw him again—Sanjoy Saksena—on our return two years later, and learned that for his students he had copied our poems in longhand, over and over, because his English department could not afford a photocopier.) While Jane was gone, Gagan Gill came to my hotel room for a long interview. She was a prizewinning poet in Urdu, whose English was particularly fine. She had visited the writers' workshop in Iowa City, and wanted to get back to the States. She was literary editor of the paper she interviewed me for, and I asked her if she had heard of the Nieman Foundation at Harvard, which gives yearlong fellowships to journalists both American and foreign. She had not heard of it. When I flew home I spoke to the director of the foundation, and a year later Gagan Gill wrote me from Cambridge. She visited the farm in June of 1993, and we spent a day with her and her husband when we flew back to New Delhi that same September.

On our second trip we added Pondicherry and Trivandrum to our itinerary, and spent a few days in Ahmadabad, talking and reading aloud. We saw many people we had seen before, including the English-language poets Dom Moraes and Nissim Ezekiel. (Nissim came from a colony of Jews that has lived forever in Bombay, doubtless a lost tribe. Dom's father was Frank Moraes, editor of the English *Times of India*, and he grew up speaking English and no Hindi or other Indian language.) In Bombay our American host JoDell Shields had a poetry party, a *baithak*, at her large apartment overlooking the sea. Seventy-five people gathered to hear a dozen of us read our poems. Jane read a poem that mentioned Ann Arbor, and after the reading a tall handsome older

man mentioned that he had spent four years in Ann Arbor studying architecture. Something prompted Jane to ask him where he
had lived—and the internationally celebrated architect Charles
Correa had lived with Jane's grandmother in her house on State
Street. Her grandmother's boarding house had specialized in Indians. Charles's brother Billy had been the favorite boarder of all
time. The next day we assembled for drinks at the Bombay Club,
where Billy and Charles reminisced about Jane as a baby visiting
her grandmother's house.

Day after day we held conversation. Day after day we received
instruction. Many interviewers recited their own poems, for Indians do not require assertiveness training. Often when we met an
Indian intellectual he or she proposed an agenda for discussion.
Entering P. Lal's Calcutta sitting room, I heard him immediately
ask, "What do you think of irony?"—and we were off. In New Delhi
I was introduced to the CEO of Procter & Gamble in India,
Gucharan Das, who wrote novels in English, who began our conversation by telling me how a group of young Indian businessmen
asked him to define contentment. His definition was "absorbed-
ness," and I agreed. In Sri Aurobindo's ashram, we talked with a
ninety-year-old Parsi poet in a wheelchair, who told us stories of
The Mother, who succeeded Sri Aurobindo. At Jane's suggestion
we each said a poem. As we left for the car and our next encounter,
I heard his sweet tender forceful old voice observe at our departing
shapes, "Jane is a *fine girl*."

The fine girl came home enthralled with India and Hin-
duism. For a time she felt religiously confused, her Christianity
confronted by another religion and culture so utterly different,
contradictory to a notion of Jesus as the way. I was equally enthralled, and more secular. I took to studying Indian history, mi-
grations, the Moguls and the Raj. We corresponded with Indian

friends and met them when they came to the United States. Our walls filled with miniatures. A bronze Ganesh, of good dimensions, stands on the Chinese chest in the parlor. Within a month of Jane's death there were memorial services — Indian friends showed the Moyers film, read her poems, and reminisced—in Allahabad, New Delhi, Bombay, and Madras.

Spring Street

December 22, 1994. After two months sleeping apart, we occupied a bed together in our Seattle apartment. In the morning Jane sat at the kitchen table to take her pills as I counted them out and put them in little plastic shot glasses. At eight-thirty Maggie Fisher arrived for Caremark. She had worked as a nurse at the Hutch, and now tended BMT outpatients at their apartments. Maggie was pretty, in her thirties, recently married, liberal in politics, and literary—a regular at the Elliott Bay readings. She told me that two years earlier, listening to NPR as she drove between patients, she heard Noah Adams interview me. When she heard talk of my liver cancer—she told me cheerfully—she said to herself, "Well, *he* won't be around for long."

Maggie understood that, although I had attended pump class, I was anxious. She watched over me as I assembled pump and tubing and programmed the pump, attached the apparatus to Jane's Hickman, and started the machine. The little pump and its gradually diminishing bag of nutrition fit into something like a briefcase with a strap that went over Jane's shoulder, so that she could move around during infusion. Putting the pieces together, I fumbled joining two parts of tubing, filter to tubing or tubing to filter. Maggie blinked her big eyes and told me, "From long experience I have observed that 'male' goes inside 'female.'" Months later, I reminded her of this observation. "It gets their attention," she said.

Jane sat at our plastic table—where I ate my meals and Jane tried to; where I wrote; where I measured out medications and assembled equipment for infusions—and Maggie drew blood for the clinic, which would measure Jane's immune system and check the blood levels of certain drugs. She inspected Jane's Hickman and took her vital signs. She went over the lists of medications and simplified our schedule. Drug bottles suggested various times between doses, so that we faced seven or eight different hours for pills. Time between doses was crucial with some; with others it was not, and Maggie calmed us down to four pill sessions a day.

Every night I made a detailed list for the next day, hour by hour, so that at proper intervals I would take Jane's temperature, rig and deliver infusions, feed pills and snacks. I reread every day dozens of sheets of instructions. I needed to keep the bags of TPN, or intravenous feeding, and hydration in the refrigerator, and take them out to warm up an hour before feeding them into Jane's bloodstream. On a pad of paper, I collected questions to ask nurses and doctors. My life was never so occupied; I lived for my work. When Maggie came by she drew Jane's blood and delivered the vial to the clinic, saving us a painful and exhausting trip. Before leaving the hospital Jane had started cyclosporine, an antirejection drug that comes in big smelly capsules difficult to swallow. Every day or two, the clinic telephoned to alter the dosage of cyclosporine, as bloodwork showed too much or too little. This drug—which saves lives by making transplants possible—has the frequent side effect of sprouting long hairs on the face and the body. To Jane's catalog of her own ugliness, she could now add facial monkey fur.

Caremark delivered bags of TPN and hydration in square white boxes. Twice a day I hooked up a bag for a major infusion. After supper, I linked tubes together, plunged the spike at one end into the sealed snout of the bag, fixed the LifeShield Protector onto the business end—the needle cunningly prevented from sticking any potential contaminant, like a caregiver, by means of green plastic arms that drew back when you thrust the needle into the line. I attached a tube to the pump's well, making sure that the red arrow was set at zero. By this device the pump audited the line for air, and if it detected Air in Line, revealed its distress by signals audible and visible. Pushing at numbers on the little pump's enumerated side, I instructed it to deliver 50 cc an hour for twelve hours. I pressed the start button to push air out of the line and was gratified to observe the first drips emerge from the needle in the Protector. The assembly was ready to go, but for now I pressed stop. Jane went to bed. At ten P.M., according to instructions, I strapped pump and bag into the canvas briefcase that carried them, and set it on a chair beside her bed. I cleaned the permeable plastic nipple at the end of her Hickman line with an alcohol wipe, pushed the needle in, pressed start—and heard the small audible purr as the liquid began to move from the bag into Jane's bloodstream. I zipped the briefcase shut, read a novel for half an hour, and went to sleep. All night, when I helped Jane to the bathroom, I carried the pump and its diminishing bag in its case, with a line that remained attached to Jane like an astronaut's tether.

At ten the next morning, without a moment's interruption all night, the Provider buzzed to tell us that it had completed its delivery. Shortly I hooked Jane up again for her intravenous feeding. She swallowed her morning pills. Applesauce helped when pills were large and hard to get down. At about eight, our home help arrived, a young woman named Darla from Kansas who was working as she attended college in Seattle. She cleaned Jane's chest around her Hickman and helped her take a shower. Maggie arrived again, to draw Jane's blood and to tutor me further, while

Darla tidied the kitchen and made the bed. Maggie left and I shopped for groceries while Darla put Jane back to bed. I returned to find Darla studying on our low sofa.

Although Maggie saved us many clinic visits, still we needed to go there. We descended to our car in the cellar, Jane with her walker, and parked near the elevator in the garage underneath the clinic. Jane required a weekly x-ray and regular visits to the nutritionist—whose name was Paula, small, dark, exact, and soft. She took Jane's weight, a vital sign, and collected the notes I kept on Jane's eating; each day I filled out a sheet, one column for solids and another for liquids, with the quantity of each. "Applesauce. Two tablespoons." "Instant Cream of Wheat. One tablespoon?" Paula gave me pages of suggestions for things to eat, together with sample cans or packages of Instant Breakfast and Ensure Plus. A physician's assistant—called a PA, usually Ernie Populus—at the clinic took other vital signs, and examined Jane again; then the current AP swept in with Jane's records for a final, usually brief encounter. Always there were symptoms to address: bone pain, mental problems, spotting, a rash, persistent emesis. Might it work to infuse Zofran for an hour *before* trying to eat?

The first thing we did, entering the clinic, was to check the mailbox and look ahead to appointments for the rest of the week. Sometimes a schedule was insane: a clinic appointment at eight-thirty in the morning followed the same day by another at eleven-thirty followed by another at four P.M.: three separate, difficult trips. Or Jane might have her weekly x-ray at Swedish on the same day as two clinic appointments—followed by two free days. It was essential to collapse the number of visits to the clinic, and I visited the desk that handled rescheduling. Before we visited the clinic, I audited medications and equipment so that I could pick up what was needed at the pharmacy and equipment dock: syringes by the case, alcohol wipes, tubing for infusions, filters, Docking Stations, LifeShield Protectors, swabs, gauze, and Duoderm. Finished, loaded down with supplies, we descended, sometimes in a wheelchair, to the Toyota six or seven floors down. Jane struggled into the car and we drove the short distance back to Spring Street. Each visit exhausted Jane, who would lie down as I assembled tubing for the next infusion, or as I set out medications and prepared something for her to eat. I bought a mixer to make Jane banana milkshakes. I bought soft bread and cream cheese. All day I suggested snacks to Jane—Ensure Plus? a baked apple? It was hard to find anything edible. Cantaloupes tasted good but added few calories. Although Jane was vegetarian she was determined to survive: Sliced turkey on soft bread with mayonnaise tasted good—and mayonnaise was excellently calorific.

Daily we consulted New Hampshire and Polly. Jane's brother Reuel arrived with his wife Dawn—Jane's old roommate—and their daughter Brianna to stay at the farm as Polly came home from Hitchcock for Christmas. Within twenty-four hours Polly relapsed and returned to a hospital bed, the local hospital this time, twelve miles away in New London. She could not speak with us on the phone. We talked with a nurse who told us Polly's eyes were rolling back. Polly thought—everyone seemed to think—that she would die almost immediately. Reuel and family visited, Philippa visited, Andrew visited, and she responded to their affection but seemed rapidly to diminish. Polly made it clear she wanted Reuel and Dawn and Bree to return to Ann Arbor. With them gone, it would be easier for her to let go. They flew back to Michigan, and Polly rallied. She took food and drink, sat in her chair, and talked with us by telephone. For almost three weeks Polly lived a conscious day without great pain, her thoughts concentrated on Jane.

Between bouts of vomiting, Jane trimmed the tree. On

Christmas Eve, Liam Rector and Tree Swenson, who had married in our back garden the year before, paid us a brief visit. They brought Jane Harvard sweats for Christmas. Jane was able to chat for half an hour, then retired to the bedroom while the rest of us finished a beer. After they left I read Jane passages from the Gospels about the birth of the child. On Christmas morning we gave each other presents. Even at such a Christmas, I wanted to give her something that exceeded good sense, something extravagant and female. What do you give your beloved when she is bald, skeletal, and probably dying? Caroline Finkelstein, talking with me on the telephone, provided the solution, and Jane opened my ill-wrapped package to find a pair of sweats from Neiman Marcus—cashmere, oatmeal-colored and soft as dandelion seed. She rubbed her fingers against the cloth. She worried for a moment that they would itch, but they were comfortable. She wore them whenever she could, and showed them off, and when we returned to the hospital her nurses pinched the cashmere with their fingertips and exclaimed. Before the BMT Jane had telephoned L. L. Bean, and I had followed her instructions not to open the box. I had a new pair of loafers.

On Christmas Day Jane vomited eight times, the Noël of the Eight Barfs. The vomiting was worse than it had been for some time, and therefore worrisome. A day or two after Christmas, when we went back to the clinic, Jane's doctors decided that she must have stomach GVHD—which was common and treatable, not likely to be fatal—and scheduled an endoscopy for December 30. The camera entering her stomach by way of her mouth would be accompanied by a device that would biopsy the stomach, retrieving cells by which a laboratory could confirm the diagnosis of GVHD. For years the standard treatment for stomach GVHD had been prednisone, which worked but often had bizarre and unpredictable mental consequences. There was now an alternative treatment, without prednisone's side effects, but it was still experimental and could not be administered without a distinct diagnosis. Endoscopy and biopsy, if they confirmed GVHD, could eliminate prednisone. Dr. George McDonald would perform the endoscopy in the Arnold Pavilion, part of the medical complex joining Swedish and the Hutch.

Before entering the hospital, Jane had endured this procedure when her doctors looked for an ulcer. It had left her panicky. On December 30, when we spoke to receptionists, nurses, and finally Dr. McDonald, both of us pleaded for a large dose of Versed. Dr. McDonald listened soberly to our anxieties and sympathized. Jane lay on a bed, as I sat beside her, in a room with Dr. McDonald, a nurse, and a resident who would manipulate the tube, Jane outfitted with a blood pressure cuff and a thumb clamp to register the oxygen in her blood. Next to her was a television monitor on which Dr. McDonald and I would witness the internal journey past the cliffs and red valleys of Jane's insides. Versed flowed into Jane's Hickman and she relaxed. With her mouth clamped open, the resident fed the tube down Jane's gullet. I watched the red passage, then heard Dr. McDonald's soft voice cajoling, "Jane, Jane," and turned to see her thrashing on the table. At the same moment Dr. McDonald watched the blood-oxygen figures plummet and I saw Jane's face turning blue. Dr. McDonald spoke quickly and clearly; the resident removed the tube and the mouthpiece and in seconds the nurse inserted cannulae carrying oxygen into Jane's nostrils. At Dr. McDonald's next words the nurse punched a button behind her on the wall and the room instantly filled with young men and women wearing white coats, maybe ten of them. Aware that I might be watching Jane die, I was silent and took care not to get in anyone's way. Dr. McDonald stood alert and commanding beside her, hands folded behind his back, and issued orders like a submarine captain with depth charges exploding around him. Someone pounded Jane's chest. A young man in a white coat suggested a tracheotomy—and Dr. McDonald gave a quick negative. He spoke again to the nurse, who fitted a nebulizer over Jane's nose and face—and her chest heaved and she began breathing. Did the whole episode last a minute? ninety seconds? She was alive, breathing—and the whole room started breathing again. Ten white coats exited quickly. Jane fell deeply asleep. Dr. McDonald told me that bronchial spasms had stopped Jane's breathing, that it resembled an asthma attack, that perhaps he had administered too great a dose of Versed—at our urging, of course, but Dr. McDonald didn't say so. Jane would be all right; she would sleep a long time. He would not attempt an endoscopy again without general anesthesia. He would confer with Jane's physicians at the Hutch. We wheeled Jane into a nearby room, and a nurse sat with her. Dr. McDonald told me to take a walk, do something, get away for a while. I took his advice, noticing that my legs had begun to quiver. I medicated myself with a Diet Coke across Madison.

(I remembered another time when I had been calm. We were flying Air India from Bombay to Calcutta on a small Airbus, and were almost halfway there when smoke infiltrated the cabin. Passengers sniffed, glancing at each other in alarm, when the pilot told us we were turning around to return to Bombay. Jane had always feared flying. She leaned back with her eyes closed, dead white, fists clutching the arms of her seat. I tried holding her hand but it did not help, nor could she listen to comforting words. Since I could do nothing for her, I concentrated fiercely on my book, and congratulated myself on my steadiness. When we landed and rolled to a stop on the tarmac, Jane sighed a huge sigh. We walked

off the plane, to transfer to a big Airbus and try again. As my feet
struck solid ground I felt my knees buckle.)

Two or three hours later Jane was groggy but awake. Her
presence was required at the clinic, where her doctors were consulting about what to do next. With a nurse pushing Jane in a
wheelchair, we descended to underground tunnels and progressed
for what seemed like a mile to an elevator deep under the clinic,
then ascended and entered a consultation room. Dr. McDonald
was there, and a Hutch AP whom I recognized. After much discussion, they decided: It was virtually certain that Jane had stomach GVHD; she could not have an endoscopy and a biopsy without
undergoing general anesthesia; in her weakened and depleted
condition, general anesthesia was not prudent; without a biopsy,
she could not be prescribed the new alternative to prednisone.
Therefore, her doctors had to prescribe prednisone. The dose
would be large, and administered in a fashion I had not witnessed
before. It entered her by injection into her Hickman—a slow
steady push on the hypodermic—and arrived in a double vial, two
liquids that were mixed together just before injection. The first
doses came at regular intervals, and a Caremark nurse (not Maggie this time) came to the apartment to mix and inject. Almost immediately, Jane's nausea and emesis diminished.

⁕

We lapsed toward the new year of 1995. Jane passed the markers
toward Day Fifty, and we slept through New Year's Eve—our annual practice. For the sick, holidays mean gaps in the omnipres-
ence of clinics and nurses, a benign relaxation, but holidays spon-
sor medical lapses also. When Maggie came back after her time
off, to draw Jane's blood on the morning of January 3, she glanced
through the report from the latest bloodwork and gasped. No one

had noticed that Jane's blood sugar had risen into the four hundreds. (One hundred is the norm.) One of the possible side effects of prednisone is an induced diabetes. With my own diabetic testing equipment, Maggie took Jane's blood sugar then and there; it was something like five hundred. After Maggie made a phone call, I ran to the clinic and brought back pure insulin which I injected into the Hickman, and for days I measured Jane's sugar every four hours day and night. Every four hours I telephoned the clinic with the figures, and at clinical instruction shot more pure insulin into her bloodstream, always a maximum dose. Then Caremark added insulin to Jane's TPN, tapering it as prednisone tapered.

A morning or two later we had appointments at the clinic with Paula for nutrition and with Dr. Devney the psychiatrist. Jane was lethargic and slow of speech as she went through her early-morning rituals of shower, pills, Cream of Wheat, and cleaning her Hickman. By the time I had parked under the clinic and fetched a wheelchair, she scarcely spoke; her eyes were open but she seemed asleep. When we left the elevator at the fourth floor we met Jane's chief clinic nurse, and when Jane spoke she sounded like a 78 rpm record played at LP speed. The nurse looked alarmed. As Dr. Devney spoke with her, Jane's ability to think was diminishing to the vanishing point, and she seemed unaware of her condition. We took Jane to a bed in the clinic's infusion room while clinicians consulted each other. A PA told Jane that she must have an MRI of her skull immediately, and have it without medication. (Not only had Jane just spasmed with Versed, but you do not give a tranquilizer to someone in Jane's mental condition.) From deep inside the cocoon of her incapacity, Jane delivered an unconditional *no*. Her panic over an unmedicated MRI remained intact. Tension and conflict surrounded Jane's bed in the clinic; she set her teeth and would not budge. I defended her intransigence. The clinic called an ambulance to return Jane to Swedish, a hundred and fifty yards as the crow flies. (An underground wheelchair ride would have been simpler, quicker, and easier; I suppose the ambulance was a matter of liability.) I rode beside her, and soon we resided again on the eleventh floor of Swedish, a few doors away from 1112. Kris Doney was still working on the floor— as was the nurse who had told us we would return at least once— and interrogated Jane in a soft and empathetic voice. What year is it? Jane thought long and hard and supplied 1994. Who is President? Jane's mental effort was perceptible: "Carter." The right party, the right initial, the wrong President. Where are you? She could not remember.

Jane went off all drugs except insulin and a gradually diminishing dose of prednisone. She would have an MRI with Versed as soon as her doctors determined it was safe. I retrieved the car from the clinic, parked it under the apartment, and walked back to Jane's bed in Swedish. We resumed the routines of separation. For me, the disappointment of her return to Swedish balanced itself with relief; she was safer out of my hapless hands, back to the intelligence and care of Carolyn, Aurora, and Kris. A neurologist examined her. Gradually her thinking returned, and after a few days she had an MRI with Versed—and nothing horrid showed in her brain. She went back to her old medications without mental side effects. The neurologist examined her again and gave us his opinion that the "loss of mentation" was the result of high sugar which was the result of prednisone. No other doctors were rash enough to explain what had happened. When there are so many drugs, and so many combinations of drugs, definite answers are impossible. It was enough to know that her brain looked clear in the MRI and that her symptoms had departed.

But now depression struck Jane. Her mother lay dying so far

away. We telephoned New London Hospital, mostly to talk not
with Polly but with her nurses. One nurse in particular ran from
the nurses' station to Polly's room to see if Polly was awake and
able to speak; often she could not speak. Jane lay on her back, staring at the ceiling or curled like a fetus. Her mother's condition carried her into the darkest place, like the old endogenous depression. Later, when she remembered this time, she said, "That's
when I wanted to die and be with my mother." A note in her hospital record speaks of "suicidal ideation without intent." In despair
she felt anger. She said, "I hate this city," gazing out the window at
the same view that she had admired all autumn. She told me that
medical personnel thought she was malingering, that her physical
therapists implied that she *could* do more PT if she wanted to.

It's possible to take urging as reproach if you are depressed
and expect reproach. With much mental aberration there is a part
of the mind that stands aside and observes the aberration, feeling
that it could exert control if it chose to. Psychotics and paranoiacs,
after recovery, sometimes claim that they were aware of what they
said or did even when their behavior was most bizarre. During this
January depression, I came back from lunch one day and Jane reported that two people from Nutrition had accused her of not trying to eat. She sounded wounded and angry, needing support. I
told her no one had ever tried harder to get well than she was trying, by physical effort and by the effort to eat, by doing everything
that she could do to help herself. She answered as if I had said the
opposite, had belittled her suffering. "I wish that for one minute,"
she said, "you could feel what I feel." I was aggrieved and immediately protested. Jane felt contrite and apologized. My hurt lingered and emerged in a nightmare as rage: Jane and I were back in
New Hampshire and Jane schemed to injure or kill me, setting a
plate of acid where it would fall on me when I pushed a door open.

She tried and failed, then tried and succeeded. With my face and upper body burning (I was feeling what Jane felt), and convinced that I was going to die, I followed Jane down I-91, Honda pursuing Saab through Vermont to Connecticut. When the dream ended I was stalking the stairway down to my mother's empty cellar, Jane crouched in terror at the bottom of the stairs, my two hands extended toward her throat and clenched to strangle her.

Kris Doney left the floor, replaced by a doctor who was more researcher than clinician. A new fellow inadvertently upset us, after we had been in residence only a few days, by cheerfully predicting that we would be discharged soon. For Jane in her depression, returning to the apartment seemed insuperably difficult, and she remained in the hospital bed. We spent two more weeks on the eleventh floor. Little things went wrong: a fall that was shocking but not damaging, a possible infection, increased weakness, increased pain and nausea. We did some circular strolling, but now Jane loathed the view from the consultation room, and she felt alert enough to be bored. Because her immune system began to function, I was permitted to take Jane on tours, pushing the wheelchair into elevators and along corridors to show her the cafeteria, the lobby, the bridge that I crossed every morning walking from the apartment. From New London, from Polly's nurses and from Mary Lyn Ray, our neighbor who spent hours sitting beside Polly, came word that Polly continued to rally. She ate, she drank. Sometimes she talked with us on the telephone, which should have been happy but wasn't; her rally only extended the wait for death. Surely the mother made an effort to stay alive for her daughter's return, scheduled now for a mere five or six weeks. Andrew and his family visited Polly. On another visit, Philippa told

Polly that Jane had eaten some Cream of Wheat, later a baked apple, and got Polly to smile. Telephoning Polly's room, Jane heard a breathing "I love you."

Usually after *MacNeil/Lehrer* Jane was ready to sleep, and I left her. Often she woke at nine-thirty or ten and lay in the dark staring upward. If Carolyn Stormer had no pressing chores at ten o'clock, she and Jane would talk. Jane loved these hours. Once when Carolyn drew blood, a drop fell on a sweater that Polly had made for Jane. Carolyn was frantic to get the blood out, but Jane told her to leave it; in the future when she saw the drop on that sweater, she would think of Carolyn. A year later, Carolyn showed me a poem she wrote after getting home at one A.M. She quoted Jane:

> I've lost my body, she announces
> I don't know where my body is . . .
> I will never lie beside my man again.
> I will never see my mother.
> I will never write.
> I will never leave this building.
> I will never find my body.

Speaking to a tender and compassionate woman, speaking to someone not her potential widower, Jane let her despair show forth more than she did when she talked with me.

Jane was depressed and could not use her old mood medicines. One drug, not usually known as an antidepressant, had helped depressives after a BMT: Ritalin, associated with the treatment of attention deficit disorder. Jane was reluctant to take another drug. Dr. Devney persuaded her to begin with a small dose. He increased it, and her mood lifted. However, she remained weak, and she felt reluctant to return to Spring Street; she felt panicky about leaving the eleventh floor. Doctors argued with us, under pressure to reduce costs. They set a time for discharge; we packed and were ready to go. At the last minute, Jane's Hickman became occluded at all three ports. There is no way short of telekinesis that Jane could have obstructed the ports of her own Hickman. Such stoppages happen from time to time, and there are ways to unblock the ports, but this time the occlusion was stubborn. Joanne Rochester was a nurse known to be good at clearing lines. She tried her best, but even she could not accomplish the trick. Jane's doctors had to give her one more day in Swedish. Not long after we were told that we would stay that night, Jane's Hickman flowed again.

The next day we returned to Spring Street, to the bleak apartment, to pumps and pills, to Maggie Fisher and Darla. Our second night at home the telephone rang at about six o'clock. I picked up the phone sitting at the little table where we ate. Jane sat, staring ahead, beside a telephone in a soft chair across the room. It was Polly's doctor calling from New London, and I addressed him by name so that Jane would pick up the phone. She heard him say that Polly had died. Jane said the one word, "Good." The next day, I spoke with Chadwick's in New London and arranged for the cremation that Polly wanted.

We resumed the routine of pills and infusions, interrupted by trips to the clinic. For a while Jane's thinking improved, and her energy rose a little. A few pages at a time, she read Alice Mattison's novel *Hilda and Pearl,* which Alice had dedicated to the two of us. She read the poems of Caroline Finkelstein's *Germany.* Sometimes I rented a movie to watch in the early afternoon. We ran to farce, to *Naked Gun* in its many manifestations. Darla told us about *Four Weddings and a Funeral,* and we discovered that a movie need not be silly. It became February, the month when we were supposed to go home. It was still difficult for Jane to eat. I pressed food upon her, tried new things, invented combinations, and she managed to swallow strange concoctions. She never threw her dinner out the window, like John Keats dying in Rome. She slept much, or sat staring ahead blankly in her big soft chair. Frequently she asked, across the room, "Perkins, am I going to *live?*" The rest of the question, unspoken, was "Or am I undergoing all this shit for nothing?" I never lied to her, didn't cheerfully assert that she would survive to write poems and climb Mount Washington again. In mortal circumstances, nothing is so repulsive as mendacious optimism. I answered her always by repeating what we knew: "That's what we're doing. That's why you go through all this." There were days and signs that were encouraging: more eating with less disgust and nausea; more walking with less fatigue. As we moved further from Cytoxan and TBI, Jane's hair started up again: a five o'clock shadow, a fuzz, an eighth of an inch, a quarter of an inch. It's when she said, "My hair will save me."

Early in the month I began to notice a new pattern. Late afternoon, usually while she was in bed resting between a movie and supper, Jane became fretful. One afternoon she suddenly worried about Gus, intuiting harm. I telephoned our house sitter, who confirmed that Gus was strong and healthy. The next day it was something else: The governor of New Hampshire had just proclaimed Jane the state's poet laureate, and in the nervous late afternoon Jane realized that she was too sick to perform the laureate's duties. I reminded her that the laureate's duties—I had done time in that office—could be accomplished by Gus the dog. Her worry subsided. The next day late in the afternoon I had a severe attack of vertigo. It came as it always did, at a convenient time, for I had just rigged Jane up for a long infusion and prepared her something to eat and there would be no pills for a while. I vomited at length into the toilet and reeled into the living room, clutching one of Jane's pink plastic barf buckets. She sat in the big soft chair. She had seen me have vertigo before, but today she would not believe it was vertigo. At first she thought it was an insulin reaction, but I persuaded her of the difference. Then in her panic she decided that I was having a heart attack or an embolism, and she reached for the telephone, saying that she would dial 911. From my prostrate position—I could not move my head without retching—I begged her not to. I *knew* this was vertigo . . . and the telephone rang as Jane's hand hovered above it. It was a nurse from the clinic (calling, I discovered the next day, to change the cyclosporine dosage), who heard Jane shout, "Don's dying! Don's having a heart attack!" The nurse said that she would dial 911. A few minutes later three young men burst into our apartment to find a bald woman sitting in panic beside a man stretched on a sofa. I said, speaking as clearly as I could, "My wife has had a BMT and thinks I'm having a heart attack. I have vertigo. Could you give me an EKG to reassure her?" The medics must have understood that confusion was common after a marrow transplant. In a few minutes they told Jane that my heart was fine, and my blood pressure. I could see terror drain from her wild eyes; she stopped panting. I asked the medics to bring me my sugar-testing equipment, to prove that I was not having an insulin reaction. Fifteen minutes after they arrived, they left and Jane was calm.

Late the next afternoon, a routine visit took us to the clinic. Quite suddenly, waiting in a consultation room for the AP, Jane was unable to stand or walk, and she was incontinent. A nurse, a PA, and I tried to walk her to a bed, but she was dead weight. Kris Doney was in the clinic, steadfast in her help, and found a chair to set underneath Jane. Then we found a wheelchair, and soon Jane was installed again in a room at Swedish. This time, her doctors understood that the problem derived from drugs and not from leukemia, so Jane went to a room on the fifth floor, a miscellaneous or catchall floor. She told a nurse that the Second Coming was under way. She was urgent that I leave her. I was stricken over her sudden madness, but I took comfort in knowing that her doctors were not alarmed. I left her in the hospital and drove back to Spring Street. At about nine Jane called me to say she had moved to another room, to give me the room number and the telephone. "I walked to this room," she told me, and then, in a tone of conspiracy, added, "The nurses *despise* me. They *hate* me." I didn't at first understand the sequitur; Jane meant that the nurses despised her because now she could walk although she had arrived unable to walk.

My sleep was fretful. I'm not sure Jane slept at all. I arrived before six the next morning to find her lying on her back with her eyes open, staring at the ceiling in wretchedness and guilt. All night, she told me in a voice that was scarcely audible, she had known that she was not sick at all; she was faking her leukemia. She had decided that Blue Cross would find her out; Blue Cross would sue us and take away Eagle Pond Farm because of her malingering. In a voice racked with misery she told me: "*I am a wicked person.*" I denied it but knew that reason or argument could not reach her. She knew what she knew: She had been unable to walk; she had walked, and she had spent all night elaborating her discovery. Later she would have no memory of this episode, so its horror was brief, but this steroid psychosis was agony for her. During the past year I had learned to measure her pain, on a scale of one to ten, by looking at her face, a dreary acquired expertise. I had seen her mouth pull down into the tragic mask under the assault of mouth pain, neuropathy, and her mother's dying. The moral pain of her guilt, in this brief madness, may have been the worst she suffered in the fifteen months.

There was nothing to do but wait for Dr. Devney. When he came to her bedside she told him what she had told me, and he asked a few questions. Did she have rapid, rushing thoughts? He prescribed two medicines, Haldol and Klonopin, the first an antipsychotic and the second described as an "evener." (It is an old anticonvulsant that has been found to stabilize moods.) While we waited for the pharmacy to deliver the pills, Jane's mood persisted. She spoke little. When a nurse brought Jane the pills, it was mid-morning. Jane had noticed my fatigue and told me to return to the apartment for a nap. Maybe I could sleep now that Jane was under medication. I slept an hour, and when I returned Jane was Jane again, with no memories of her brief insanity. She went off Ritalin now, and briefly off other medications, like morphine, that could have combined with Ritalin to produce the psychotic episode.

We returned to Spring Street the next morning and started again where we had left off only two or three days before: food in small but calorific quantities six times a day, decreasing TPN and hydration; daily workouts with a physical therapist; daily walks around our second floor, and on the mildest days walks outside. Every afternoon we watched a movie. Unintentionally we twice watched Debra Winger die of cancer: *Terms of Endearment* and *Shadowlands*. The second was more upsetting than the first—it was truer, and its characters were literary. It was upsetting to me, at least; I wept. Jane, who used to weep at any movie, watched these films without a tear.

At the clinic, Paula reported—glancing at the food and drink sheets I filled out—that one day I had persuaded three thousand five hundred calories into Jane. It was difficult and unpleasant to eat, but Jane was determined. She was past depression now, and again expressed her amazement at how much she wanted to live. We finished watching Ken Burns's *Baseball*, which we had interrupted to enter the hospital in November—and the clinic began its discharge routine: sampling Jane's skin for evidence of chronic GVHD (there was none, and we were overjoyed; maybe it would have been better if her GVHD had been chronic); checking her lung capacity, her teeth, her musculature against the measures taken in October; consulting with a gynecologist about menstruation, stopped by chemicals for more than a year; attending together meetings to prepare us for departure.

It was hard to believe that we would fly home. Our discharge date was set for February 22. The airline reservations I had made back in October were for February 24, so I let the date stand. I packed up everything acquired in Seattle. I had saved the stout square white cardboard boxes in which Caremark delivered its bags of hydration and TPN, and now filled them one by one. When I had a batch I drove to a UPS place nearby. The day before we flew, I packed up the boom box and VCR in their cartons and sent them as well.

Jane was sick, sick—weaker, thinner, and frailer than she had been at any point in New Hampshire. At best, she could walk a hundred yards. Two days before we left, we drove out on Madison Avenue to Madison Park, as we had done in our previous Seattle outing—but this time Jane brought her walker; this time we walked five minutes only. On that same day we took part in a miracle: There would be no more infusions, no more chemo into her catheter, so that Jane no longer required her Hickman. The contents of a thousand bags had entered her bloodstream through these plastic teats. Now, in ten seconds of a steady gentle pull, Dianne Stayboldt removed Jane's line. A Band-Aid covered the wound of thirteen months. We said goodbye to Dianne, to Ernie Populus, to the receptionists we had come to know. We left the clinic for the last time, as lighthearted as lovers at the end of a movie.

On the day before flying, I visited Kris Doney in the morning at her office and we talked about our four months, as if I could provide help by feedback. In retrospect, I marvel at the purity or naiveté of my joy, our joy. I *knew* the leukemia was likely to return; I *knew* Jane's chances were poor. Or I should have known; I had read the books. But even Kris, who knew these matters intimately, seemed optimistic. In the afternoon Carolyn Stormer came to our apartment for a cup of tea and to say goodbye. I took photographs of the two friends, Jane with her emerging crewcut, the white swatch of hair over her forehead rising intact in stubble. After tea, we watched Carolyn disappear with regret, but we regretted little.

Our ride to the airport was due at ten. We were packed and ready to leave by nine. I paced. Used to such pacing, Jane sat quietly girding herself for the difficult, wonderful day of return to the house of poetry and Gus the dog. Our suitcases waited downstairs in the little foyer. At least ten minutes early, Jane took my arm and we walked to the elevator. Our volunteer driver was already parked by the curb. We were first on the plane. The equipment took off this time, the long flight to Pittsburgh. Our carry-ons were medical and nutritional, overpacked with my usual obsession about contingencies. (Jane said that my autobiography should be titled *The Foresight Saga*.) I had packed her medicines for the flight, together with cups of applesauce for help in swallowing cyclosporine. I had swiped a spoon from the apartment—in case first-class USAir ran out of spoons—and cans of Ensure Plus. Who could tell what the airline would serve us, or if Jane could eat anything provided? I packed a week's supply of pills—in case a February blizzard kept us in the Pittsburgh Airport for a week, or diverted us to Sri Lanka.

We landed in Pittsburgh ahead of schedule, met by a young woman with a wheelchair who pushed Jane to the gate for Manchester, New Hampshire. We were first on the plane again, and again the airplane took off, no blizzards in sight, and we landed in New Hampshire on schedule. Jane's extra half-Klonopin had relaxed her enough so that she slept a little, something she normally could not do on an airplane because of her anxiety over flying. Later, Jane announced that she had discovered a little-known side effect of a bone marrow transplant: It removed the fear of flying. We walked off the plane with Jane holding my arm, determined to arrive in New Hampshire on her own two legs. Behind the glass partition we saw my children leaping and cheering. Philippa and Jerry waved cards of welcome that their children had made. Andrew jumped and ran, waving a placard his three children had collaborated on, with WELCOME HOME JANE FROM SEATTLE! in big letters. For the thirty or forty yards from jetway to children, Jane walked on my arm, smiling more broadly—out of her pale face, under her wig—than she had smiled in thirteen months. Then she sat in an airport wheelchair, overcome with joy and surrounded by the joy of others, ten-thirty P.M. on February 24, 1995. We took the elevator down to the luggage carousel. Jerry and I retrieved six suitcases while Andrew fetched his car and warmed it up curbside. Philippa and Jane talked gaily.

Jerry and I wheeled and carried suitcases to Andrew's car and installed Jane, wrapped against New Hampshire's cold, in the warm front seat. We hugged Jerry and Philippa, and Andrew drove us home. All lights were on as we stopped in front of the house. We had thought so often of Gus's ecstasy in seeing Jane again, and now it would happen. Our house sitter opened the door and Gus exploded outside to examine the visitors. Understanding our desire for privacy, our house sitter had loaded her car and as soon as we arrived told us goodbye and departed. While Jane stood gaining her balance in the cold night bright with stars, Gus sniffed her carefully, thoroughly. I had expected him to leap over the roof, but it was clear that he required nasal certainty. He could scarcely believe his olfactory equipment. Could it be fraud? Could this woman possibly be the winner of a Jane Kenyon smell-alike contest? Gradually he believed, and began cautiously to sing, little high-pitched notes. He wriggled, his hindquarters dancing to one tune and his forepaws to another. Andrew and I helped Jane inside. I asked if she wanted to go straight to bed. She said she was too excited, and would lie on the sofa for a moment. Andrew and I brought the suitcases in, and listened as Gus gave vent to profundities of rapture. With Jane on the couch, her whole body was at nose level. He sang, he sang, he sang. If the humpback whale sings a mysterious song, Gus sang an entire opera that night, a contratenor playing the roles of a hundred angels, scored by Schönberg for instruments never invented. I suggested that Andrew sleep in the parlor and leave in the morning, but he was too high to sleep. He would drive two hours home in his excitement.

He left, and Jane and I were alone again in our house with our dog and cat. Even Ada the cat showed enthusiasm over our return. When Gussie had quieted to an occasional yelp, I helped Jane undress. In one of our suitcases I found the blue-striped flannel nightgown that Caroline had given her, and slipped it over her head. The happiness we felt that night was the greatest ever felt.

1993

THE LAST YEAR of our healthy life together was the busiest of our twenty-three, unprecedented in its constant motion, hectic with activity, breathless with a clutter of pleasures. We complained that we were doing too much, being too public, missing out on silence and solitude—but we kept at it. It was a good year for writing. Jane's *Constance* came out in 1993, yet her posthumous *Otherwise* starts with twenty poems finished after she put *Constance* together. Some began in 1992, others in the busy year of 1993—when we did a book tour and were interviewed by Bill Moyers and acted in *Love Letters* and returned to India.

We started the year by visiting my mother in Connecticut, January 4. For these monthly visits I picked up mail at the post office at ten, and we drove west through Claremont, eating lunch at Todofrali's, and crossed the Connecticut River into Vermont, then drove down I-91 by the river past Brattleboro into Massachusetts, past Springfield where traffic began, into Connecticut through Hartford to an exit in Hamden three miles from my mother's house. She was eighty-nine, living alone, reading books and writing letters and fashioning nylon scrubs to keep her hands busy. For two or three days before we arrived, Lucy cooked a pot of American chop suey in five-minute hobbles to the kitchen: two big cans of Franco-American spaghetti, copious sliced onion, crumbled hamburger browned in a quarter pound of butter. Before dinner, Bob McIntosh joined us from his house across the street, where he had been the big kid when I was little. I made the drinks. Lucy sipped two Scotch and sodas and smoked multiple Kents. The second day, Jane and I did errands, mostly an expedition to Stop & Shop for the month's groceries. We sat and visited with Lucy, then in the afternoon Jane left for Alice Mattison's house in New Haven, where the two friends walked and talked. For supper the second night I fetched us a pizza from Sorrento's. We slept in the guest room, and after breakfast the next day drove north along the river home. January 6, we got home in time for a five-thirty potluck at church.

Some years, these Connecticut visits comprised most of the time we spent away from Eagle Pond. But this year, on January 14 we flew to Louisville, Kentucky, to read our poems at Bellarmine College, staying with our friend Bert Hornback. We did two joint readings, going ABAB in fifteen-minute segments. We never conspired about which poems we would read, and sometimes changed our plans to read a poem that conversed with a poem that the other had just read. Each of us read one poem by the other. Usually Jane read "The Long River," which I wrote in Ann Arbor when she was ten years old on the other side of town. Usually I read "Twilight: After Haying," one of the poems of Jane's breakthrough early in the 1980s. Saturday morning in Kentucky we drove an hour to stay with Wendell and Tanya Berry, where we told stories, laughed, and walked with Wendell as he did chores—the fastest farmer I have ever followed around. We drank malt whiskey and ate the Berrys' home-grown beef and lamb—Jane turned corpse-eater for love of the Berrys—and stayed up talking late. Jane said that Wendell's laugh was the most beautiful noise she had ever heard.

We spent a week back home, then drove down to Amherst in Massachusetts for the twenty-first and twenty-second, where Jane

workshopped with Alice Mattison and Joyce Peseroff. After my
liver cancer the year before, Jane and I were uncomfortable being
apart. We took a room at the Lord Jeffrey Inn, next to Joyce and
Alice's room; I read and wrote alone all day while the three friends
worked and challenged one another. The four of us ate dinner and
visited Emily Dickinson. The day after Jane and I returned, Bill
Moyers and a television crew of ten arrived from New York. The
result was *A Life Together*, which PBS broadcast at the end of the
year. Tentative filming had started the September before, when
Jane and I read poems and talked at the Dodge Poetry Festival in
New Jersey, a biennial do that assembles dozens of poets for an audience of high school students, their teachers, and poetry's public.
David Grubin, a television producer who loves poetry, filmed us
there as we read our poems in a huge tent and talked poetry with
small groups of students. We had been told that if Moyers could
raise the money, he would visit the farm and interview us. Big cars
from New York, full of equipment and technicians, pulled into our
driveway and cased our house for filming the next day. Saturday
morning the crew emptied out our living room, filled it with cables
and cameras, and positioned two dining room chairs for the interviews. The crew hung plastic curtains at the outside edge of our
porch and set lights inside the curtains shining through our long
windows into the living room, so that the light on our faces remained steady. Beginning the interviews, Moyers calmed us down
as soon as the cameras rolled. Moyers himself may be tense—people who work with him say so—but he injects calm into panicky
subjects. He and I talked on camera for two hours. After Moyers
walked for twenty minutes on Route 4, he returned to talk with
Jane for another two hours. Asking questions, he looked into our
eyes, not at notes, and quoted chunks of our work from memory.
(Maybe he would remember nothing a day later; he remembered

when he had to remember.) He stayed alert to what we were saying, not bound to a script in his head; the show's structure would
come out of editing, the final fifty-six minutes snipped and shaped
out of thirty-five hours. Moyers's command and intimacy allowed
us actually to converse with him. At one point, he noticed something about one of my poems that permitted me to understand an
image that had always mystified me. My understanding came live,
on camera.

Interviews done, Jane and I tried to relax before a poetry
reading that night at Wilmot's town hall, the building where we
voted, where the Grange meets, and where Wilmot sometimes
puts on a play. Moyers wanted to film us reading to the neighbors.
A precious painted curtain fronts the stage, and tonight it would
serve as a backdrop when Jane and I stood at a podium in front. It
was my turn to read first, in our ABAB. As we drove the three and
a half miles from our house, Jane drank a viscous liquid, honey
and tea, because her mouth was dry from terror and antidepres-
sants. The Honda bounded off a frost heave and a sweet stain
oozed over her dress. We changed plans; we would go AB, and I do
my half hour first while she drove home and changed. She
dropped me off and I took the platform. Dave Grubin's two cameras followed me and the colorful assemblage of neighbor faces—
Jane's mother looking perky, an old minister of ours, a newspaper
editor and his wife and their young son, shopkeepers and librarians and carpenters, longtime friends, and strangers from other
towns. When I had done my thirty minutes, Jane had not returned. I read another poem, and another, feeling increasingly
anxious: Jane was in a hurry, the roads were icy, maybe she lay in a
ditch somewhere. I could hold my anxiety back no longer and told
the audience what was happening. I started on yet another poem,
and halfway through looked up and saw Jane, pale and out of

breath, enter the town hall. She sat for a moment while I finished the poem I had begun. When she stood at the podium she explained: She had decided on a dress to replace the stained one, and found it quickly—but she could not undo the knot in its sash. (I see her struggling to tear the knot apart with trembling fingers.) When she gave up she decided that another dress would do—but it needed ironing. In the television show, as the camera cuts back and forth between poet and audience, each of us appears in a reaction shot, listening to the other. I look benign and supportive, smiling, but while I am reading Jane looks disturbed—wild-eyed, her lips trembling. She had just parked the car.

The next morning was church, and in the film I pass the hat. Jane and I sing hymns. We were miked, and I belt out stanzas although I cannot hold a tune. After church two great cars wended their way south, and Jane and I took a long nap. Back in New York the filmmakers studied what they had gathered and took notes and set forth a tentative plan or story line. Before filming, they had notions of emphasis, and asked us to read certain poems; thus, the film looks closely at Jane's assimilation to house, family, and culture, a problem that had occupied her and her poems eighteen years before. They had me read poems that embodied the rural society in which we lived. Another topic that loomed throughout was my recent cancer and imminent death. In June the film's editor, David Stewart, visited us with a cameraman and photographed us in another season, so that we can see Jane in the ice of the January back garden and at the same trellis in June.

(I have watched the show since Jane's death, with more pleasure than pain: Here is Jane at the height of her powers, energetic and confident, with the beauty that accrued to her in her forties. Only at the end of the film do I get weepy. In the last shot, Jane and I walk red Gus through our green hayfield, disappearing down a hill as Jane's voice says "Otherwise," ending, "But one day, I know / it will be otherwise." When she was sick, Jane remembered the final sequence in the film and said, "My head went first.")

The 1993 calendar continues with dentist's appointments, Jane's handwriting saying "Shop with Mom," Jane's lunches with friends in New London, and weekend visits from couples. We took a bus to a rehearsal of the Boston Symphony; Jane spoke to a literacy group; we visited my mother again in February; Jane accompanied me as I did a reading in Pittsburgh. The next day we flew on to Washington, where I performed as councilor for the National Endowment for the Arts. While I sat with other councilors around a boring table, Jane spent the days looking at great paintings in great museums. I had been appointed to the NEA by Bush the First in 1991, an oddity conceived by Liam Rector, who is a First Amendment freak. The NEA had been attacked and diminished by conservatives, Jesse Helms at the forefront, who used photographs by Robert Mapplethorpe and Andres Serrano (exhibited by museums under grants from the NEA) to attack art and its governmental support. NEA councilors and administrators had sometimes been craven in their responses to assault, and Liam wanted to enlist me in the cause of free speech. John Sununu, who was running the White House, had been governor of New Hampshire, and it was his advocacy of everything New Hampshire that put David Souter on the Supreme Court. Sununu and I had met when I was the state poet laureate. Liam suggested that I ask Sununu to appoint me to the council. I did. Six months or so after I wrote him, when I had forgotten my request, I heard from the NEA that the President had submitted my name to the Senate. An FBI man from Concord took to hanging around the local gas station, saying that Donald Hall was up for a presidential appointment and did anyone know of a reason why I shouldn't be preferred? (He heard some smart answers.) The same FBI man interviewed me, my name was advanced to the Senate, and the Senate confirmed my appointment. I signed on for quarterly visits to Washington, and to oceanic boredom.

At first, things were sometimes interesting. I arrived after the great Mapplethorpe-Serrano fracas, but the agency remained under attack, and there were frequent small crises over grants to organizations that showed pictures—or sponsored performances or printed poems—that appeared to tolerate or even celebrate sexual activity. Panels of artists had approved these grants and sometimes a cowardly council rescinded them. Other councilors included artists—the painter William Bailey and the dancer Tricia Brown were two—but more often councilors were administrators of the arts, gallery directors, and directors of art organizations. Many were sharp; some were merely rich and political donors or supporters—maybe trustees of an orchestra or a museum—and received this presidential appointment as a public reward by which they could do little harm. Like some people on all committees, there were councilors who were devoted to the music of their own voices. Temporizing soliloquies of stultifying repetitious empty sentences contaminated Washington days in the Old Post Office Building. We were reminded to be "proactive." Some councilors were genuine honorable conservatives, but others were censors out of strategy, not conviction, fearful that Jesse Helms would destroy the NEA entirely. I argued that it would be better to expire of assault than to wither of timidity. On occasion, I spoke for the constituency of letters, which I claimed was underfunded, but mostly I defended freedom of expression—sometimes known as pornography. I was on the losing side of 13–7 votes. One vote was

17–1 against a grant to Franklin Furnace—a New York gallery and performance space—and I was proud to be singular. Even out-voted 17–1, I knew that one dissent was useful. *Somebody* defended art against the assaults of prudery.

The meetings were public, the audience a shifting population that included the press, which in those days found it useful to cover NEA meetings. There was also security, beefy fellows, increased sometimes if there was a rumor of a demonstration, maybe by Act Up. (Homophobia was a permanent component of conservative attacks.) When an acting chair vetoed a grant to an MIT gallery, a show called "Body Parts," which featured a wallpaper of repeated penises, I raised my hand to protest. The acting chair addressed me as "Don," and at the conclusion of my statement changed my name to "Mr. Hall." The veto stood, but Aerosmith ponied up money to fund the show and I wrote an introduction to the catalog. "Body Parts" increased my standing with my granddaughters, since at the opening I met Steve Tyler.

Later in February Jane and I went to New York, where I read at NYU. Back home, my granddaughter Abigail was christened in the South Danbury Christian Church. In March we went to town meeting; we visited my mother in Connecticut again; we read together at Dean Junior College in Massachusetts. Then we flew to Norfolk, Virginia, where the Association of Writers and Writing Programs held its annual meeting. The AWP put together a tribute to me, a year after my liver operation—one of several anticipatory memorial events in 1993. Louis Simpson flew in from Long Island, Robert Bly came down from Minnesota, Galway Kinnell from New York. Jane took part, puzzling some people by speaking of one "Perkins." Later that month I read in West Virginia; Jane read and ran a workshop in Vermont; I spent a week visiting four Indiana campuses. In April we went to Connecticut for my mother's ninetieth birthday. Jane read in Manchester and I in Boston. In May we drove to Ann Arbor for a joint reading and for my honorary Michigan degree, before we went back to the NEA and I sat through more dull speeches.

Liam Rector and Tree Swenson drove up from Somerville to be married in our back garden. We had known them before they met each other, separately connected with Liam the poet and Tree the book designer and publisher. Our particular acquaintanceships morphed into a deep couple-friendship. Liam decreed that he and I—best man—would wear tails and red sneakers. His daughter Virginia flew to attend. Tree brought Anne Hirondelle, closest friend from her old life in Port Townsend, Washington, to stand up with her. Jane arranged for a woman friend, who was a Unitarian minister, to perform the service. It was a mild, pretty day, seven people gathered among peonies. After the ceremony, Liam was reading "Little Gidding" aloud when the rain shower started. The dining room adjoins the garden, and he finished the Quartet inside.

It was Jane's birthday on May 23. Then Gagan Gill from New Delhi visited us; we drove back to my mother's again; Jane's workshop met at our house. In June Jane climbed Mount Washington; I flew to Albuquerque for a reading; we had dinner in Hanover with Galway Kinnell and Bobbie Bristol; we saw Louis Simpson at Bennington; we had lunch with Charlie Simic in Concord. After the July visit to Connecticut, Jane and I took a brief holiday north of the White Mountains at The Balsams—where we learned that my mother was in the hospital again after an episode of congestive heart failure. We drove to her at the New Haven Hospital and later arranged her removal to Clough Extended Care, nearby in New London.

Then a theater man telephoned asking if we would act in

Love Letters. A. B. Gurney's play for two characters is a man and a woman sitting onstage reading aloud the letters they have written each other. To act it, one does not need to memorize a part, and therefore many couples—known as couples and not as professional actors—have performed the script. I love to act, and wanted to accept—but I knew that Jane would refuse. She was already complaining that we were too busy, and we were about to return to India. But all marriages build their own myths, and one of ours—that Jane invented and I accepted—was that Perkins always wanted to do *everything,* more dates and engagements, and that in order to survive, Jane had to resist my urgencies. Jane was the reticent one who desired only silence and solitude. When I told the producer that I would call him back, I had small hope that we would act on a stage together—at a small summer theater, the Papermill, in the White Mountains. When I asked Jane, I began by saying that I *knew* she wouldn't want to do it—and discovered to the contrary that she wanted very much to do it. After twenty-one years of marriage I gradually came to realize that the myth—Jane passive, me aggressive—was no longer entirely true. Maybe Jane in her twenties took cover in my shadow, but at forty-six she cast her own lively shadow. We bought the script of the play and studied it together, then rehearsed with the director, who gave us notes. We played it with enthusiasm and some success—Jane was much better than I was—with Jane's visiting brother and family in the audience, and friends who drove up from Boston. The theater director from Colby-Sawyer College in New London attended, and booked us for a second run over Valentine's Day next year.

Two days after our show went dark, Jane and I drove to Boston, the last day of August, and at WGBH recorded an interview with Terry Gross for *Fresh Air.* We taxied from the studio to Logan Airport and flew all night to Frankfurt on our way to New

Delhi. For three weeks we revisited India and chatted with people we had met two years before. Again we read our poems and lectured and were interviewed and ate wonderful food and walked in markets and among monuments. We flew home, exhausted, and did two joint poetry readings in three days. Joy Harjo came calling; we heard Phil Levine read at Dartmouth; we took Polly to New York to celebrate her eightieth birthday; we saw a rough cut of the Moyers film. I flew to Kansas for a reading; Noah Adams came to the house to interview me for NPR; Stewe Claeson, Swedish translator of *The One Day,* visited to ask about idioms; we visited my mother in her room fifteen minutes away; we each did bookstore signings.

In Washington we read together at Chapters, then had dinner with Dan and Pat Ellsberg. I flew to New Jersey one morning, did an afternoon reading, and flew back at night. We flew to Chicago, then Minneapolis for radio interviews and bookstore signings—a double mini-tour for *Constance* and *Life Work*—and continued to Des Moines and Iowa City. Then it was New York, where *The Museum of Clear Ideas* had been nominated for the National Book Award. Jane and I had lunch with Louis Begley, and I was a bridesmaid as Archie Ammons took the award. Flying back to Boston, we went to a BSO rehearsal; the next day we were interviewed for a *Globe* Sunday magazine piece, occasioned by the Moyers show; the next day we flew to Miami and read at its book fair. Jane and I read at a church in Sanbornton, New Hampshire, as we did every year; we read at Proctor Academy, just down the road in Andover. Wendell and Tanya Berry, with whom we had begun the year in Kentucky, flew to New Hampshire to visit us in return. The Moyers show went national on PBS, December 17, and we watched it with my mother at Clough. The church program, carols and children's pageant, came two days later. The calendar for December 23 says, "Pick up turkey." Polly had Christmas dinner with us, and the next day we ate with children and grandchildren at my son's house. Wes and Diane McNair came calling, and the newlyweds Liam and Tree, and Joyce Peseroff with her husband Jeff. We slept through New Year's Eve, and it was January 1994—the month when leukemia came to our house.

The Best Day the Worst Day

On February 25, 1995—a year after Jane's first remission—we woke in our own bed at Eagle Pond. It was a Saturday, and Gus was asking to be fed, asking to go outside, asking that we wake and pay him some notice. It would be a long time before Jane could again walk him up New Canada Road. Today he danced beside me, second best, as I trudged with him on Walker Brook Road. It was a slow, quiet, calm day after the intensity of our cross-country return. We talked with friends on the telephone but no one came calling. We breathed the thin high air of relief—but everywhere in the house we found Polly: Her coats hung by the door; a book she had been reading lay beside the chair she had been sitting in; her soft woolen berets and her dresses remained in the parlor where she had slept. Here were her tapes of old PBS programs; here were pieces of sewing equipment, with magazines and books about sewing; in the bathroom lay her toothbrush and toothpaste. While Jane took a long nap, I bundled Polly's things and took them upstairs to the guest room, where I had stacked my mother's caftans and music boxes. When she woke Jane looked around her and realized what I had done. "Thank you, Perkins."

On Sunday we visited church for a few minutes, to the cheers of friends and neighbors. Jane could not sit for long in the hard pew. In the afternoon Philippa and family visited from Concord. Monday we continued to rest, and I baked a meatloaf for my vegetarian wife, who was determined to gain weight. On Tuesday we

211

went back to Dartmouth-Hitchcock for bloodwork, regularly required. We were due at eight for the blood-drawing, nine for consultation with Letha Mills and her assistant Diane. We woke that morning to a freezing drizzle, yet we never considered postponing our hospital visit. We drove an hour through an ice storm, cars decorating ditches alongside us, and fulfilled our appointment on a day when the hospital phones were lively with cancellations. One needn't be phobic to fear driving I-89 in an ice storm. Two years earlier, we would not have made the journey. Yet Jane sat beside me calm and easy, as she had sat beside me on the long flight from Seattle to Manchester. At Hitchcock a tech drew blood from her arm. We walked to the elevator—no wheelchair today—and waited at Hem/Onc for results from the lab. Letha and Diane and the clinic nurses burst out to the waiting room to welcome us back, triumphant survivors returned to the port we had sailed from. When the report from the bloodwork was good, we were free to leave, and I borrowed a wheelchair to roll Jane back down to the Bubble, where our nurses Kate and Mary, Sharon and Shari, hugged and congratulated her. On the drive home, sunshine had melted the ice.

Pill-taking was arduous still. Bactrim was two large pills that were hard to swallow even when broken in half. Mostly, Jane slept or rested. Many afternoons I rented a film, and we caught up on twenty years of neglected movies. Jane's great blue chair moved over beside mine in front of the TV. On the far side of Jane's chair she kept the bookstand that her father had used. Jane read two books of short stories, Wendell Berry's *Fidelity* and John Updike's *The Afterlife*. She saved Alice Munro's new book for later; its stories were longer. Every day by tiny but discernible steps she was getting better. Jean Frey visited us daily, a nurse's assistant who bathed Jane in bed or helped her take a shower, and rubbed her down. The visiting nurse called on us, and a physical therapist for Jane's general body strength. Three times a week occupational therapy arrived in the shape of Linda Lucas, married to Don Lucas who cut our hayfields, who came to help Jane's hands, crippled by cyclosporine. Carole Colburn, who had cleaned for us for years, came at least twice a week, and helped Jane feel that the house was under control when she could do little to control it. I cooked and kept track of Jane's calories. Neighbors left cornucopia baskets on the porch. Twice a week we went to the clinic, and Jane still underwent painful procedures. She would have two more lumbar punctures to infuse methotrexate into her spinal column; then she would have had as much as she could tolerate in a lifetime. She still required bone marrow biopsies, as she would in the future but at longer intervals. We would begin to diminish the dosage of cyclosporine when we had finished—happy day—with prednisone.

The second week was a good one, March 6 to 12. We understood that it would take a year, maybe two years, before Jane was *well*. But maybe in four months, or five, she would drive the car, go shopping, eat lunch with a friend. As I thought happily of old life returning, I understood with a lurch of shame that I would miss taking care of her—miss being requisite, miss her dependency. Now I was still needed: to drive the car, to shop, to medicate. One day, on our way back from the clinic, we parked for a moment outside Cricenti's so I could pick up groceries. Jane waited in the car, bundled up. We stopped at the bank and I helped Jane inside to have her signature notarized on a State of New Hampshire document where she swore to perform her duties as poet laureate. The next day was anxious for me, although Jane was doing well, because I would leave her for eight hours. Our friend Mary Jane Ogmundson would stay with her while I drove to my son Andrew's in Massachusetts and we went to the Boston Garden to watch the

Celtics play the Knicks. Sports had fastened father and son together through nasty times. When I returned at one or two in the
morning, I found a sheet of paper, lines in an unfamiliar hand, on
the bookstand next to Jane's chair. I recognized Jane's language:
She had dictated to Mary Jane her last, unfinished poem—"The
Sick Wife"—about sitting in the car, the day before, while I bought
groceries. In the morning I asked her, "Did you dictate to Mary
Jane, instead of to me, because you were afraid I'd think it was terrible?" "I thought of that," said Jane. Typed up, the poem lay on the
tilted bookstand. Sometimes Jane's head swiveled to read it
through. She would hand it to me for revision. "Change 'cloud
over' to 'steam up,'" she would say. Over the next several days she
altered four or five words.

Jane ate more, she did more. Changes budged in the right direction. I made an appointment for my annual colonoscopy. I
found someone professional to make sense of our medical bills,
Blue Cross and the hospitals tangled like yarn. Because the Honda
had started to fail the summer before, I drove to Concord—a
friend stayed with Jane—and shopped for a new one. Jane and I
went through piles of medical detritus, discarding supplies no
longer needed. From one box I pulled out a plastic bag full of
Jane's long curly haircut a year earlier. "Throw it away," said Jane.

Philippa and her family came again on Sunday the twelfth.
Whenever we saw the people we loved, our relief and optimism
gave everybody energy. Then it was Monday, the thirteenth of
March, which was surprisingly a spring day. There had been little
snow in New Hampshire that winter, and today was positively
warm, the sunlight that pale buttery tint of early spring. Jane
loved such a day because it carried the prospect of snowdrops, daffodils, tulips, peonies, lilies, and roses. Normally, it would carry

the promise of long exhausting days in the garden. This year it would be frustrating, because she would be able to do little. But doing a little would give her strength, and next year she could begin to apply herself, to bring the garden back to its standard. After our early nap, the day was at its brightest and warmest. To my surprise and delight Jane suggested walking Gus together, a short walk by necessity, but the first New Hampshire walk together. In past years, Gus usually enjoyed two walks a day. Jane took him up-mountain early in the morning, between breakfast and work, and after a nap I walked him myself, often on another quiet road. In high summer's long light we sometimes took him out together in early evening—*three walks in one day!*—and he was ecstatic to go with us both. The warm noontime of March 13, when Gus realized that we were taking him for his first double walk in almost two years, he sang and danced as he had done when he welcomed Jane home. We parked near Mary Lyn's house, where the narrow road runs flat for two hundred and fifty yards, a patch where stone walls have escaped frost's tumbling and stand high and intact the way they stood when they were built a century and a half ago. We walked our dog, maybe a hundred and fifty yards down and a hundred and fifty yards back, and we were as happy as Gus was. Driving back to the farm I could feel energy radiating from Jane's skinny body. She was more confident than I had seen her since the June before, when she worked on poems and we buried my mother. "Maybe, after I rest," she told me, "we could go to Tilton." In Tilton lived Uncle Dick and Aunt Nan. Nan was my mother's kid sister, eighty-four now; she had been poorly for several years after a series of small strokes; she had lost the power of speech. When Jane had been well, we visited them once a week. Nan was generally shy to have visitors, ashamed because she could not speak or attend to her appearance, but our visits pleased her. If she could not follow what we said, the tune of our talk made a music that pleased her.

Jane rested in our bed for forty minutes and announced that she could go to Tilton. I telephoned ahead, Jane put on her wig, and we drove seventeen miles in the warm sun over small familiar roads. Nan smiled, seeing us for the first time since August, and the brief visit was another restitution of the old life. As we drove home we stopped at the Dairy Queen between Tilton and Franklin, where we had stopped before, and we each ordered a Peanut Buster Parfait. I finished mine. As with so many old pleasures, Jane's sundae did not taste right and she took only a few bites. Driving toward East Andover we gazed again at a vista we had loved together for twenty years—a great upward-tilting swoop of hayfield, just greening up, interrupted by a farmhouse with a red door. "It's still there," said Jane. It was the best day.

Soon after we returned, Jane was assaulted by sudden extreme abdominal pain. Appendix? The pain seemed misplaced for an appendix. The thought struck me (as I'm sure it struck Jane) that GVHD had afflicted or shut down some vital abdominal organ—liver? spleen? I called Letha, who told us to drive to Emergency again, and our great day ended as Jane sat beside me, doubled over in agony, and I drove as fast as I dared to the well-remembered portals of Hitchcock's Emergency entrance.

When Jane described her pain, it reminded me of something I had felt long ago—before I knew Jane—when my gallbladder went berserk and was removed in 1969. I had never heard of GVHD causing gallbladder problems, and it seemed impossible that Jane, recovering from leukemia and a bone marrow transplant, should be afflicted by a new and unrelated disease. In Emergency—where you lie for hours answering the same questions from nurses and medical students and finally doctors—it became gradually apparent that Jane was indeed suffering from gall-stones. After two or three hours, the pain stopped as quickly as it had started, typical of a gallbladder attack. I learned that the dis-ease was not unconnected to her leukemia, deriving as usual not from the disease but from its treatment. For the past thirteen months, Jane had consumed enormous life-sustaining quantities of TPN. TPN is fatty, and many patients who imbibe much TPN develop a sludge of gallstones.

A surgeon named Meg Mooney diagnosed and attended to Jane, Letha was consulted, and Jane was admitted to the surgical floor, I presumed for observation and consultation. The first thing was massive continual drips of antibiotics, for gallstones cause in-fections and Jane's immune system was inadequate. I arranged for care of the animals. I reserved a room at the Days Inn and drove home to pack the car again: Jane's clothes, boom box with CDs, and a golden cardboard box that had inhabited many hospital rooms with Jane's address book, pen, and notebook. I telephoned my children. I arranged with Bert again to bring me mail and typ-ing. I canceled my colonoscopy, telephoning the friends who were going to drive me; I canceled my Honda engagement. After the glorious plupart of March 13, we ended the day massively retro-gressed. The best day became the worst day.

In the morning when I entered Jane's room I was alarmed to see the wrappings that inflate to protect a patient's legs from blood clots during surgery. Jane was scheduled for the knife this morn-ing. Had Letha agreed to this procedure? Surgeons always want to cut. The operation would be the laparoscopy, far less devastating than the major abdominal surgery I had endured twenty-five years earlier, but invasive and frightening. Because of the fear of infec-tion and hemorrhage, post-BMTs are supposed to avoid having their teeth cleaned, much less their abdomens opened up. I needed to know that Hematology and Surgery were in agreement. I ran from Hem/Onc to Bubble to Hem/Onc—and found Letha, who put a stop to plans for immediate surgery and moved Jane down to the Bubble again, to nurses familiar with leukemia and BMTs.

Then followed a week of antibiotics and medical ambivalence. The danger of surgery was infection. The danger of no surgery was infection. With a laparoscopy Jane would lose the gallbladder that otherwise might infect her, but she would be cut open and she would wear a tube dripping bile from her side. Physicians from Surgery, Gastroenterology, and Hematology conferred. At first they decided to keep Jane on intravenous antibiotics a few more days, then send her home on a gallbladder diet. A dietitian visited with sheets of instructions. The diet was a problem, because a gallbladder diet eliminates fat; I was feeding Jane Ensure Plus and mayonnaise . . . I telephoned Kris Doney, who talked to Dr. McDonald, who counseled caution; he didn't seem to believe in the prudence of cutting, and said TPN sludge wasn't always worth removing. Then the Jane Kenyon Gallbladder Committee met again, and this time decided that the procedure of a laparoscopy was less dangerous than no procedure.

Now I wheeled Jane to the limbo where surgical patients receive their general anesthesia, as Jane had done when I lost half my liver three years earlier. I paced in the room where caregivers wait, where Jane had waited. After three hours, Meg Mooney's co-surgeon gave me audience and told me the procedure had gone as desired, and the gallstones looked like the result of TPN. Two hours later I was allowed to visit a groggy Jane in the recovery room, and next day sat beside her in the Bubble again, this time watching her recover from a new and different pain. She developed herpes zoster again, which had been something to worry about in the summer of 1994; by 1995 shingles were scarcely worth attending to. It was hard to believe that a week earlier we had walked the dog and visited Tilton. Jane was set back six weeks, as if we had returned to January in Seattle, depressed and discouraged.

But we came home, after eleven or twelve days in the hospital. We got Gus back. Jane had lost weight, and I concentrated again on fattening her up. We went back to the clinic on March 30, and the bloodwork was satisfactory. On Saturday, April 1, we heard bad family news. When my cousin Peter Powers had married Nancy, both were aware that she could not conceive a child. Then she became pregnant and they were overjoyed. Now, three days after the birth, their baby son Curtis died in Nancy's arms. SIDS. We knew them well, had attended their wedding, and were horrified. A memorial service and a burial would take place on Wednesday, April 5, at three o'clock.

Our next clinic appointment had been scheduled for April 4, but we had it changed to the third because on the fourth I needed to drive south to Exeter, where the school would give me its annual award to an alumnus. (Exeter had been trying to give it to me for six months.) On April 3 Jane's blood counts had risen again, and our next visit to the clinic was scheduled for April 11. The day after I returned from Exeter Jane felt weaker and was in pain. It was a cold, cold day with a high wind—and Curtis Powers would be buried at three P.M. It was insane for Jane to go but she was adamant; I could not touch her resolve. I bundled her heavily and brought a chair for her. We parked beside the road shortly before the service, and Jane held to my arm as we walked into a desperate wind over the frozen grass of the graveyard. Wearing wig and scarves, she showed only a portion of her face, as pale as the scraps of snow that still lay on the north side of gravestones. As we approached neighbors and cousins standing around the grave in the frigid wind, they parted like the Red Sea to let us through. Jane was heavy, heavy on my arm, struggling to walk. I set down the folding metal chair beside the little hole and Jane collapsed onto it weeping for Curtis, for Nancy and Peter. Everyone looked at Jane with astonishment; someone spoke of her courage. Everyone was horrified to see Jane look as she looked. They guessed what occasion would gather them next.

The rest of the week was further setbacks, as the bone pain continued and Jane felt weaker. We thought we had underestimated the effects of the latest affliction. While a friend sat with Jane, I picked out a new Accord with leather seats and a sliding roof. Jane wanted me to buy a Miata, indulging Perkins, but Miatas are not known for performance in snow. The new car would be ready on Monday the tenth. In New Hampshire, we register our cars in our birthday months. We kept the titles of both our cars in Jane's name, saving me an errand; Jane visited the town clerk in May to register both vehicles. This time, I didn't think Jane should waste her energy riding to Concord to sign the papers. The dealer in Concord allowed me to let ownership remain flexible until the car's pickup on Monday morning. Monday morning Jane insisted that we pick up the car together, and that she sign as owner. She felt wretched and we set out. It was the weekly day off for the personable saleswoman with whom I had dealt, and who knew about Jane's illness. Our new car was ready, black-green and smelling of leather, and a fill-in salesman handled the paperwork for us, a young man who normally did intake in the service department.

We exchanged keys, and he presented papers for Jane as owner—Jane unsteady on her feet, pale, weak, mostly silent, wearing her wig. The young man addressed questions to me not to Jane, and would not look her in the eye. He was awkward or embarrassed in the face of death, like most of us until we have practiced. It took her five minutes of concentration to sign her name. When we walked outside to our new car, Jane said slowly, "He didn't think I was all there."

The next morning we drove our new car the habitual journey to Hitchcock, blood-drawing at nine and consultation at ten. I wanted to fetch Jane a wheelchair at the hospital entrance, but she said she would walk; she needed to build her strength back. She sat in the foyer while I parked, and held my arm as we walked to the blood-testing place and took the elevator upstairs to Hem/Onc. We sat on the green plastic chairs out front, but Jane was hurting; an hour of waiting in a chair was too much. I found an unused bed in the infusion room and Jane dozed as I sat beside her. I went downstairs to Au Bon Pain for coffee and a muffin. I wandered little because I was worried; I must not miss Letha's visit. A nurse came by to take Jane's vital signs. Letha's assistant Diane stopped by for a preliminary chat before the lab finished analyzing her blood. I told about Jane's bone pain, fatigue, and increased weakness. Diane left and we waited, longer than usual, I suppose because the lab was double-checking with Pathology. Then a nurse told us that Dr. Mills wanted to see us in a consultation room this morning. It was unusual, but it did not occur to me why she wanted privacy. Jane and I sat together on small chairs beside the doctor's desk in the tiny room. Letha walked in and sat against the far wall, with Diane standing behind us leaning against the closed door. Letha took a breath, looked at us directly, and spoke the words we had imagined over fifteen months, the worst words: "I have terrible news. The leukemia is back. There's nothing to do."

Jane bent her head and tears started. I reached for a box of tissues. Letha said we could put Jane in the hospital right now, and treat her a little, but it would only delay . . . Jane's head shook its negative; as ever, we were in agreement. I asked, "Did the gall-bladder . . . ?" I worried that Jane's recent trauma, depressing her immune system, might have allowed the cancer to multiply. But if residual leukemia cells survived rejection by the donor's T-cells, leukemia would inevitably have found its way back. "No," said Letha, weeping. I mumbled something about the Hutch, about anything *new*. Letha said, "There's not much out there." I asked Letha how long, not a question that could receive a definitive answer. She said, "Maybe a month. Or so." Jane asked Letha only one question: "Can I die at home?" Letha said she didn't know why not.

Maybe we were in the consultation room ten minutes. There was nothing to say. I watched Jane compose herself, trying to go cold, to begin to let go. (Jane died in eleven days—rather than in "a month. Or so.") Diane fetched a wheelchair; there was no longer reason to gain strength. I wheeled Jane out of the clinic the back way, down the familiar route of elevator and hallway, past troops of patients and staff. Anyone looking at us must have known what news we had heard. I left Jane at the hospital's front door, with the attendant, retrieved the new car with its leather smell, and tucked Jane in. I put the box of tissues between us and we drove home. I cried and Jane was dry-eyed.

The Caldecott Room

Our first years at Eagle Pond, we interrupted our usual day, of work and reading aloud, to explore the country. We found roads nearby that we had never taken, and improvised an afternoon's travel, aiming the car so we would get back to Route 4, not knowing what we would encounter on the way. We collected handsome villages and landscapes, varying with the season. Before we put in central heat, our winter trips were brief or we would return to a frigid house. In warmer weather we drove farther afield. Our second year in residence, we looped over to the coast of southern Maine and drove through the village of Perkins Cove. Jane was amused to see the street and store signs. As she told it later, "There was Perkins Avenue and Perkins Lane, Perkins Pharmacy, Dr. Perkins, Attorney Perkins, and Perkins Dry Goods Store. This Perkins," she said, "must be quite a fellow." From that day on, "Perkins" became my name. She used it when she teased me—"Perkins, dim your lights!"—but also on tender occasions. Maybe "Donald Hall" and even "Don" were brand names, professor and local poet of Ann Arbor; "Perkins" was husband and lover.

By 1977, our intimacy had grown stronger than it had ever been. We worked all day apart, and ate dinner with wine by candlelight. As we loved each other without irony or reserve, as we together concentrated on loved things around us, we felt more married than we had felt in the Ann Arbor years that began in a judge's chambers. Five years after that wedding, two years after our move to Eagle Pond, we met on a Saturday afternoon in April with our minister Jack Jensen in the dark cool South Danbury church at two in the afternoon. Jack led us through the wedding ceremony. He had brought flowers. He had brought three glasses and a split of champagne. While my horrified teetotal ancestors watched, we toasted our marriage, five years after it started, in the shadowy church.

Jane worked hard every day on her poems but at first made little money; at times she felt that she let down the female side. One year in the early 1980s she took a job teaching at a small college not far away, one class in creative writing, but Jane was not born to be a teacher. She had trouble with authority, on both sides of the desk. She had written poems about rebellious feelings as a child in her one-room school; now she wrote about being too strict or sarcastic with her creative writers. The students at this college were dedicated to partying; many signed up for writing as an easy course; Jane was enraged when they didn't do assignments or came late to class. She quit after one term, vowing that if she needed a job she would bag groceries rather than teach. She never needed to take a job, and increasingly contributed to the family income by selling poems and doing poetry readings. For me, making a living by writing seemed so unlikely that it carried the charm of the illicit; I had the pleasure of getting away with something, as well as the pleasure of providing. Jane said she lived on a perpetual "Hall"—as in "Fulbright" or "Guggenheim"—so that she could write poems.

Jane loved to cook, but so did I, and in our first years here we fought over who got to make dinner each night. Otherwise, we both avoided drudgery. We brought a dishwasher with us. Jane didn't like housecleaning and didn't feel obliged to be especially tidy, but sometimes she stopped writing to clean house. I was uncomfortable seeing her vacuum and pick up, but not uncomfortable enough to do it myself. When our finances became stable, I persuaded Jane to hire help with housekeeping so that she could keep to the desk. Our first whole summer, she put in an asparagus patch that still produces. We grew a big vegetable garden, nominally my territory as flowers were hers. It was across Route 4, so in dry times we carried water in buckets across macadam. But raccoons harvested our corn and woodchucks gobbled our beans. I relished killing predatory woodchucks. When I was a boy I had sat for hours with my .22, waiting to blast off a furry head poking out of the ground in my grandparents' vegetable garden. As an adult I was too impatient to sit. I baited a Havahart trap, and when I captured a woodchuck I whacked it. Every year when I shot my first woodchuck, I remembered my cousin Freeman, who in decades past ate an annual woodchuck fattened on his peas. (My grandmother Kate baked it in the oven, holding her nose.) *Joy of Cooking* contained a woodchuck recipe, which I read annually as the inaugural corpse lay in its merciful trap. When Irma Rombauer reminded me that, skinning the beast, I should wear rubber gloves against the mites, I walked across the road carrying a shovel. As the years went on, I found myself forgetting to weed the garden. I was infuriated by the depredations of deer and rabbits and even birds, who pecked holes in tomatoes just as they ripened. Then John Clough opened a stand in New London that sold his own fresh corn, ripe tomatoes, leeks, and everything good. Our vegetable garden shrank like a spill of water on the top of a woodstove.

Meantime Jane's flowers thrived. In the winter she read Gertrude Jekyll's gardening books and studied the catalog from

White Flower Farm, plotting her spring planting. I would see her staring out the window at borders of ice and snow, lost in ambitious daydreams of peonies and lilies and hollyhocks. On warm days in late March she would clean up for spring, waiting for April and the daffodils. Every fall she planted more bulbs; every April the bright yellow cups would hallelujah out of the ground, and late snow would fill their blossoms. In the heaviest gardening time, May and June, black flies made outdoors miserable. Jane wore a mesh beekeeper's mask and heavy socks rolled over the bottom of her jeans. She planted; she transplanted. She attended to colors and their proximity, loathing a yellow patch at the end of our lawn because it clashed with nearby orange. Gradually she moved my grandmother's perennials, which tended not to be colorful, to peripheral sites, and created a magnanimous row of peonies in front of the porch, the triumph of June, superseded by famous hollyhocks in July. While the dew was still thick on the petals, early in the day, she wrote at her desk. Then she donned her gardening gear and gathered her tools and lost herself in dirt and blossoms. She interrupted her labors for lunch and our daily nap, then labored until it was too dark to see. On several occasions I aimed the car's headlights so that she could finish a task she had set herself. It was a passion never fully satisfied. Winter's imagined garden always shone brighter than summer's real one, which was subject to moles and chipmunks, to drought and thunderstorm.

Jane had other devotions, even in summer. We made it down to Fenway Park once or twice a year, starting with the first game of the 1975 World Series, when we sat in the bleachers and observed Luis Tiant's tonsils as he swiveled toward us in his eccentric windup. We watched Ted Williams in an old-timers' game. I umpired for Danbury school baseball. We judged Danbury Prize

Speaking together, and she was my dresser when I performed Santa Claus. Sunday morning at church was the one moment of the week, each week, when we knew what we would be doing. The congregation gathered at sunrise on Easter morning outside Ansel and Edna's house, sang hymns, then went inside to eat the hot cross buns that Ansel baked, with scrambled eggs, and bacon cured from a hog fed all summer and dressed in the fall. We both cooked for the church fair in July, where I helped with the auction that ended the day.

In September of 1978, three years after the return, I was fifty years old. Andrew was at the University of Wisconsin, Philippa just down the road at the University of New Hampshire, so she could join Jane and me for my birthday. We had given Philippa our old Plymouth 6 when she went to college, a car that had trouble from time to time with its linkages. I was not surprised when she telephoned, the morning of my birthday, to tell me that the Plymouth would not start and she couldn't come. Predictably I said, "I'll come and get you." It was only an hour and a half, and I loved sitting beside her talking on the drive back. As we approached the farm we came over a little rise, just a hundred and twenty yards south of the house—and I saw the cousin cars and pickups parked in our hayfield. Philippa and Jane had conspired to get me out of the house so the surprise party could assemble. It was a happy ritual of return and acceptance, as our neighbors and friends potlucked a party and chipped in to buy me a cardigan.

Then I discovered that I had become an adult-onset diabetic. Jane set out to become a diabetic cook. (Discouraged, I cooked little now; my recipes had started with two cups of olive oil.) I lost twenty-five pounds, paused, and lost twenty-five more pounds. My relative skinniness not only benefited my diabetes; I stopped having trick knees and lower-back spasms. I felt younger, with a new body, and I wanted to make further changes. For twelve years I had worn a large unkempt black beard, which fitted my old shape and not my new. I plotted shaving my beard. At Christmas both mothers were with us, and my two children. In the dead midmorning of Christmas—presents done, turkey cooking—I secreted myself in the bathroom carrying a paper bag with shaving equipment I had not used for a dozen years. I was nervous: You don't *have* to do this, I told myself. But I did it. I scissored off as much of my beard as I could, then lathered and scraped. After struggling for twenty minutes I gave up, with strange tufts of hair still deranging a shaved face. I opened the door and emerged. Only Philippa was in the living room. She screamed. Lucy rounded from the kitchen, and screamed. Polly screamed. Jane screamed. Only Andrew remained calm. My mother had hated beards, and for twelve years tried not to look at my face. For her the change was all good; for everyone else, as for me, the change was stunning and comical. No one in New Hampshire, except for cousins who remembered a very young face, was acquainted with the skin of my jaw. There were friends who refused to believe that it was me. (I showed ID.) At the other end of things, there were a few who noticed something different, but couldn't say just what it was.

One midmorning unscheduled lust overcame me, Jane reciprocated, and we enjoyed an impetuous moment on the sofa. It was so impetuous that we had neglected to take precautions—and Jane missed a period for the only time in her life before leukemia. For a few weeks we thought we were pregnant. Although Jane favored the legality of abortion, she would not have aborted her baby. In daydream and night dream, I found myself cheerful at the notion of our child. Jane did not. When she had been a girl in high school, before we knew each other—it had nothing to do with my age—she understood with clarity that she should have no children, and now, in night and day dreams, she continued to feel the same way. After she menstruated I had a vasectomy.

A recurrent pleasure of our return to Eagle Pond Farm was the sight of the farm's three daughters—Lucy, Caroline, Nan—reunited on the sofa in the house where they grew up. My mother drove up regularly from Connecticut. Nan lived with her husband Dick only seventeen miles away, and we frequently double-dated—a woman in her twenties and a man in his forties sitting with a couple in their sixties—laughing and drinking cocktails together in a vernacular restaurant halfway between our houses. Caroline and her husband Everett lived a little farther away, in southern New Hampshire. I always loved my Aunt Caroline, and when Jane had first been my student, I told her she made me think of Caroline. When they met, they took to each other. Caroline had MS. When she was diagnosed in her thirties, she had told her mother and her sisters, who fretted her by their attentions. Then her doctor told her that the initial diagnosis had been false, that she did not have MS; her family's relief removed a burden. When her doctor with embarrassed apologies reinstated the diagnosis, Caroline kept it to herself—except that she needed to tell someone, and she told me. Now and again I would see her walking stiffly, and I knew that she was losing sensation in her lower limbs. Then she would go into remission again. Shortly after I shaved my beard Everett called from Jaffrey. Caroline, who was seventy-seven, was in the hospital after a mild heart attack. I drove down to see her, revealing the skin of my face. (She was pleased for Lucy.) Caroline was skeptical of her illness: "I don't know about this heart business." It was the same as her father's—Wesley died at seventy-seven when a valve failed—and two days later Caroline died of a heart attack in her hospital bed. I mourned an icon of my childhood.

Then, in the natural way of things, losses continued. The old ladies of the church congregation died away, one face after another disappearing from the pews. Maybelle Wells, widow of my grandfather's brother Forrest, died late in her eighties. She and Jane had picked dandelion greens in the spring of 1976. Too soon afterward, unexpected and devastating, her daughter Edna died in her early seventies of a blood clot after surgery. We thought that Edna would live to be older than her mother, and we missed her. She worked at the Danbury elementary school, and was the soul of the church, warm and forthright and massively affectionate, politically a staunch Democrat islanded in a conservative Republican sea. Her widower Ansel still came to church, strangely alone, and we watched her daughter Bertha grow more and more to resemble Edna, and to take her place at the elementary school. Edna's cousin Audrey, and her sister Martha, who both taught Sunday school, sustained the gene pool and the church community.

Jack Jensen was not only minister but also friend. He and his wife Jo came to dinner; we drank Scotch and argued all night. Sometimes we partied with a third couple, the husband chairman of English at Colby-Sawyer College, where Jack taught religion and philosophy. Jack wrote his sermons on Saturday afternoons, useful if he was hung over the next morning. Then Jack, who was younger than I was, developed a tumor in his abdomen. There was an operation and chemotherapy. He lost his hair. I determined to shave my head but Jack spoiled my gesture by wearing an elegant wig. He preached sitting on a barstool, grew stronger again—and a year later the cancer returned. All night before he died Jane and Mary Lyn stood by his bed, repeating over and over, "Lord have

mercy upon us, Christ have mercy upon us, Lord have mercy upon us, and grant us Thy peace." At six in the morning Jane came home to bed, and I replaced her as Jack died. He was fifty-seven.

We kept busy improving our house. When we moved in, there was already indoor plumbing—water came to the kitchen from a gravity well just up Ragged—but we added an artesian well, because we brought to the house a dishwasher and a clothes washer. The bathroom was 1938 Sears, Roebuck. Earlier in the 1930s, when I visited the farm with my parents, we used a five-holer at the end of the woodshed, a good solution if you must have an outhouse because we could walk there under cover in the snows of winter, from kitchen through toolshed through woodshed. When the bathroom was installed next to the dining room, my grandfather never felt comfortable with it. There was something shameful about defecation inside the house. He continued to crouch under the barn, where he kept toilet paper, and night soil accumulated beside the mountain range of Holstein manure. For the rest of us, the 1938 bathroom served its purposes, but it was not well made or well placed. It was perpetually grimy, cold in winter, with pipes prone to freeze, and in summer populated by spiders. As soon as we moved in, Jane and I began to think about a new bathroom. We figured out what to do, but at first it was too expensive to undertake.

Our bedroom had been my grandparents' and my great-grandparents', fairly small and with no closets. It was in the northeast corner of the house, and a door led from it west to a bedroom beside it, which had been my room as a child and now became my study. We would make the old master bedroom into bathroom and laundry; we would extend a new bedroom, with closets, from the

north end of the house. The door from the living room, which led into our bedroom now, would begin a corridor to the new bedroom, my study opening to its left, the new bathroom to its right. Building it would cost five times as much money as we had in the bank.

Money was a concern. Until I went freelance, during years of academic salary and benefits, I took pleasure in knowing nothing about finance. I was thrifty but ignorant of savings, health insurance, and retirement. I read two newspapers a day and never glanced at a business section. The moment I went off salary, I bewildered myself daily with the *Boston Globe*'s financial pages. What did 401(k) mean? What was a mutual fund? Joyce Peseroff's husband Jeff is a financial adviser, and became Virgil to my Dante through money's inferno. Right away, he had me saving three hundred dollars a month, a hundred each in three mutual funds, whether I had three hundred or not. Annually I received two large checks from the sales of a textbook, and otherwise there were small sums from dozens of sources. (If you have fifty bosses you have no boss.) I read manuscripts for university presses; I edited poetry for *Harvard Magazine* and *Country Journal;* I wrote about Gertrude Stein's Ford roadsters for *Ford Times;* I did poetry readings; I edited *The Oxford Book of American Literary Anecdotes;* I wrote book reviews for the *New York Times Book Review,* the *National Review,* the *Nation,* the *Atlantic,* the *Boston Globe,* the *TLS;* I wrote children's books; I wrote for the sports section of the *New York Times,* for *Sports Illustrated,* for *Playboy,* and for *Esquire;* I wrote pieces for *Yankee;* I published poems in *The New Yorker;* I collected essays on poetry into books that paid small royalties. Nothing but my textbook *Writing Well* produced much reward, but many small checks accumulated enough income for comfort— interrupted occasionally by panic. There were tuitions to pay, as

well as taxes and a mortgage. When the offer of a contract coincided with a panic, I contracted to do a thousand-page three-genre literature text.

One afternoon my cousins Paul and Bertha Fenton came calling. Paul was my grandfather's nephew, a little younger than my mother, and resembled my grandfather more than anyone else I knew. Like Wesley, Paul loved to tell stories. When a grin spread on Paul's face, you knew he had remembered a story. Paul had been a farmer, with a herd of registered Holsteins that his son Dennis continued to milk. He had been a schoolteacher, and as a stout Democrat he had also taken political jobs; for a while he ran the county farm for Merrimack County. Sitting on our sofa, a Sunday afternoon, he grinned and started, "Did you ever hear the one about the fellow, lived around here, every year in the fall he loaded up his ox cart with what the farm made or grew all year, and . . ." The man with the ox cart walked by his animal's head to Portsmouth Market and sold everything out of the cart ". . . and then he sold his ox, and then he walked home." When Paul delivered the kicker—ox cart sold, man hiking home to begin the cycle again—I felt the familiar spine-tingling which means that a story or a phrase has struck deep. The next day, elated by the notion of human life rounded like a perennial plant, I began a poem called "Ox-Cart Man." When I had finished it, ten months later, I had the notion that if I told the same story in different words, and with the help of an illustrator, Paul's tale would make a picture book for small children. I asked Paul's permission to steal his story, and wrote the children's book quickly. Harper and Row (my chief publisher then) instantly rejected it, and my agent sent it to the Viking Press, which instantly bought it. Viking asked if Barbara Cooney would do as an illustrator. She would do, and she did, and a couple of years later *Ox-Cart Man* was published in an edition of twenty thousand in September. By the end of the year it had sold most of the first printing. In January Viking got word that the American Library Association was awarding *Ox-Cart Man* the Caldecott Medal (for the year's best children's picture book)—and ordered a second printing of sixty thousand copies. The next summer we had our new bedroom, and our old bedroom became our new bathroom and laundry, with a little plaque over the doorway: CALDE-COTT ROOM.

My cousin Forrest was carpenter, who had earlier fixed up the kitchen, installed bookshelves, and rebuilt the woodshed. The new bedroom was bright, windows on three sides, closets, sweater drawers, and a floor of pine planks a yard wide. When the house extended itself another twenty feet north, the addition left an area shielded from the road. Ragged Mountain had sloped down to the house, sometimes flooding the rootcellar, and Jane came up with the notion of bulldozing this area flat, using stones from the rootcellar to build a retaining wall at the foot of the hill. She created a hidden garden, and planted the hillside with bulbs, and laid bricks for a patio. We set chairs outside and in summer sat in privacy, reading and taking supper.

Upstairs was a bedroom that my grandmother had called "the best room"—big, with large northern windows, from the 1803 part of the house. Her brother Luther used it when he slept at the house. Twenty-two years older than his sister, a widower and a minister retired back home from Connecticut, Luther lived mostly in a small cottage down Route 4. If he needed his sister's care, he walked uphill to the farm where he had been a boy—and slept in the best room, because ministers deserved the best, on a remarkable double bed he brought with him from Connecticut. This bed is a dark brown with floral designs painted on it in black and gold, with bees and peacocks and an owl and a dragonfly—and the legend *Sleep Balmy Sleep*. Jane and I marveled at the bed's eccentric beauty, but it would not do for sleeping in, because it caved vastly into its middle. Then one December when I was on the road Jane spirited it away to a cabinetmaker, and presented me for Christmas a rebuilt, comfortable, painted bed for two, which became our bed. Jane died there.

My diabetes remained mild and controlled without great difficulty, no problems with kidneys or circulation or eyesight. Early on, however, I developed a symptom that was not mortal but heavy. Thirty percent of males with adult-onset diabetes become impotent. (The word is used for different conditions. I was orgasmic but could not sustain an erection.) At first I was intermittent and then I was no longer intermittent. We made alternative love, and Jane was kind, but she was not content with our curtailment—a monogamous woman in her thirties for whom lovemaking was primary. At this time it was well known—to internists, to psychologists—that impotence in a fifty-year-old man was psychological ninety percent of the time and physical only ten percent. (Shortly it would become known that the percentages were in fact reversed.) Out of vanity and shame, I did not speak of my condition to my doctor; maybe it would go away. Then our doctor during a general examination idly asked Jane about her sex life. She burst into tears and told him. I saw him the next day and he sent me to a psychotherapist. The condition persisted, and our dejection. Then I read a magazine article in which a surgeon spoke of physical causes for impotence, and of surgical solutions. My doctor consulted a urologist who said, yes, there were many physical causes—for instance, was I diabetic? I saw the urologist, who tested me and confirmed that my trouble was physical—almost certainly a result of diabetes. He told me about penile implants. Together, Jane and I visited the urologist and pondered choices among prostheses. There was a gadget by which one could pump up an erection; we decided to avoid movable parts. A different device left a permanent hard-on—but the penis could swivel down, so that it would not stick out and be embarrassing. I arranged for an operation to insert a bionic erection—general anesthesia, incision, insertion of stainless steel surrounded by plastic—in January of 1985. The first days were painful, and for two weeks I felt jittery, perpetually on edge. A permanent hard-on is nerve-racking; it feels like a permanent hard-on. A couple of weeks after the procedure, we assayed a first, tentative use . . . a second, a third, a fourth, fifth sixth seventh eighth. For the rest of her life, Jane said, "Perkins, what you did for me!" In vain did I insist that I did it not only for her. For the impotent period of middle life, I had lived in a steady gray mild (compared to Jane) depression, and my poems turned passive, accepting or welcoming old age. I quoted Meister Eckhart's "repose" like a mantra. Now, prosthetic manliness brought vigor back to my poems. I was able to finish *The One Day.* Surgery benefited Jane's poetry as it did mine; our use of the implant relieved her melancholy for hours.

But Jane's depression was chronic. We flailed about to improve the conditions she labored under. We put in central heat, with an oil furnace in the rootcellar, and we could leave the house in winter without hiring a sitter to tend the stoves. I missed the routine of feeding the fires, a break in the writing routine, a time to stretch and do a minimal chore. (Something always told me when a stove needed attention, the way a mother knows her baby is about to cry for milk.) I swore I would keep on burning wood and then didn't. The house's thermostat decorated a wall directly across from the living room Glenwood, so that if I kept a fire there, the rest of the house became frigid. And our new routine had its charms. Before, I had waked at five to clean ashes out of the stoves that burned overnight, fill them up with wood, and open the drafts. Now a touch of the thermostat and the house was quickly warm. I missed minding the stoves but liked my comfort, and liked getting earlier to the desk.

After Jane's father died, Polly had stayed on in the Ann Arbor house as long as she could, on Social Security and savings. Then she sold the house on a land contract that gave her a few years of income. She settled in a small Ann Arbor condominium for a while, as she grew older and arthritic. Late in the 1980s it became clear that she could no longer afford the condo. Jane looked for housing near us and found an apartment in Wilmot Flat. We drove to Ann Arbor, helped her pack up, and moved her to New Hampshire, Jane driving Polly's Ford while I went ahead to await the moving van. In New Hampshire Polly thrived—attending church, shopping with her daughter.

Late in the 1980s, Jane spent two weeks in the Soviet Union, a group tour sponsored by Bridges for Peace. Her general love for Russian literature, as well as her years of work on Akhmatova, drew her to visit the country. On the tour the group would meet Soviet citizens and spend a week in Estonia. (Six months later, Estonians visited us in New Hampshire.) Jane was thrilled by the prospect of her trip, but I dreaded the notion of two weeks in an empty house. Even when Jane went off on a poetry reading, I felt restless and moody. Therefore I came up with the idea that I would visit London while she traveled in Russia. I could see old Oxford friends. I could go to the theater and to museums. I arrived in England the day Jane flew to Moscow, and immediately collapsed into depression. I did not telephone anyone. I walked out on a Maggie Smith play after the first act. I lay down to read a book and after two pages stood up to take a walk. I walked a block and returned to my hotel room and a novel I could not attend to. After two weeks of relentless boredom and melancholy, I flew home the day Jane did. As I heard her stories from Russia, I suddenly burst into tears. I was hurt that she had gone without me. She was surprised, taken aback; what had she done wrong? She looked down, without speaking, and, after a pause, quietly said, "I am cold, like my mother." Jane was not cold, but she was less needy than I was. In most marriages I have known, the husbands have been needier than their wives.

Early and late, we had small social life. Cocktail parties and dinner parties were rare. On occasion, social events at Dartmouth sent us home happy to be away from a university. Ann Arbor visited us not only in old friends, but also in the shape of Jane's family. Her brother Reuel, her sister-in-law and old roommate Dawn, and her niece Bree made annual summer visits, staying in the cottage down the road, which we had bought—the only house we could see from our place. My children visited, in early years coming from school or college, then with friends of the opposite sex, then with spouses, eventually with babies. Five years apart in age, my children had their first children four days apart. Emily Hall was born in New York on July 30, 1988, Allison Smith on August 3 in New Hampshire. It took us a week to get to Manhattan. We encountered Allison when she was two hours old. I took a roll of photographs, daughter with daughter's daughter, and was much too impatient for one-hour developing. I rushed out of Concord Hospital, bought a Polaroid, and rushed back. I took the camera to Manhattan and photographed Emily. Then my son's family moved from New York to Massachusetts, and it was easy to spend days with both families. We studied infant character as the babies developed and acquired language. Ariana Hall was born, Abigail Smith, and Peter Hall. Jane, who had not wanted to be a mother, held babies on her shoulder. She made clothespin dolls and played games with little children. I had written, long before, that I wanted to live in this house as "somebody's grandfather." Somebody became five children, and their presence on visits—they loved exploring the old house: spinning wheels of their ancestors, highchairs more than a century old—rounded the circle of my life as I entered old age.

Eleven Days

On April 11, 1995, Gussie greeted us with enthusiasm when we returned from the hospital, then turned quickly doleful. I helped Jane to bed. On the wall of our bedroom was a sampler that Alice Mattison had stitched: "You're going to live!" (Alice had said so on the telephone; Jane told her: "Work that in cross-stitch, would you?" Alice worked it in cross-stitch.) Seeing it now, I erupted in bitterness, "I'm going to take Alice's sampler down!" Jane said quietly, "No. No. Leave it there."

As soon as Jane was in bed, I took the phone off the hook. I could not bear the notion of someone calling to ask how we were doing. I would wait until night to make the calls. I threw away Jane's medicines. I lay down beside her and we held each other. From time to time I cried and Jane did not. She lay thinking, thinking. She told me that she did not fear punishment when she died. I could not answer, "But we will love each other in Paradise!" Dying, she could not affirm an afterlife as she had done in "Notes from the Other Side."

That afternoon remains in my memory, interminable and timeless, as if it were a dream I dreamed this morning. "What will happen to Perkins?" Jane said and briefly wept. I told her that my children and our grandchildren would be loving and tender, that our friends would look after me, that I would remain in our house with our animals. In the mail came a writers' magazine with a photograph of the two of us on the cover, and the joint interview conducted two years before in Virginia, when the AWP had performed my rites. We rose from bed midafternoon to watch one last movie, and fittingly it was the worst movie ever committed. Our cherished auteur Mel Brooks starred in a hideous aberration called *Life Stinks*.

In the next few days, I concentrated on being there—to look at, to touch—yet otherwise tried as hard as I could to let her go, because I knew (from her poems as well as from common sense) that my anguish to hold on to her could do nothing but cause more pain. When she was still fully present she lost herself to wild grief on only two occasions. Once she said, "Dying is nothing, but . . . *the separation!*"—and howled. Another time, I think Friday morning, I was talking about things we had done together. I talked about our trips, excursions to England and Italy, months in India. I talked about the more important things—summer afternoons by the pond, ping-pong, reading Henry James aloud, driving to Connecticut while we listened to tapes of T. S. Eliot and Geoffrey Hill. I talked about twenty years of writing poetry together. Then I spoke of lovemaking on this bed. Her face convulsed. "No more fucking!" she wailed. "No more fucking!"

Jane told me things that she had been planning to tell me, if this moment should arrive. She wanted her papers to go to the University of New Hampshire, where mine reside. We spoke of what we would do in the days remaining: We would choose poems for her posthumous new-and-selected poems, write her obituary together, and plan her funeral. She told me where, in her workroom, I would find copies of the poems she had finished since *Constance*. I brought them downstairs, together with photocopies of poems from her books—I had already assembled them—so that we could begin work tomorrow on the posthumous volume. Late afternoon Linda Lucas parked in the drive, to help Jane recover the use of her hands. I met her at the door and sent her away weeping. Tomorrow, Carole Colburn would come to clean and I would tell her the news—she and Jane were fond of each other—but today was not a time for unnecessary announcements. It was a time for long thoughts and few words. I ate a sandwich when irrelevant hunger overtook me. Out of one long thoughtful silence I heard Jane say: "We did the right thing. I would do it again."

The brutal day elapsed. I made myself supper. Jane felt hunger and swallowed something to ease it, though eating was ironic. She was ready to sleep early, and I tucked her in by six-thirty and turned out her lights and went to sit in my living room chair. Every few minutes I walked to the bedroom to hear her breathe. I did not want to call anyone until I had told my son and daughter, and I did not want to call them until they had put their children to bed. I read over letters that I had dictated the day before and added postscripts. I dictated new letters for typing the next day, writing people whom I would not telephone. Then I picked up the phone and broke the news to Andrew and Philippa: *Jane is going to die.* In mini-denial I changed "a month or so" to "a month or two." Their long anxiety, softened after Seattle, ascended to anguish. (The next day, when the grandchildren heard, each wanted us to go back to Seattle. "Seattle" had become the redemptive place.) I told poor Joyce. I left a message for Alice to call me. Alice heard my message, feared the sound of my voice, and dialed Joyce to hear the news. I told Caroline. Everyone began planning a last goodbye. I could not reach Jane's brother and family, who had no answering machine. I called them at six-thirty the next morning, and they made reservations to fly to her bedside.

When Jane woke we began work on her book. Her mind was alert and concentrated. She drank and ate a little; she could still walk. I faxed driving directions to Letha, who would pay a house call. For two hours or more, Jane and I attended to *Otherwise*. I suggested the title, after the poem she wrote when I was supposed to die. There were more new poems than she had remembered, including a small, beautiful poem I had never seen, "In the Nursing Home," about my mother at ninety. "I didn't think that little thing amounted to anything," she said. When I read it aloud she changed her mind. I suggested an order for her new poems, beginning with "Happiness" and ending with "Reading Aloud to My Father." Of the twenty new poems, fourteen had not gone out to magazines, many of them revised or finished during her brief patch of work in May and June the year before. I asked her where I should send them. She wanted me to show them to Alice Quinn at *The New Yorker*, who had long admired her work, to Peter Davison at the *Atlantic*, to Joseph Parisi at *Poetry*, and to Liam Rector, who had succeeded me as poetry editor at *Harvard Magazine*. The next day I faxed fourteen poems to Alice Quinn, with a note about the circumstances.

We agreed on the order of the twenty new poems. Then we would print selections from her four published volumes, from the earliest to the most recent. I made a preliminary choice among these volumes, because I remembered the poems Jane had come to dislike. I read aloud the titles of poems I suggested including. Sometimes when I said a title she would say no, not that one; I would read it aloud, and argue with her. If she persisted I stopped arguing, but with a few poems my advocacy persuaded her to keep them in. From her first book I wanted her to print "Cages," a love poem out of our early marriage, but she was adamant: "Puppy love," she said. When we had gone through the poems I tentatively selected, we went over the poems I tentatively omitted. We restored one or two. Eight years separated *From Room to Room* from its successor, *The Boat of Quiet Hours*, the first book published by Graywolf. With this second volume it became harder to leave poems out. We dropped some because they were small, others because they bore resemblance to later poems that were better. During these eight years Jane had completed her study of Keats and her apprenticeship-by-translation to Anna Akhmatova. When we finished the selection from *Boat* we started on *Let Evening Come,* and midway through this book Jane was overcome by devastating fatigue. We had to stop.

Now the florists' vans began to pull into the driveway. Lilies arrived, tulips, roses, bouquets that were tight and hard, bouquets that were lavish and gorgeous. I had faxed the news to a friend in Bombay, and flowers arrived from Indian friends. In Jane's journal, when she trained to be a hospice worker in 1981, she answered questions put by her teacher. She had been asked: What would you want to do in your last days if you knew you were dying? In 1981 she wrote that she would want flowers about her, but the reality was opposite. Flowers were a major adhesion to the world Jane was leaving. She would not look at them. When I brought them into the bedroom, she had me take them away. Soon the kitchen and the dining room were overrun by cities of petal and bloom. She would not look at flowers nor allow me to play her favorite CDs. These things tied her to what she had to part from. In "Reading Aloud to My Father," she told how her father, dying, asked her to turn off a Chopin piano concerto.

Letha came to visit, this day or the next. Charles Solow came. Each time someone dear came calling, I left the bedroom so her visitors could remain alone with her. She could not endure long visits. She napped, and I sat or lay beside her. On the telephone I scheduled farewells. On Thursday, when Jane had bathed with Jean's help and taken a little nourishment, she seemed too tired to work again on *Otherwise.* I said, "Let's not try to do it today. Let's wait until you feel stronger." (Why would I think she would feel stronger?) "No," said Jane. "We'll do it now. We'll do it now." She was right. We did it now, as her body started to desert her. She was eating little, and the leukemia permitted less and less oxygen to reach her brain. She still walked to the bathroom and showered, but her thin limbs grew thinner. On Maundy Thursday we finished choosing the poems for *Otherwise,* and agreed that I would show the manuscript for approval to Alice and Joyce. What if they differed with the omissions Jane had made? I suggested that each of the friends could add one poem that Jane had omitted, and she liked the idea, which made her closest friends part of the process of selection. I had a further thought: We both knew that "The Sick Wife" was unfinished, that if she had lived she would have revised the poem. I asked her, "If I can find a way to print it as an unfinished poem, and say so, may I print it?" She thought hard and said yes. When I wrote the Afterword to her posthumous book I found the place to speak of "The Sick Wife" and to print it, so that Jane's words ended the volume.

While Jane slept I drafted an obituary, working from her vita. My assistant put it on the computer, and Friday Jane and I worked it over. Jane wanted to be sure that the Guggenheim was mentioned. In the manner of essay writers I put the Guggenheim at the climactic end of a paragraph, but I had forgotten the manner of newspapers. When the *New York Times* needed to cut a line, Jane's Guggenheim went unmentioned. That she had been named poet laureate of New Hampshire meant little to Jane, but the label would mean something to newspapers. I called Jane Poet Laureate at the top of the notice. As the obituary was reprinted throughout the East, and sporadically through the rest of the country, it was headed by varieties of POET LAUREATE OF NEW HAMPSHIRE DIES. The next day, and the next, we continued to revise the obituary. When she handed it back to me at the last, no further corrections, she said, "Wasn't that fun, working together?"

We worked together on plans for her funeral. Attention to details of her death distracted us for a moment from her death. With a copy of the hymnal she chose four hymns that she loved. For recitation she picked Psalm 139: "If I take the wings of the morning, and dwell in the uttermost parts of the sea, even there shall thy hand lead me, and thy right hand shall hold me." We decided to ask Alice Ling to sing one of the hymns a cappella. I would ask Liam to read aloud "Let Evening Come" and "Otherwise." I asked Jane how we should dress her for the coffin. She said she hadn't thought; did I have a notion? I did. "The white salwar kameez," I said, a silk she had bought in Pondicherry, in September of 1993, product of Sri Aurobindo's ashram. She had worn it in a photograph taken in Allahabad, when we had breakfasted in a rich man's garden. She had worn it at the Plaza, the November following, at the National Book Awards dinner. "Oh, that's good," she said, "yes." I did not tell her when I first conceived the idea. It was a year before, after seeing my mother in the coffin at Chadwick's, that I had flashed a waking dream of Jane in her coffin—and she was wearing her white salwar kameez.

Later that day—because Jane had spoken about working together—I brought her a poem of my own again, the last time I would do it. As I read the poem aloud to her that afternoon, she screwed her face up in concentration. I was asking a lot but I was right to ask it. She listened, thought, nodded her head twice, and said, "There's something left out. There's something you haven't said." She was right. Four or five months later, following her direction, I discovered what was missing and supplied it, to finish that poem. Meanwhile the planner inside me still needed to plan. At one point I shot forth, "I know what I'll do! When Gussie dies I'll have him cremated and put his ashes on your grave." As quickly as I spoke, she answered with enthusiasm, "That will be good for the daffodils!" Then she pulled back from our bizarre dialogue and laughed. "Perkins, what will you think of next?" But I had my instructions. The next autumn Alice Goodman and Geoffrey Hill and I planted dozens of bulbs, from Jane's White Flower Farm, over the double plot of our graves.

After a nap I sat with her and we talked. She fretted again about what would happen to me. I was not then dwelling on my own fate; there would be the rest of my life for that. I dwelt on the dying present to avoid the dead future. We told each other that we loved each other. Now and then I howled, but I did not beg her to stay alive. We had done her book and her obituary, planned her funeral, and chosen what she would wear in the coffin. We would follow the tradition of calling hours, the night before the funeral, when friends and neighbors could see her body in its coffin at Chadwick's. We agreed that her coffin would be closed at the funeral in the South Danbury Christian Church. There were people we loved who would have been upset by the open coffin.

This weekend Philippa and Jerry would visit; Andrew would come on Monday. Later in the week Alice and Edward would drive up, Liam and Tree, Joyce, and Caroline. A visiting nurse came by, and Jean Frey twice a day. I made a note to call Joseph Parisi at *Poetry* on Monday. In Jane's obituary we were listing the annual award *Poetry* gave her two years before, but we could not remember its name. Jane and I discussed the disposition of her estate—so much to her brother and family, so much to my children, the rest to me. It was a small estate, an IRA and some mutual funds, which she had assembled from poetry readings and magazine publications. Jeff White, our financial adviser for almost twenty years, read over Jane's will and found a tactical error in it. When Jane and I made our wills, we assumed Jane would survive her elderly husband, and paid small attention to the possibility of her dying first. In the wording of her will, some of Jane's estate would be tax-able by the State of New Hampshire, taxes that an expedient could avoid. Working quickly with Jeff, our attorney drafted a new will, which arrived by fax on Friday afternoon. Saturday morning a branch of the Lake Sunapee Bank opened next to the Kearsarge Mini-Mart, where we pumped gas and bought skim milk. While Jean stayed with Jane, I went to the bank to see if the manager could notarize the new will. Even she, whom I knew only to nod to, knew what was happening. She told me I could bring Jane at any moment, and she would recruit witnesses from the Mini-Mart. Back home Jane put on her wig one last time and I bundled her into warm slippers and a winter coat over her sweats. She leaned on my arm to step down from the kitchen, and rode the wheelchair to the car. I settled her in the new car, stowed wheelchair in trunk, and drove her the two familiar miles. Outside the bank I brought the wheelchair to the car door while the manager solicited wit-nesses. I pushed Jane to the desk. Two women whom we had known for years, with whom we had joshed while buying bananas, stood on either side of the chair. Jane took minutes to sign her name. It was silent in the little room, filled with dolor as the three women watched a fourth sign her name. No one seemed awkward or frightened. I thought of the young man at the Honda dealer-ship, just the Monday before, who could not look in Jane's face.

Home again, I resumed my station beside the bed. Friends wanted to talk with Jane, but she felt too tired and found it hard to hold the phone or to raise her voice. Jeff White sent us a speaker phone by FedEx, but by the time it arrived Jane no longer spoke. I think it was later on Saturday when she first had trouble with speech. She would miss a word, search and search but not find it.

Once she said, clearly and straight out, "I have something important to tell you." I waited. She said, "I want . . ." and she lay staring upward, fiercely concentrating, searching the word, "I want . . . I want . . ." until at last she blurted out "spinach"—and shook her head disgustedly from side to side. It was not spinach she wanted. I questioned, "Something to eat?" A shake of the head. "Are you thirsty?" I would never learn what it was, important, that she had to tell me.

Because her failure to find the word annoyed her, she chose mostly not to speak. I tried to avoid asking questions that required her to make reply. Since I needed constantly to say "I love you," I learned to add, "And I know you love me too." The effort to speak, and the failure, bothered her more than her pain did. She felt bone pain still, and neuropathies, and maybe the pain of shingles, but I had grown accustomed over fifteen months to gauging the degree of her pain. On a scale of one to ten, her pain looked no worse than a three. She continued to swallow morphine, MS Contin, as long as she could swallow. Then an infusion service strapped a morphine needle to her left thigh. When she made a moaning sound I pressed the bolus.

Saturday Philippa and Jerry came to say goodbye, and Jane could speak a little. Philippa was incapacitated by grief, and incapacity was appropriate: There was nothing to say. We could only have accepted: *Hold everything! There's a cure!* Or: *Sure Evidence of Afterlife!* Jane lay pale and silent and terminal, flesh dropping away and the strong facial bones struck in increasing relief. She looked like her mother Polly, when Philippa had visited Polly in the New London Hospital only two months before. Philippa and Jerry and Jane sat and looked at each other. Philippa held Jane's hand. They spoke in fragments of Allison and Abigail, left with a sitter. It would have been terrible for the children to visit her now.

Sunday was Easter. Alice Ling and her husband stopped on the way to church. We prayed and Alice made communion for us all, using bread she had baked. It was Jane's last communion, because when Alice returned later in the week Jane could no longer swallow. Monday was our twenty-third wedding anniversary. Jane told me to look on the back stairs, which led to her workroom, for a box from L. L. Bean. By telephone she had ordered me a braided belt, but she had ordered by my dimensions of fifteen years earlier, when my waist was six inches bigger. Quietly, in the distant toolshed, I pounded a nail through the braid to make a new hole. I showed her the lavender summer dress I had ordered her from Texas, then put it back in its box. She said it was pretty. Flowers arrived. Casseroles appeared on the porch. The phone rang. Andrew left work in Boston and drove to see us late in the afternoon. On Thursday he and his family would fly to Texas, a long-arranged reunion of Natalie's people. We would talk every day while he was gone and he would fly back at any moment when I needed him. He and his family would return on Monday the twenty-fourth. It was becoming clear that Jane would die soon. I made a note in my Day-Timer that we should not bury her until Tuesday the twenty-fifth at the earliest, and I knew that we would avoid Thursday the twenty-seventh because it would be Abigail's third birthday. Maybe Tuesday or Wednesday for the funeral, I planned as I gazed into her living eyes.

Andrew sat with Jane for as much as half an hour, the two of them alone together, speaking little, Jane moving into sleep and out again. I assembled something from the baskets of food that neighbors brought, and Andrew and I ate supper holding plates on our knees by the bed. When I finished eating I remembered my insulin shot, which I normally took before supper, and hoisted myself to announce my purpose. Jane's eyes were closed as Andrew admonished me: "You've got to take care of yourself." Jane opened her eyes and made the thumbs-up sign. When Andrew left—he told me later—he walked for an hour by the pond before driving home. At home he wrote Jane a letter on his computer which he faxed the next morning. Jane asked me to read it aloud many times.

Tuesday morning Liam and Tree drove up from Somerville. They brought their little dog Kenyon with them. We gathered in the bedroom, and Tree asked Jane if she had notions for the cover of *Otherwise,* which Tree would design. Haltingly, Jane said that she knew the painting she wanted—but she could not remember the name of the painter or the painting or the title of the book in which she had found it. She let us know that the book was in the living room. Because she no longer walked, I brought the wheelchair to her bedside and helped her into it. I wheeled her down the corridor into our living room for the last time. She pointed to *The Impressionist Garden,* on the floor beside a bookshelf where I had piled it after unpacking our Seattle boxes. Someone—I cannot remember who it was—had sent her the book at Christmas. I remembered Jane leafing through it while she sat on her big soft Seattle chair, saying that she had found the painting she wanted for her next cover. Now I trolled through the book slowly, holding it in front of her eyes until her hand reached forward and stopped my hand. She had found *Le Jardin Potager, Yerres* by Gustave Caillebotte, and when I saw it I remembered it. Thus Jane contributed to the design of *Otherwise.* When Tree went home with *The Impressionist Garden,* she worked as rapidly as she could to draft the cover, hoping that Jane might live to see it. Tree brought a mockup to the funeral eight days later.

When Liam and Tree departed they parked by the pond and walked there for an hour, just as Andrew had done the day before.

In the afternoon Philippa brought Reuel and Dawn and Bree from the Manchester Airport, and popped into the bedroom before leaving Jane with her family. Jane spoke more easily for a moment. Her family would stay at Polly's old apartment, which we were still renting, three months after Polly's death, because no one had been able to clear it out. Dawn and Bree had return reservations in a week, and Reuel would stay on, emptying his mother's flat.

Wednesday was hard, because Jane was conscious but rapidly declining. The catheter in her side, which still collected bile from the gallbladder operation, leaked on the bed. I made a telephone call; a visiting nurse pulled the tube out and bandaged the hole. Mary Lyn Ray visited. Joyce and Jeff visited. Letha telephoned. Kris Doney and Carolyn Stormer called from Seattle. That night and early Thursday were the hardest time. In the dark I woke continually to hear Jane struggling out of bed. Incontinent, she was trying to reach the commode beside her. Each time I pulled up her nightgown and set her on the commode, she raised her arms around my neck as I embraced and lifted her, and murmured, "Mama, Mama." I wiped her, helped her into a clean nightgown, and set dry pads over the wet sheets. At six she was sleeping and I rose to feed Gus and Ada. When I returned she had left her bed and was sitting in a chair across the room. I was terrified that she would fall—she could not stand up without my help, yet she had crossed the bedroom—and break a limb and cause herself more pain. In sudden panic I determined that I could not handle her; she would have to go to the hospital. I called Letha at her house, who told me she would arrange for the room, and I should call the ambulance. I made a quick list of things to pack. Jean Frey arrived and I told her what I had done and why. She offered to pick up pads that morning; we could keep Jane diapered. Still panicked, I thought only of Jane falling and breaking a bone. She woke, making sense, and I told her I was calling an ambulance and Letha was arranging a bed at Hitchcock. For the first time in days I saw her face screw up with tears. "Do we have to?" she said in sorrow. Instantly I converted: "No!" I said. "No!" I called Letha, apologizing, and she calmly canceled the bed. In the last days it was the only time I lost my wits.

Jane never left her bed again, or tried to. Jean Frey changed the bedsheets and brought pads from the VNA. Once when Jean was in attendance, I drove away for twenty minutes—to buy some milk or juice—and when I came back Jean told me that Jane thought in my absence that I was dead. I didn't leave her again, except to piss or make a sandwich—and if I left her side I announced what I was doing. I think she understood me; speaking goes first and seeing next (she never asked for her glasses now), but hearing continues until close to the end. Late Thursday afternoon, Alice and Edward Mattison arrived and Alice spent time alone with Jane. They stayed nearby overnight and Alice returned early Friday morning. When she did, Jean was giving Jane a sponge bath in bed, and Alice helped to hold her up while Jean washed Jane's back. "It's not much fun, is it?" said Alice, and Jane said "No," her only word. After Alice left, Caroline Finkelstein arrived, driving up from the Cape. Jane knew she was there. When Caroline drove home she was ticketed for speeding, the wages of rage. At noon as I prepared to leave Jane for a minute, I said to her, loud and clear, "I'm going to put these letters in the box." She answered, in a matter-of-fact tone, as if speech were no problem, "Okay." Such as it was, it was Jane's last word.

Friday afternoon a fax arrived from Alice Quinn at *The New Yorker:* She would buy four of the new poems. Jane did not respond; I think she heard me. When the mail came, I read her letters from friends. Bill Moyers, who had already written her longhand, sent by FedEx a bound galley of *The Language of Life* with its full-page picture of Jane. I held it up before her. Now her hands emerged from the covers and remained clenched at the level of her ears. Many years ago a friend had given Jane a china figurine, a Greek goddess whose hands were clenched and raised where they must once have held a spear or staff. The friend said the goddess made her think of Jane, and now Jane's clenched, raised hands resembled the goddess's. Jane's breathing altered into a Cheyne-Stokes rhythm. She took three short breaths, a pause, and then a deep breath, her breathing controlled by the surviving stem of the brain. Late afternoon Letha Mills drove down from Dartmouth-Hitchcock after her long week. She took Jane's pulse and bustled about. There was nothing she could do for Jane, but her presence itself was a comfort; she said Jane knew she was there.

After the Cheyne-Stokes breathing started, we knew it would not be long. Jean Frey, changing Jane again, offered to spend the night, but I wanted to be alone with Jane. "Perkins, be with me when I die." I sat beside her, alone with her, watching her chest in its rhythmic heaves. Now and then, I touched her upraised fists. Her hands and her face were pale white and cool. Her big face had always been strong in its bones—chin, cheekbones, nose—and now that she had so little flesh, her bones pushed themselves forth like an abstracted line drawing and exaggerated her features. Her wide brown eyes seemed bigger than ever; she did not blink. Rarely, one of her clenched fists flicked in the direction of her face; just in case, I scratched her nose. In the darkness of eight o'clock, I leaned over her to kiss her once more, a light or fleeting kiss, and was astonished when her lips puckered and budged to peck me back. I don't believe that a peck is autonomic.

All night I slept in fits, twenty-minute naps lying beside her in our old bed, from which I woke checking that she still breathed:

three short breaths, a pause, and a long breath. In the morning I woke and dressed beside her. Then Jane's breathing altered again, from the Cheyne-Stokes rhythm to a series of rapid pants. I remembered sitting beside my grandmother Kate, dying at ninety-seven, when the quick panting began. I watched Jane's chest move, shallow breaths, and never took my eyes away. Motion stopped. No pulse, no breath. With my thumbs I pulled down the lids of her brown eyes.

Postscript 2005

THE MORNING after the funeral, I woke early. I picked up the *Globe* at the store and, instead of returning home, drove two miles farther to the graveyard. It was six o'clock, the hour at which for twenty years I poured Jane a cup of coffee to set beside her bed so that she could entice herself awake by the aroma. Today it was as if I brought coffee to her grave. When I stood there in the dawn twilight, I saw something I had missed the night before. In the middle of the oblong of fresh earth, set there as if on purpose, was a bright penny. I picked it up and put it in my shirt pocket.

Thus began the after life. I had a task, because it was April 27, my granddaughter Abigail's third birthday. After lunch I drove to Concord to look for presents. A month earlier, before we knew Jane would die, Abigail had spoken of a piggy bank. At Toys R Us I found a huge hideous pink plastic pig with a slit in its spine and dropped into it the penny I found that morning. I drove to my daughter's house in Concord on South Main. Allison, who was six, hugged me but could not speak; Philippa and I wept together. I gave Abigail her store-wrapped packages, and she liked best a mechanical horse called High Stepper, Barbie's mount, with a mane both platinum and insanely long. I found batteries in the glove box of my car, and High Stepper stepped high for enraptured Abigail. She shook her piggy bank, smiling, and rattled the single penny. I gave Philippa the ring that Jane named Please Don't Die when I gave it to her on our wedding anniversary, a year earlier at

256

leukemia's onset. Dying, Jane had wanted me to give it to Philippa, but I should have waited until later; I was not in my right mind.

Everything I did, those first weeks and months, I did deliberately, with lunatic clarity and without judgment. Before driving home that day, for no reason, I visited the new Concord Wal-Mart. I pushed a cart around and bought nothing. *Who am I and what am I doing here?* When I turned the cart into one aisle I suddenly wept. It was office supplies—pads and pens, Post-its, clasped envelopes—writerly objects that Jane and I had given each other as tokens of affection. When I returned from a trip, I might bring Jane a package of fancy striped paper clips; when Jane came back from a poetry reading, she might hand me a lined pad with Elvis on the cover. Driving home from Wal-Mart, I suffered the onslaught of a new emotion; I felt intense, overwhelming, permeating shame. I remember it still, the way one remembers certain nightmares. I drowned under shame's ocean, crying and heartsick as I drove up I-93. No thought or recollection set me off. What did I feel shame for? For letting her die? It reminded me of one thing only: waking in the morning, twenty-five years earlier in Michigan, desolate between marriages; I had been drunk the night before, and knew I had done something unspeakable but had no notion of what I had done.

For the next years I lived a scattery and hectic life, full of misadventure, content only when I wrote Jane grieving letter-poems. I talked about her to everyone I met, and to a dog. I paced; I screamed; I went to the grave four times a day. The public response to Jane's death pleased and distracted me. There were celebrations of her life and work in Boston, New York, and Minneapolis. *Otherwise* went into printing after printing, followed by a collection of Jane's prose.

Today, ten years after her death, her poems endure. So do I, still at Eagle Pond Farm, where Jane fills the air around me like a rainy day. Her handwriting labels jars of spices and lists telephone numbers. I fry Italian sausage in her skillet and boil spaghetti in her saucepan and drain it in her colander. I look at her photographed face as I move from room to room. But I no longer howl; rarely do I weep. I drive to her grave only when I introduce her to a visitor. I show the polished black marble of her monument, incised with lines Jane wrote in 1992 when she anticipated my death:

> I BELIEVE IN THE MIRACLES OF ART BUT WHAT
> PRODIGY WILL KEEP YOU SAFE BESIDE ME

Another inscription—my name and the year of my birth—answers the question.

The landscape I inhabit resembles the countryside before leukemia, but I live in a solitude of one. My life after Jane's death has come to resemble the life of the only child and adolescent who feasted on solitude and wrote poems. I wake in our bed, I gaze at Mount Kearsarge and walk on New Canada Road. Much of the time I am reclusive—but I love a woman who lives an hour away, with whom I spend a day and night each week. I am old, hobbling through my eighth decade, but I do not fret about dying. I am able to love and to work.